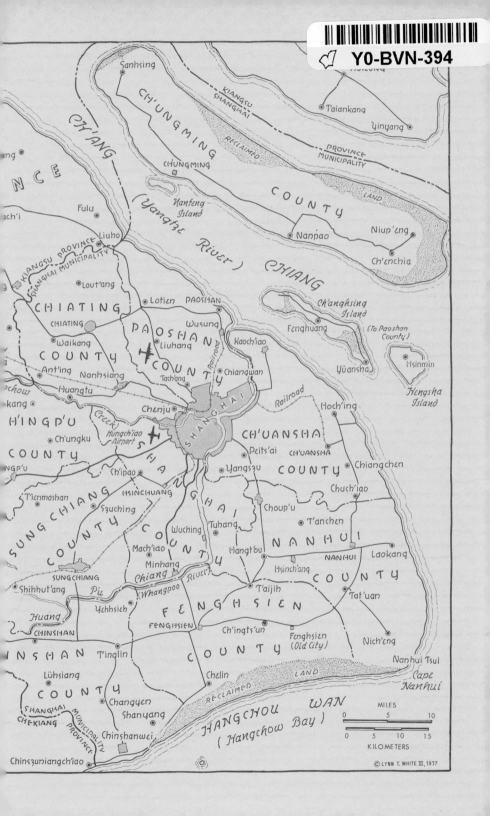

Sanhsing

CH'UNGMING

KIANGSU
SHANGHAI

RECLAIMED

Holtung

Taiankang

Yinyang

CH'IANG

CHUNGMING

COUNTY

PROVINCE
MUNICIPALITY

LAND

ng

NCE

Fulu

ch'i

Liuho

(Yangtze River)

Nanfeng
Island

Nanpao

Niup'eng

Ch'enchia

CHIANG

KIANGSU PROVINCE
SHANGHAI MUNICIPALITY

Lout'ang

Lotien

PAOSHAN

Ch'anghsing
Island

CHIATING

CHIATING

Waikang

PAOSHAN

Wusung

Fenghuang

(To Paoshan
County)

COUNTY

Liuhang

Kaochiao

Yüansha

Hsinmin

Ant'ing

Nanhsiang

Tach'ang

Chiangwan

Hengsha
Island

chow

Huangtu

Chenju

SHANGHAI

Railroad

Hoch'ing

kang

H'INGP'U

Creek

Hungch'iao
Airport

CH'UANSHA

Ch'ungku

Peits'ai

CH'UANSHA

Chiangchen

COUNTY

NGP'U

Ch'ipao

Yangszu

COUNTY

Chuch'iao

Tienmashan

HSINCHUANG

Choup'u

SUNGCHIANG

Szuching

Wuching

Tuhang

T'anchen

NANHUI

Mach'iao

Hangtou

COUNTY

Minhang

Chiang

River

Hsinch'ang

NANHUI

Laokang

SUNGCHIANG

Pu

Whangpoo

T'aijih

COUNTY

Shihhut'ang

Uchhsieh

FENGHSIEN

Tat'uan

Huang

Ch'ingts'un

Fenghsien
(Old City)

Nich'eng

CHINSHAN

FENGHSIEN

Nanhui Tsui

INSHAN

T'inglin

COUNTY

Chelin

RECLAIMED

LAND

Cape
Nanhui

Lühsiang

SHANGHAI

Changyen

Shanyang

HANGCHOU

WAN

MILES

0   5   10

CHEKIANG
PROVINCE
MUNICIPALITY

Chinshanwei

(Hangchow Bay)

0   5   10   15
KILOMETERS

Chinszuniangch'iao

© LYNN T. WHITE III, 1977

CAREERS IN SHANGHAI

This volume is sponsored by the
CENTER FOR CHINESE STUDIES
University of California, Berkeley

THE CENTER FOR CHINESE STUDIES at the University of California, Berkeley, supported by the Ford Foundation, the Institute of International Studies (University of California, Berkeley), and the State of California, is the unifying organization for social science and interdisciplinary research on contemporary China.

RECENT PUBLICATIONS:

LOWELL DITTMER
Liu Shao-ch'i and the Chinese Cultural Revolution
The Politics of Mass Criticism

TETSUYA KATAOKA
Resistance and Revolution in China
The Communists and the Second United Front

EDWARD E. RICE
Mao's Way

FREDERIC WAKEMAN, JR.
History and Will
Philosophical Perspectives of Mao Tse'tung's Thought

JAMES L. WATSON
Emigration and the Chinese Lineage
The Mans *in Hong Kong and London*

LYNN T. WHITE III

Careers in Shanghai

The Social Guidance of Personal Energies in a
Developing Chinese City, 1949-1966

UNIVERSITY OF CALIFORNIA PRESS
Berkeley   Los Angeles   London

University of California Press
Berkeley and Los Angeles, California

University of California Press, Ltd.
London, England

Copyright © 1978 by
The Regents of the University of California

ISBN 0-520-03361-2
Library of Congress Catalog Card Number: 76-48369
Printed in the United States of America

For Barbara-Sue

Eagles dart
  across the wide sky,
Fish swim
  in the shallows—
All display their freedom
  in the frosty air.
Bewildered by the immensity,
I ask the vast grey earth:
"Who decides men's destinies?"

—Mao Tse-tung

From "Ch'angsha," translated in Jerome Ch'en,
Mao and the Chinese Revolution
(Oxford: Oxford University Press, 1967), p. 320.

CONTENTS

A NOTE ON ROMANIZATION

This book uses the Wade-Giles transliteration system, rather than the *pinyin* system of the People's Republic of China, because most Western readers come with preconceptions that the sound value of a romanized letter should bear some relationship to its pronunciation in major Western languages. *Pinyin* does not meet this test, although it is good for teaching Mandarin to Chinese who speak other dialects. This book drops hyphens, because they are unnecessary when spellings like *ah* (rather than *a*) and *yi* (rather than *i* and parallel with normal Wade-Giles *yin* and *wu*) are employed. The postal system supplies names for provinces and major cities.

TABLES

MAPS

ix

ABBREVIATIONS

CB	*Current Background,* Hong Kong, U.S. Consulate-General.
CFCP	*Chiehfangchün pao* (Liberation army news), Peking.
CFJP	*Chiehfang jihpao* (Liberation daily), Shanghai.
CKCN	*Chungkuo ch'ingnien* (China youth), Peking.
CKCNP	*Chungkuo ch'ingnien pao* (China youth news), Peking.
CNP	*Ch'ingnien pao* (Youth news), Shanghai.
CNS	*China News Summary,* Hong Kong.
ECMM	*Extracts from China Mainland Magazines,* Hong Kong, U.S. Consulate.
HkTKP	*Takung pao (L'Impartial),* Hong Kong.
HkWHP	*Wenhui pao (Documentary news),* Hong Kong.
HMPWK	*Hsinmin pao wank'an* (New people's evening gazette), Shanghai.
HMWP	*Hsinmin wanpao* (New people's evening news), Shanghai.
HWJP	*Hsinwen jihpao* (News daily), Shanghai.
JMJP	*Jenmin jihpao* (People's daily), Peking.
JPRS	Joint Publications Research Service, Department of Commerce, Washington, D.C.
KJJP	*Kungjen jihpao* (Workers' daily), Peking.
KMJP	*Kuangming jihpao* (Bright daily), Peking.
LTP	*Laotung pao* (Labor news), Shanghai.
NCNA	New China News Agency, wire service, various cities as noted.

PkTKP	*Takung pao (L'Impartial),* Peking.
PR	*Peking Review,* Peking.
SCMM	*Selections from China Mainland Magazines,* Hong Kong, U.S. Consulate.
SCMP	*Survey of the China Mainland Press,* Hong Kong, U.S. Consulate.
SHNL	"Shanghai Newsletter" column in *South China Morning Post,* Hong Kong.
SN	*Shanghai News,* Shanghai.
SHWP	*Shanghai wanpao* (Shanghai evening news), Shanghai.
URI	Union Research Institute Library, Hong Kong.
URS	*Union Research Service,* Hong Kong.
WHP	*Wenhui pao* (Literary news), Shanghai.

ACKNOWLEDGMENTS

The idea that I should study Shanghai came up in correspondence with Professor Chalmers A. Johnson of the University of California at Berkeley, who has provided unstinting help and good advice for this project since its inception. I owe him deep thanks.

Many Chinese were also of essential aid in answering interview questions, assisting directly with research, and taking the trouble in countless conversations to correct my wrong ideas. Among those who can be named here, the author expresses gratitude to Tisa Ho, Liu Teh-lan, Lu Hui-chu, Ng Lok-yan, T'ang Yüan-yü, Yang Shih-chang, and "Dai Hsiao-ai." The quotation from Mao Tse-tung's poem "Ch'angsha" is translated in Jerome Ch'en, *Mao and the Chinese Revolution* (Oxford, 1967), p. 320, and is used by permission of the Oxford University Press.

The manuscript has been read and very usefully criticized by Joel Glassman, C. S. Hsü, Chalmers A. Johnson, Gilbert Rozman, Robert A. Scalapino, and Frederic Wakeman, Jr. Both of the anonymous readers for University of California Press also offered voluminous and very constructive comments on the draft. All these people stirred me to make improvements. Mervyn Adams Seldon did what she could to correct my ungainly style, and I am deeply appreciative of the excellent and extensive work she put into this project. William J. McClung, Jr., expertly saw the book through the press. I am solely responsible for what remains and am grateful to each of these colleagues.

Institutions helped, as well as individuals. The Foreign Area Fellowship Program generously financed this Shanghai research. The Center for Chinese Studies of the University of California at Berkeley, in whose publication series the book appears, supported

xiv   *Acknowledgments*

the author as a fledgling sinologue. The Universities Service Centre
provided a desk, light, library, and stimulating company in Hong
Kong, as did the Center for Southeast Asian Studies of Kyōto
University in Japan. The Union Research Institute in Hong Kong
supplied help in terms of interviews and an incomparable library
for this subject. The Center of International Studies of the Woodrow Wilson School and the Committee on Research in the Humanities and Social Sciences arranged for clerical services at Princeton
University. Some final editing was accomplished while I was
supported by the Joint Committee on Contemporary China of the
Social Science Research Council and the American Council of
Learned Societies. There is no relation between the specific policies
of these institutions and the content of this book, but without their
help, it would not exist.

My family—Barbara-Sue, Jeremy, and Kevin—sacrificed a great
deal for this book, and I am more thankful to them than I can
express here.

LYNN T. WHITE III

Princeton, New Jersey
October 1975

CAREERS AND SHANGHAI:
AN INTRODUCTION

This book is about the effects of modernization on the daily lives of people in China's largest city. Its primary focus is on the ways authorities have used resources and incentives to direct career patterns and on the responses of ordinary citizens to these efforts. There is a career guidance system in Shanghai, involving household registrations, school admission procedures, housing policies, the rustication of youths, and job availability. This system directs the energies of individuals toward collective goals. Each chapter is an effort to show how this happens in terms of a specific career stage or resource. Access to each resource can be seen both as a spur to individuals' action in Shanghai and as a means by which the government seeks to control personal energies for social ends.

Although this book is a local study, it is not a complete one. It concerns career patterns, rather than other aspects of the city. Shanghai's role in China is not its main subject, nor is this mainly a story of the origins of the Cultural Revolution. By looking at career patterns within the context of a local study, several topics that have usually been treated separately can be newly related. The synthesis, even if it is loose, may be more important than any single one of its parts.

Shanghai was chosen as the locus for this study because, with its differentiated economy, articulate press, and literate population, it is like an open laboratory for the use of career guidance systems in a modernizing country.[1] Within Shanghai, the unit of analysis is the

1. Interested readers might also consult Ezra F. Vogel, *Canton Under Communism: Programs and Politics in a Provincial Capital, 1949-1968* (Cambridge,

individual and his or her response to state policies that influence
career opportunities. The concerns of individual citizens have
generally been neglected in recent studies of China, and they
deserve new attention.

THE PLAN OF THE BOOK

The order of chapters parallels the order in which a typical citizen
of Shanghai faces career decisions. A child's first major project in
society at large is to obtain an education that will equip him or her
for later work. In the main, such preparation is the task of young
people, but this book is not exactly an "ages of man" analysis.
There are many levels of schooling and many ages at which people
can study for careers. The point is that education, at any level or
age, comes as a first prerequisite to work in society. The chapter
dealing with it comes first in this book.

Before careers begin, another prerequisite must also be met.
There are many names for this social hurdle—respectability, ma-
turity, full citizenship, the outcome of a symbolic rite of passage
that precedes a regular career. This is chiefly a problem for adolescents. Chapter 2 will thus emphasize the mix of ideals and pressures
that stir Shanghai youths to "rusticate" (*hsiafang* or *hsiahsiang*) in
rural parts of China, before some of them return to take up
respectable places in urban life. Again, this kind of rite is not in
principle tied to a person's age. During the latter part of the
Cultural Revolution, many high bureaucrats in China went
through similar experiences in May 7 Cadre Schools prior to their
resumption of office. The point is that full citizenship, in a
political sense, is now a prerequisite for many specific careers. State
policies for access to respectability can affect careers and have
consequences for economic development.

Mass.: Harvard University Press, 1969), a masterful study of the successive waves of
campaigns that swept over a Chinese province and city. The main current books in
English on Shanghai are an historical geography by Rhoads Murphey, *Shanghai:
Key to Modern China* (Cambridge, Mass.: Harvard University Press, 1953), and a
blow-by-blow account of the Cultural Revolution by Neale Hunter, *Shanghai Journal* (New York: Praeger, 1969). I have published several articles, listed
in the bibliography, about other aspects of Shanghai and plan to publish other
books about certain topics related to that city which are minimally covered here.

A third constraint on individual careers in the city is an aggregate and economic one. Jobs must be available, and acceptable to the applicants. The number of posts of any specific type in Shanghai is determined by the long-term effects of political decisions and by economic factors such as the amount of capital in the city, its effect on the productivity of various sorts of labor, and market demands. All these are deeply influenced by government policies. The problem of finding employment is especially keen for persons in their most productive, middle years, when they are raising families (or considering the possibility of doing so), and when they need incomes for both material and social reasons. In principle, however, job seeking is also not directly related to age. It is better analyzed as a career stage, coming after the attainment of the educational and symbolic requisites mentioned earlier. The government can guide the energies of whole categories of Shanghai's people by making specific kinds of jobs available, or not available, to specific kinds of applicants. In fact, this is done, and the career guidance effects are largely by-products of other policies whose main purposes lie elsewhere. The needs of the development process can conflict with a vision of China as a workers' state. If economic incentives are stratified for greater productivity, proletarian solidarity can suffer. The origins of the Cultural Revolution in Shanghai can partly be explained in terms of the growth of different types of political consciousness among different sorts of workers, almost as if these groups began to resemble social classes.

A fourth stage in the Shanghai career cycle is an individual's ability to maintain himself as a resident in the city. The household registration system certifies people for legal residence in any Chinese urban area. This procedure, along with the commodity rationing system and other policies related to it, allows the government to influence indirectly decisions on where people work. Food, housing, and other facilities for urban residence are officially rationed. In some periods, it has been difficult for people to remain in the city without them. Such controls on residence apply most evidently to unemployed workers, who have no enterprises or schools to certify their reasons for being in the city. Chapter 4 thus considers a wide variety of apparently disparate but really interrelated policies, which act in concert to channel desires for urban residence toward social uses.

The effectiveness of government guidance appears to be greatest in the early stages of residents' careers and to decline thereafter. Admission to education for large numbers of children, for example, is something that the government can determine directly and effectively. At the other extreme, the government has been less successful in its attempts to control residence in the city through the ration system. The congerie of policies discussed in this book is partly, not wholly, effective for development ends.

The last chapter does not restate or summarize the argument of the book, but it raises some related questions and suggests some answers. To what extent does a career guidance system exist? During what periods has it been most effective? Under what conditions can these urban career policies serve the interests of social development? When do they become ineffective for that end? For reasons to be discussed in the concluding chapter, the answers depend largely on the level of urban economic prosperity. Generally speaking, individuals have had most incentive to take up government-approved careers in times of medium economic well-being. They have had less incentive to do so in times of either scarcity or good supply. From the viewpoint of the state, career guidance policies have been relatively effective in periods of middle level prosperity, and less so in poorer or more prosperous times.

The conclusion also explores a link between economic change in the mid-1960s and the spread of the Cultural Revolution in Shanghai. But pre-Cultural Revolution data are sufficient to answer the main questions of the book, as raised above. For this reason, and because the mix of material and ideal career incentives altered importantly after 1966, the book ends with the Cultural Revolution. The career guidance system before then generally worked for social goals, and it inevitably restricted individuals. Inefficiencies in this system do not seem to have overwhelmed its positive effects for collective economic growth, but, because of the increasing stress on propaganda incentives after 1966, this book concentrates on the unified structure of other incentives that prevailed before then.

SOURCES

What career choices do urban Chinese face? A high hurdle must be jumped in any attempt to answer this question. Our most reliable sources of data are official ones. They concern policies and publishable outcomes. Their viewpoint is collective and governmental to a fault. It is sometimes necessary to make great leaps (so to speak) in order to guess at the motives of individual citizens on the basis of censored data. Some misinterpretations are unavoidable, but the inductive approach used here should allow us to see maximum life in the quasi-governmental publications that still provide most data for research in the contemporary China field.

Local newspaper sources are the basis of this book. National statements are cited mainly when their effect on Shanghai seems to have been greater than that of local statements. Interviews were used whenever qualified informants could be found, but documentary information remained most important. The documents included wire-service and radio transcripts, as well as Party newspapers like *Jenmin jihpao* in Peking and *Chiehfang jihpao* in East China. Especially important were daily papers for less official readerships; their firm loyalty could be taken less for granted than that of the regular readers of the Party organs. Examples of newspapers in this category are the national *Kuangming jihpao*, Shanghai's *Wenhui pao* and *Hsinwen jihpao*, Canton's *Yangch'eng wanpao*, and the *Takung pao*, which is published in various cities. These papers of course follow official policies, but they have often printed frank articles to interest their subscribers—most of whom are of bourgeois origin—lest such people read no daily press at all. Primary reliance on non-Party papers from Shanghai has allowed coverage of some fresh topics and has complemented other research in this field.

For the most part, the techniques of "Pekingology" have not been used to interpret these newspapers. Such methods are less necessary for gathering factual information from a local press about the content of urban policies than they would be, for instance, in a study of elite politics, or in a study based on materials printed largely for Communists. The method of scanning newspapers in time is, however, important. If we gather evidence about specific topics mainly during the periods of their reform from the top, when patterns are being actively changed, then political movements are inevitably the focus of analysis. The distribution of power along a spectrum of central and local authorities thus easily becomes the overriding question of research. This book, however, attempts to complement such work by gathering the somewhat scanty data that local papers offer about sections of society that are not in the midst of campaigns in the hope of revealing a more balanced picture of behavior. All available issues of Shanghai local papers were read for information about sectors that were not being reformed, as well as for the more accessible data about campaigns. In reporting all this, there has been an attempt to give relatively continuous histories of certain issues through the Communist period in Shanghai. Sectors and functions, rather than campaigns, are the focus of this study, which can thus try to assess how much effect campaigns really have on the goals and behavior that prevail at other times.

APPROACH

One of the most important trends of modern political science—a trend into which this book does not fall—treats matters as politically important when they go up, for example, up to a black box, up to the mayor of a city, up to a legitimate decision-making process. In these studies, the quintessential question of politics is who governs, especially in high places. Some major progress has been made toward answering that kind of question, and many aspects of the politics of individuals and small units can also be approached in these terms. "Mass" politics can often be related to "elite" politics, because the former can be studied with reference to the ways in which popular cultures and types of authority in small units affect the stability and variety of high regimes.

The present book stands in a different tradition, no less viable or interesting than the one described above, but still a bit less usual, especially in the Chinese field. Its starting point and main questions are not the same as in an elite study. This tradition looks at voting behavior, public opinion, or other expressions of politics at the bottom. Its first assumption is that public action and reaction at low levels can be as political as anything that transpires at high ones. This book looks at Shanghai in terms of its citizens, as well as its government. The city fathers have done much to alter the opportunity structure available to the city's people, but their capacities to foresee the consequences of various reforms in career policy are limited. In fact, the residents of Shanghai also alter the structure of opportunities available to the city fathers.

A second perspective to be explored in this book is that social action in China derives from both individualist and communitarian motives. Our problem is to find the relation between them in specific cases. This research on careers is all about exchanges of repression at some levels for freedom at others. It is not easy to make any general moral judgment about such tradeoffs, because each of the various levels of a polity contributes to the creation and development of each of the others, and these exchanges need more structural study before pontifical statements can be made about them. It would be too easy to choose words like "dictatorship" and "repression" or, alternatively, words like "liberation" and "guidance," to describe the topic of this book. The consistent use of either set of terms would belie the fact that these are two sides of the same coin. It is definitely possible and eventually necessary to judge, criticize, or praise the efficiency and justice of this system as a whole. Our prior job is nonetheless to find its shape. To understand what makes Shanghai work, to find the motives and hopes of the people who live there, it seems useful to try to limit the range of political assumptions and to deal first with new kinds of data. We must try to discover general and specific things that we did not know before, even implicitly.

Does an emphasis on localities and sublocalities, and on the interplay of individualist and communitarian motives in social action, controvert the widespread idea that the People's Republic of China is a centralized hierarchy? This book takes no general position on that issue, which involves both conceptual and practical problems. The very notion of politics implies an interplay of groups, and those in lower offices influence the substance of the directives they receive.[2] From a practical point of view, leaders in

2. See my article, "Local Autonomy in China During the Cultural Revolution: The Theoretical Uses of an Atypical Case," *American Political Science Review* LXX: No. 2 (June 1976), 479-491, and my more abstract model, which distinguishes administrative and political levels sharply, "Shanghai's Polity in Cultural Revolution," in John W. Lewis, ed., *The City in Communist China* (Stanford, Calif.: Stanford University Press, 1971), especially pp. 357-369. A recent book on the careers of Soviet bureaucrats is William Taubman, *Governing Soviet Cities: Bureaucratic Politics and Urban Development in the U.S.S.R.* (New York: Praeger, 1973). This

Peking need strong friends in the provinces and municipalities, or else they find themselves leading only their secretaries in the capital. Central policies need strong, imaginative local implementers, or they soon become dead letters. Local leaders and local interests also require constant support from the center; in Communist Shanghai, they have often been able to obtain it. To pretend to resolve central-local tensions either way is unrealistic. China is not completely totalistic, nor are any of its parts completely free. There can be a good deal of inconsistency or ambiguity among the different goals held by a single political actor at a single time. Central interests can be used for local purposes. Local resources are affected by what the center tells adjacent localities to do. The spirit of nationalism can sometimes transfigure local advantages and make their practical exercise seem patriotic. The behavioral approach, at least in its original sense of trying to find out what goes on throughout a polity, is the broad and natural approach to politics on many levels, center and city as well as citizen.

The focus on low-level politics does create problems, however, for the study of socialist countries where it is not possible to conduct surveys and interviews. The main effort to approach their politics from this direction has been found in studies of psychology and socialization, whose concepts often cause problems, despite the fact that they raise important questions. Work has also been done on political participation. This book will add to that literature, with emphasis on the reactions of individuals to certain policies from high government levels.

Some treatments of Communist China have neglected the analysis of low-level politics on grounds of a supposed lack of data. Published materials from China have not exactly stressed the fact that different opinions arise in different levels of politics there. Even worse, China scholars have too frequently been asked by others to spend their best efforts explaining the latest headlines. Today's arrangement of factions in Peking has been our most durable interest. Speculation about tomorrow's arrangement has

local elite study refines, and often conflicts with, Merle Fainsod's classic on Smolensk, *How Russia Is Ruled*, rev. ed. (Cambridge, Mass.: Harvard University Press, 1963). See also my "Leadership in Shanghai, 1955-1969," in Robert A. Scalapino, ed., *Elites in the People's Republic of China* (Seattle: University of Washington Press, 1972).

been our most popular product. We have had too few recourses during the times when the well of information went completely dry. As a wry colleague disclosed sagely, at one of his more desperate moments, "The situation bears watching."

THE LITERATURE

The main comparative studies of the relationship between personal careers and public action elsewhere have been of little help here. Such works have mostly dealt with elite politics. A classic in this field is Harold Lasswell's *Power and Personality*.[3] More recent contributions include Joseph A. Schlesinger's *Ambition and Politics*[4] and Kenneth Prewitt's *Recruitment of Political Leaders*.[5] There are also many case studies of leadership careers. For the sake of brevity, only one will be mentioned here (by authors who have also worked in the China field), Alexander and Juliette George's *Woodrow Wilson and Colonel House*.[6] These books are concerned with the careers and ideas of politicians who make decisions at the top of a political system.

The careers of the masses and their effects on political decisions at all levels are less well explored. For China, the bibliography on "mass line" techniques is extensive.[7] These books examine low-level reactions to high policies from the viewpoint of leadership principles. They are as much about the "line" as about the "mass," but they serve better than any other body of work to integrate the concerns of this book with those of elite studies. Low-level emphasis, such as is attempted here, is more common in articles discussing specific policies than in books. Nevertheless, one recent example of the perspective used here is sociologist Martin K. Whyte's *Small Groups and Political Rituals in China*.[8] His book on small groups allows this study to focus on some alternative and concurrent forms

3. (New York: Norton, 1948).
4. (Chicago: Rand McNally, 1966).
5. (Indianapolis, Ind.: Bobbs-Merrill, 1970).
6. (New York: Day, 1956).
7. No attempt will be made here to cite all the relevant works in this area, even for China. The best book is still John W. Lewis, *Leadership in Communist China* (Ithaca, N. Y.: Cornell University Press, 1963). In a different vein, many essays by Lenin and Mao are also pertinent.
8. (Berkeley and Los Angeles: University of California Press, 1974).

of social control. Other distinguished works in this area include
James R. Townsend's *Political Participation in Communist
China*[9] and Franz Schurmann's *Ideology and Organization in
Communist China.*[10]

Such books on China must interact with similar research on
political development in other countries. Detailed local information from socialist Shanghai may be more useful in suggesting ways
to broaden current comparative theory than in trying to make
premature comparisons on the basis of superficial data. The citizens of China's largest city during the past two decades have been
under collectively organized social pressures of an intensity that
cannot be matched during that period in any other metropolis of its
size. Many developing countries have had to face problems of rapid
migration to cities, of motivating labor to fill particular jobs, and of
alleviating the frustrations of claimants to higher levels of education. These matters are not peculiar to Shanghai or to China. The
words "Communist" or "socialist" are absent from the title of this
book because career guidance issues in Shanghai resemble those in
other quickly developing cities. Other modernizing countries must
also find ways to mobilize the talented residents of big cities more
directly for national goals. The similarities between their problems
and China's now may become even more evident, with the death of
Chairman Mao Tse-tung. In effect, this book describes a government policy option for collective progress through the use of
certain career incentives, and the popular response to that option.
Shanghai's experience may be relevant elsewhere, even if the career
policies of other modernizing countries take different courses. It is
hoped that this book on Shanghai will stimulate similar studies of
other cities and comparative work on the role of career guidance
systems in modernization.

    9. (Berkeley and Los Angeles: University of California Press, 1967).
    10. (Berkeley and Los Angeles: University of California Press, 1966).

1

EDUCATIONAL INCENTIVES TO SOCIALIST CAREERS

The daily lives of many Shanghai citizens are largely determined by political decisions on the content and duration of schooling, the kinds of persons to receive it, the academic and social standards to be met for admission, and the criteria for obtaining diplomas.

Like many other components of the city government's overall policy on career patterns, educational plans are linked with long-range strategies for China's economic development. Decisions regarding promotions and curriculum influence the local economy heavily. Such decisions have changed frequently at the level of high policy in Peking, but their implementation at provincial and local levels has been less radically cyclical.[1] Such decisions help set the

1. Government administration in China, during most of the period since 1954, has been carried out through the following territorial levels: First, there is the central apparatus of ministries and agencies in Peking, under the State Council. Second, there are provinces, "autonomous regions," and "directly ruled cities" (*chihhsia shih*, such as Shanghai, which thus has province-level status). Third, most provinces have subprovincial cities and have usually been divided into "special districts". In Shanghai, these units have not existed, so that the third level of government in the main built-up area has comprised "urban districts" (*shih ch'ü*, ten of them during most of this period). In the rural parts of Shanghai, the third level has comprised "counties" (*hsien*, also ten of them since 1959), centered on major market towns (often "townships," *chen*) which near the metropolis are in fact small cities. The fourth major level of rural Shanghai government since 1958 has been the "people's commune." On lower urban levels, see note 3. The relative importance of each of

speed with which the urban economy, and that of its hinterland, can expand over the long term. The high quality of Shanghai's labor force is one of the city's major arguments for partial retention of its tax revenues as local investment. Technical manpower allows Shanghai to produce some kinds of goods that would be more difficult to make elsewhere.

The general relation between education and development in poor countries is a moot topic in comparative studies. Scholars such as Frederick Harbison, M. J. Bowman, and C. A. Anderson generally conclude that there is a positive but loose correlation between literacy and production. They also warn, however, that poor countries can easily spend their education budgets wastefully in terms of development. They propose and test many hypotheses which relate particular sorts of investment in human resources directly with economic growth.[2] This chapter discusses only a particular kind of indirect relationship between education and development. School policies constitute a career control: access to, or denial of, particular kinds of education can be used as an incentive for citizens to work toward state-defined community goals.

Shanghai has two different sets of schools. The regular system includes primary, junior middle, and senior middle schools, technical colleges, universities, and specialized institutes. The duration of schooling at different levels has varied from time to time. This regular system is run by the city government's Education Bureau, which makes decisions about curricula, academic schedules, and textbooks. Education offices in each of the city's urban districts and rural counties administer these policies locally and make or approve most personnel decisions. These organs are supposed to apply national directives to the local situation.

these levels has changed from time to time. Concerning China's rather formal legislative system, see note 29. Administrative levels of the Communist Party have not always been identical with the government units, but Party units exist at all the levels mentioned above, and the occasional short-lived extra-Party levels will be mentioned in the text only when they are relevant.

2. Frederick H. Harbison, *Human Resources as the Wealth of Nations* (New York: Oxford University Press, 1973); and Mary Jean Bowman and Charles Arnold Anderson, "Concerning the Role of Education in Development," in Clifford F. Geertz, ed., *Old Societies and New States: The Quest for Modernity in Asia and Africa* (New York: The Free Press, 1963), especially pp. 276-279.

The regular, city-run system is supplemented by citizen-run (*minpan*) and factory schools, which are partly autonomous, or dependent only on local street committees or economic firms.[3] *Minpan* and factory schools can have either part-time programs during working hours or spare-time programs after working hours. In addition, various short-term training courses are financed by government offices or state corporations. The duration of individuals' schooling in this supplementary system has also varied from period to period.

This variety of training programs affects the structure of incentives that can be used in the city. Because Shanghai's universities serve a wide area of East China, and because the city's industrial and commercial development serves the whole nation in many specialized fields, there are often national motives behind local school decisions. The objectives of Shanghai's education system are not entirely limited to local economic needs, but its planning has important effects on local stratification because many students who come to the city try to stay there after graduation.

EDUCATION IN THE EARLY YEARS AND MID-1950s

During the first years of Communist rule, the "pressing desires of the masses for education" far outran the facilities with which the government could satisfy them. The Shanghai government's doubts about the economic value of many kinds of education were probably as well founded as was its appreciation of the political desirability of meeting some immediate demands for education. The problem was to reconcile Shanghai's development needs with popular pressures for schooling and jobs, and to make sure that Shanghai's educational system served national purposes.

In the early years, most of the demand for schooling was at the primary level. From 1949 to 1952, children's primary enrollment

3. Note 1, above, refers to the urban districts (*shih ch'ü*) in Shanghai, which are the main subprovincial units in built-up parts of the city proper. Under each urban district, there are street committees (*chiehtao weiyüanhui*, sometimes called "neighborhoods"), which despite their title usually have jurisdiction over wide areas, each containing several streets and lanes. Below street committees are residents' committees (*chümin weiyüanhui*), very local organizations which may take some initiatives in economic and other fields, and to which the state agencies mentioned in note 1 often send representatives for special purposes.

increased 83 percent—from 312,000 to 570,000; in the fall of 1952, it was reported that 95 percent of Shanghai's primary-school-age children were being educated. These efforts produced some 62,000 graduates by the spring of 1953. That summer, more than 66,000 children (including some who had been out of school for a time) sat for the junior middle entrance exams. Only 30,000 slots had been planned that year, but the demand was so great that 43,000 students were actually admitted.[4] Their promotion seems to have been decided on academic grounds. There are no data on the use of political criteria in admissions policies at this time, but probably no students were barred from early grades on the basis of bourgeois family background. Government policies clearly bowed to popular hopes for education.

Rising primary enrollment meant increased pressure on authorities to create more middle schools or to find occupations for more primary graduates, who are often as old as fourteen. Of 104,000 students who received degrees at all levels in Shanghai during mid-1953, no less than 59 percent came out of primary schools. Only 23 percent were graduates of junior middle schools, and 18 percent were from senior middle schools or equivalent technical or normal schools.[5] Local newspapers complained about "the pressing problem of primary and junior graduates who cannot continue their studies."[6] *Wenhui pao* said that "all government organs, public bodies, and state and private industrial and mining enterprises [should ask] permission to establish junior middle schools and supplementary literacy schools." It was hoped that the additional classes would take pressure off the labor market in the short run, even if graduates from these new institutions would inevitably put more pressure on it later.

Efforts were also made to educate the working population. After February 1950, the municipal Education Bureau set up 49 factory schools for 17,400 students in "large" factories. Trade unions ran

---

4. *SN*, October 12, 1952; *WHP*, September 14, 1953. *WHP* was so eager to avoid emphasizing the tight supply that it rounded the 65 percent to "almost 70 percent," even though this obscured the government's real generosity in exceeding its original plan for the number of entrants. See also Barry Richman, *Industrial Society in Communist China* (New York: Random House, 1969), pp. 128-129.

5. The exact figures for 1953 graduates were: primary, 61,563; junior middle, 23,409; senior middle and equivalent, 18,741.

6. *WHP*, September 14, 1953.

another 106 schools for student-workers. In December 1953, the central government approved further establishment of *minpan* schools, which came in many varieties and served both children and adults.[7]

At the university level in Shanghai, there were more entrants during the early years of the People's Republic than there were senior middle graduates. The need to train new functionaries in a hurry made the Party call for direct admissions of many leftist organization men, who before Liberation would not have attended such high level institutions. For many years, Shanghai has had more regular university vacancies than senior middle graduates. Any direct comparison of these two numbers is meaningless, however, because Shanghai's universities draw applications from all over China. Some of its graduates from other places are able to obtain jobs in the city after leaving school. The Korean War in some ways increased Shanghai's prosperity. At this time before labor market controls were strict, individuals might keep jobs in the city if they could find them. A career guidance system for Shanghai, insofar as schools could administer it, was only beginning in the early period of Communist rule.

EDUCATION DURING THE TRANSITION TO SOCIALISM AND THE GREAT LEAP FORWARD

In Shanghai's local economic history, there is no way to distinguish sharply between the causes of the transition to socialism and those of the Great Leap Forward.[8] In many ways, the transition of 1956 is a more important watershed than 1958. Shanghai's Great Leap really began then. Changes in the city's economic management structure at that time spurred some corresponding new emphases in the local educational system.[9] Politically, there was

7. *LTP*, September 8, 1950; *JMJP*, December 14, 1953.
8. I plan to develop this point at much greater length in future writings.
9. The "transition to socialism" of 1956 was a movement in which the "joint state-private" (*kungszu hoying*) sector of China's economy expanded rapidly. Firms in similar commodity or service lines had already been officially grouped into guilds (*t'ungyeh*) of a traditional sort in the years immediately after Liberation. These were converted to large "joint state-private" commodity corporations in 1956. Enterprises of this sort fell under state planning procedures more than before the transition to socialism. Private managers still had some role, and even a nominal legal stake, in

a new emphasis on a student's class background. Economically, the schools stressed technical subjects and lower levels of education even more than before, although educational openings at higher levels also increased. Administratively, education was decentralized, with new schools established in factories and in new suburban residential areas.

ADMISSIONS AND PROMOTIONS, 1956-1959

Educational planning before the Great Leap grew out of Communist ideals and favored more schooling for the proletariat. Already by mid-1957, more than 70 percent of the students in Shanghai's primary schools came from officially designated workers' or peasants' families.[10] Out of this pool of lower-class talents came students with the academic credentials to push many capitalist background students off middle school matriculation lists. Moreover, the promotion policies of district-level admission committees began to favor students of worker and peasant backgrounds. Even well before the Leap, students of bourgeois family origin were complaining about this bias. During the Hundred Flowers campaign in 1956-1957, when the government encouraged people to criticize its policies and performance, bulletins were posted in the canteen of T'ungchi University to criticize the ease with which formerly lower-class students were promoted. Applicants from

---

the firms they had previously owned. State officials were assigned to the joint corporations (and to their large branches) to oversee the new public interest in them. These arrangements varied greatly, according to the commodity or service type, the supply of trained economic cadres, and other factors. Some joint firms, as well as some fully nationalized ones, had existed in previous years, but the 1956 transition to socialism greatly increased their number. By creating a large new group of state businessmen, it affected investment, education, and many other local policies discussed in this book.

The Great Leap Forward, beginning in 1958, was mainly a rural movement to establish "people's communes" (*jenmin kungshe*, low-level state agencies that engaged in economic work largely through their subsidiary production brigades and production teams). In cities such as Shanghai, the Leap had certain policy effects whose origins this book will in many cases trace to the mid-1950s. Its main local effect was to lower urban imports from rural areas between 1959 and 1962.

10. NCNA, Shanghai, July 10, 1957. A person's "family origin" (*chiat'ing ch'ushen*) is his or her social class label, which is determined by the source of income of his or her household during childhood. It is officially recorded, for an urban resident, in a "household registration book," about which Chapter 4 will provide further information.

special "accelerated middle schools" were especially favored. These were institutions from which proletarians might enter a university without being examined, under a policy of "direct, untested promotion for excellent students" (*yuhsiu sheng mienshih chih sheng*). Shen Chien-ju, a counselor (*futao laoshih*) at T'ungchi University, called this "a way to invoice and sell students that is similar to unified distribution in the wholesale business for commercial goods."[11] The local newspaper *Hsinwen jihpao* reported:

Posters objected that the students from accelerated middle schools are given priority even when their academic results are identical with those of students from elsewhere. The posters also advocated that accelerated middle school students should go back to their work posts. When students who had attended these schools entered the university canteen, they were shouted at and told to get out.[12]

The worker-background students were also accused in Marxist language of being "sectarian," a charge that brought a prompt response from pupils in the Worker-Peasant Accelerated Middle School attached to Futan University. They issued statements against Shen Chien-ju and others who agreed with her, but the reasonable tone of their counterattacks suggested that she had hit a sensitive nerve. As a second-year student from Shen's own department said:

The state tries its best to educate an intelligentsia of workers and peasants, but it has not exploited the landlords and capitalists by taking away from their children a right to education. There has been no sectarianism.[13]

After the transition to socialism and during the Great Leap in Shanghai, there was a drive to advance social equality within the city's educational system and to break down the wall of separation between students' lives and those of workers and peasants. This campaign was congruent with other efforts at the same time to make schools economically more useful. Educational policy during the Leap generally furthered the dominance of technical courses over general and cultural courses (except in the field of politics). It also placed more emphasis on low-level education and less on higher levels, although it would be difficult to prove that

11. *HWJP*, June 25, 1957.
12. *Ibid.*
13. *HWJP*, June 26, 1957.

many semitrained technical workers are more effective than fewer well-trained ones for the purpose of industrial development. All the slogans about "democratic management" and "triple combinations" would have been even more meaningless than they were, without a body of at least semieducated workers at the basic level.[14]

The goal of social equality was to be achieved by combining education with productive labor. Students were supposed to learn mainly the skills that would allow them to participate in economic work. Entrance to higher education remained limited, even under these conditions. One set of national figures implies that as many as 90,000 senior middle school graduates were refused admission to a university in 1957. There were 1.8 committee-approved applicants for every higher education vacancy in China that year.[15] These figures suggest that in 1957 more than 200,000 students throughout the country applied for only 110,000 university vacancies. Popular pressure for education continued apace with official efforts to relieve it.

SCHOOLS, STUDENTS, AND CURRICULA, 1956-1959

Especially at the lower levels of education, one solution to the demand for diplomas and jobs was to supplement the regular city-run system with spare-time schools in factories or residential areas. The Great Leap encouraged the establishment of many new secondary schools and workers' universities, which were usually attached to existing enterprises or offices. The restoration of a powerful (now socialist) business class in Shanghai after 1956, and the subsequent Hundred Flowers, antirightist, and administrative streamlining campaigns of 1957 caused middle level administrative units to become more important for many purposes.[16] The sizes

14. "Democratic management" (*minchu kuanli*) was a term much emphasized in late 1957; it implied both that cadre officials should participate in manual labor and that workers should have some voice in industrial administration. The term "triple combination" (*san chieh ho*) was first used in 1958 to suggest that workers, as well as officials and technicians, should participate in industrial innovation decisions. (This phrase became very prominent again during the Cultural Revolution, when it acquired many additional and alternative meanings.)

15. Estimated from figures in URS, Vol. 36, No. 13 (1964), based on the editorial of *JMJP*, April 25, 1957. No Shanghai local series on annual graduations from senior middle schools was found, unfortunately.

16. The antirightist and administrative streamlining campaigns of late 1957 and early 1958 were the government's reactions to criticisms during the Hundred Flowers

of these units differed according to the nature of their tasks. Personnel were sent to, and resources were retained in, middle level units with more regularity than before. Sometimes subsidies from higher authorities were reduced at this time, but control from higher organs also receded. Later, during the Leap, socialized companies and government offices were under pressure from their staffs for access to education, and they were able to set up their own in-house schools.

Some residential units, particularly at the street neighborhood (*chiehtao*) level just below the urban districts, enjoyed similar new collective freedoms. A major cultural effect of the Leap was to further the longstanding goal of universal education by allowing purely local committees to establish, finance, and run new middle schools in parts of the city where postprimary educational coverage had previously been slight. Public schools coexisted alongside factory and street schools. This was part of the famous Great Leap policy of "walking on two legs."[17]

This aspect of the Leap, like many others, had begun before 1958. Local financing had been a feature of the 1956-1957 literacy campaign, during which many Shanghai people paid their own tuitions. For example, the Yangp'u District First Employees' Sparetime Primary School (Yangp'u Ch'ü Tiyi Chihkung Yehyü Hsiaohsüeh) began as a subsidized institution in early 1956. It offered 36 classes with an average enrollment of 55 pupils. Soon thereafter the Education Bureau apparently decided to reduce or eliminate its subsidy. The tuition charged at this school in 1956 was 7.50 yüan per term.[18] Fee waivers for some students, which had

---

movement. On one hand, "rightists" who had been critical of official policies were gathered together for ideological reform. On the other hand, many of the officials they had been criticizing were sent to do more manual work, and especially to take administrative posts in rural areas. Both of these campaigns, whether by planning or by accident, provided bases for the start of the Great Leap Forward.

17. The policy of "walking on two legs" promoted the simultaneous development of a modern sector and a sector based on locally available resources, popular energies, and traditional tools.

18. *Shanghai saomang*, May 9, 1957, states that the school had 1,818 tuition-paying students (92 percent of its total enrollment) during 1956 and that receipts were 11,280 yüan. The tuition per student per session in each year must therefore have been 7.50 yüan. These figures also imply that scholarships, for 8 percent of the student body in 1956, were abolished in 1957. The tuitions were quite low, and they sufficed to support the school because class size was large. An estimate of 55 students

existed in 1956, were abolished in 1957. In addition, there was a 30 percent increase in the school's small "donation to the state," apparently to the district government as a kind of overhead charge. Many "civilian-run" (*minpan*) schools, like this one, survived because of student's tuitions; others received larger subsidies from their local factories or offices. The reduction of both subsidies and controls, in combination with the nearly insatiable demand of Shanghai's people to educate themselves, allowed hundreds of rather independent *minpan* schools to flourish during the Leap.

During the 1958-1959 academic year, Shanghai had roughly 1,800 "people's" schools, most of which were administered at least nominally by neighborhood committees.[19] These *minpan* schools were set up for several different kinds of students during the Leap. Primary and literacy programs were most numerous. Neighborhood committees increasingly got into the business of running "spare-time middle schools" and "middle vocational schools" (*yehyü chunghsüeh, chungteng chuanyeh hsüehhsiao*). Some neighborhoods even established "higher vocational schools" (*kaoteng chuanyeh hsüehhsiao*), a term that almost suggests their equivalence to universities.

The Leap increase in the number of primary and middle schools of all sorts provided places for half a million new Shanghai pupils in the autumn of 1958. This was half again as many as had entered the system during the previous boom year, 1957. Shanghai's government during the Leap claimed that junior middle school registration was now "virtually universal." No less than 53 percent of Shanghai's secondary schools were *minpan*, and 47 percent were in the regular system (the absolute numbers of institutions in each category were 1,800 and 1,565), but total enrollment at the citizen-run academies during late 1958 was probably still well below that in the regular city-run schools.[20] Moreover, the number of schools

---

per meeting was computed from the published enrollment and class numbers. (The Chinese yüan has been valued at roughly one-half to one-third of the U.S. dollar; its nominal exchange rate, determined by official policies and by the particular basket of internationally traded commodities, is not a good indicator of its value to the people who spend it.)

19. *HWJP*, October 12, 1958. At this time, the schools were also sometimes called "lane self-run" (*lilung tzupan ti*). The term *minpan* can be used of any organization that is run by a collective, rather than by a state office.

20. NCNA, Shanghai, October 5, 1958.

under *minpan* administration apparently decreased somewhat in 1959. By the end of that year, Shanghai street committees were reporting a total of 1,694 schools with 236,000 students (an average of about 140 per school). A large new neighborhood-administered school system had nonetheless been established. These figures do not include the part-time schools set up in many economic institutions. Shanghai factories and stores reported they were running 5,000 schools with no fewer than 1,090,000 students, or at least 200 per school.

In Shanghai's rural suburban communes (where 265,000 students were enrolled at the end of 1958), 53 percent (141,000) were at the primary level. Only 9 percent were middle school students, and 1.5 percent were in "red-and-expert" schools for cadres. A newspaper report on this topic did not account for the remaining 36.5 percent of the students, presumably because they were taking elementary courses.[21]

Although the main emphasis of this period was on primary and secondary technical education, efforts were also made to provide more advanced training for middle school graduates, thereby enhancing their career possibilities and potential utility in China's development. During the summer of 1959, the government boasted that new Leap universities, in conjunction with older Shanghai institutions, were now providing places for 95 percent of Shanghai senior middle school graduates.[22] Only two years earlier, in 1957, nearly half of the qualified university applicants in China could not matriculate. Shanghai, because of its relatively large—and largely bourgeois-background—pool of academically competent candidates, and because of the quick expansion of "university" facilities in the Leap, was able to reduce this career bottleneck dramatically in 1959. From one girls' middle school, for example, 90 percent of the graduates matriculated at universities to study applied science—70 percent in natural sciences and engineering, and 20 percent in medicine and agriculture. Even bourgeois students with unspectacular grades could receive substantial training

21. *HWJP*, January 1, 1959.
22. NCNA, Shanghai, July 4, 1959. This article reports that Shanghai had 23,000 senior middle graduates that summer, and that 22,000 would be admitted to "higher educational institutions throughout the country." Free tuition and dormitory space were provided for all who needed them.

and vocational university degrees during the Leap, if only they were willing to help production.

The fully respectable high-quality university system expanded in this period alongside the less prestigious colleges. In mid-1959, Shanghai had 24 institutions of higher education in the regular, full-time, city-run system. These enrolled 45,000 students in academic courses from which they would receive degrees that would be very useful to their careers. Eight of these relatively good universities had been founded in the previous two years.

The most important of the new institutions was the Shanghai University of Science and Technology, established in 1958 by the local branch of the Chinese Academy of Sciences.[23] It was quite exclusive, enrolling only 300 students in the summer of 1959. Other selective institutions of higher education included the seven "full-time" engineering colleges set up during 1959 by various municipal bureaus in 24 large Shanghai factories. These colleges admitted only 1,200 select senior middle school graduates. They were called "factory-run schools" (*ch'angpan hsüehhsiao*). Although these colleges were nominally "full-time," the students in fact spent two-thirds of their time in classrooms and the rest in productive labor. Faculty members were mainly factory technicians.[24] After completing fixed three-year courses, the graduates could be assured of quick advancement in their sponsoring enterprises.

The continuous flow of educational policy in Shanghai during the transition and Leap, from 1956 to 1959, led to the creation of many new kinds of schools. During most of this period, the city's

23. NCNA, Shanghai, June 18, 1959. The top-flight Shanghai higher educational institutions in mid-1959 included three full universities with distinguished pre-Liberation heritages. Chiaot'ung (Communications) University had by 1959 developed into a polytechnic institute for Shanghai's heavy industry. Futan (Aurora) University maintained its traditional specialties of literature, social science, and natural science. T'ungchi University was strongest in its engineering departments, especially architecture and civil engineering. Other important colleges and institutions were almost all specialized, and academically most of them were as good as any other Chinese institutions in their fields: First and Second medical colleges, College of Chinese Medicine, College of Textiles, College of Chemical Engineering, College of Aquatic Products, College of Social Sciences, College of Foreign Languages, College of Physical Education, College of Drama, Shanghai Teachers' College, East China Teachers' University, Conservatory of Music. Some of these professional schools also have long and distinguished histories.

24. NCNA, Shanghai, February 3, 1960.

economy was expanding because of the increased power of local business cadres after 1956. Somewhat paradoxically, overall state control over educational career incentives decreased. The disputes over proletarian school admissions in 1956-1957 were overwhelmed by the expansion and variety of schools that emerged from the enthusiastic Leap.

POST-LEAP RETRENCHMENT, 1960-1963

As a result of educational efforts in the 1950s, it was reported at the end of 1958 that 90 percent of larger Shanghai's population was literate, although no precise definition of literacy was offered.[25] By early 1960, the total number of Shanghai residents in educational institutions of all kinds was about 3.5 million, or roughly half the city's population. Fully 40 percent of these were adults, most of whom were in literacy classes and lower schools. Their attendance rates are unclear.[26]

This vast expansion of primary schooling was maintained in the 1960s. It exacerbated and accompanied an increasing demand for secondary education. At the same time, the economic recession and a shortage of funds necessitated some restructuring of the school system. In 1961, vertical leadership was somewhat strengthened over regular schools. The enrollment of worker-students in primary and secondary classes was encouraged, in part because productive work could not be found for them during those hours. Vocational and political subjects were stressed at the expense of other programs for more general self-cultivation. Government efforts to ensure the economic usefulness of graduates of regular institutions increased, while continuing student demand for education led to the expansion of spare-time courses in factories, on a correspondence basis, and on radio and television.

25. *HWJP*, December 31, 1958, says that 90.2 percent of Shanghai's people could then read. The author, on a trip to China in February 1976, was told that city folk must be able to read 2,000 characters before they are counted as "literate," whereas rural dwellers need only master 1,400. It is unlikely that this or any other standard definition has been applied regularly in China at all times and places.

26. NCNA, Shanghai, February 11, 1960, says that there were 1.4 million "adults" studying at that time. The age-limit definition of the category is not given.

POST-LEAP ADMISSIONS AND PROMOTIONS

By the early to mid-1960s, admissions procedures had generally become standardized throughout the country. In 1961, Peking launched a policy of "unified admissions" (*t'ungyi chaosheng*), which strengthened central controls over all levels of the school system, including the entrance process. In both educational and economic terms, the nation became more "like a single chess board," to use Shanghai Mayor K'o Ch'ing-shih's phrase. Earlier localization of authority over the school system was reversed in several policy areas. By 1963, it was possible for the national government to mandate that greater preference be given to worker and peasant applicants to the levels of education that were still selective.

At the primary school level (where attendance had become nearly universal in Shanghai by the early 1950s), decisions for admission were made by neighborhood schools. In urban Shanghai, regular middle school enrollment was approved at the district level. In the suburbs, approval was at the county level; and *minpan* middle schools in rural areas were generally under the control of communes. Outside agencies did not order the admission of specific students but had some say in making policies.[27] Enrollment criteria for higher education were supposed to be under unified admissions policy, but national directives calling for social class quotas, scholastic quality, and good physical health gave the Shanghai Higher Education Admissions Committee much leeway for interpretation.[28]

A look at enrollment procedures for the university level will shed light on the processes all Shanghai students had to follow. There were some differences between secondary school and university admission procedures, but the latter give a surprisingly good idea of the process at all levels.

1. Before a student could apply for higher education, he was usually required to show that he had completed the equivalent of a senior middle school or technical school education. For a graduate

27. *JMJP*, October 12, 1963; *HMWP*, July 2, 1964. Most Shanghai children enter primary school at the age of seven.

28. NCNA, Peking, May 12, 1961. Cf. *HMWP*, June 5, 1964, whose report of an admission committee meeting suggested this interpretation.

or prospective graduate of such a school, the middle or technical institution would provide a voucher. A city resident who had no such connection might obtain this kind of certificate from the education office of his urban district people's congress.[29] A rural person might get certification from his county education office if it felt that he or she deserved a chance to try for university entrance. Working personnel of Party, government, army, mass, or business organizations also had to obtain written permission (in fact, strong testimonials) from the heads of their units before they could take any university entrance exams. Discharged soldiers in civilian jobs could improve their chances of entrance if they had strong recommendations from their local civil affairs departments, as well as from their old military units. Returned Overseas Chinese, including those from Hong Kong and Macau, needed testimonials issued by Overseas Chinese affairs organs if they wanted to sit for the exams in competition with domestic students without going through any special preparatory courses. In practice, almost all applicants were in the process of graduating from senior middle schools.[30]

2. Local education bureaus administered the examinations, usually in late July, to all such certified applicants. The test questions were composed in the Ministry of Education and were identical for university entrance throughout China. The importance of test scores for admissions varied from year to year, but informants generally agree that the academic tests (when they were given at all) were significant in determining success. Students certainly regarded the exams as serious tests of their education.

All candidates had to take four sets of tests. Three were in Chinese, a foreign language, and politics. The fourth set was chosen from one of three broad fields of specialization, into which Chinese universities are grouped. Students hoping for entrance to

---

29. The national, provincial, directly ruled city, urban district, and county units described in note 1 above all have people's congresses. Each congress above the urban district or rural county elects representatives to the congress at the next level, culminating in the National People's Congress, which ratifies state actions and programs.

30. Interview with an ex-cadre not from Shanghai in Hong Kong, November 1969. This informant reported that there was no distinction between city residents and village dwellers, or discrimination against either group, in university admissions.

an engineering curriculum (*kung k'o*), including many applied
and some natural science majors, took their fourth set of exams in
mathematics, physics, and chemistry. (In Shanghai, Chiaot'ung
University generally had the most distinguished engineering departments.) Students applying for a physical science curriculum (*li
k'o*), including medical, agricultural, and some other sciences, took
their fourth set of exams in physics, chemistry, and biology.
(T'ungchi University was most famous in Shanghai for its physical
science departments, as well as for some construction courses.)
Finally, people who wanted to concentrate on a humanities curriculum (*wen k'o*), including literature, history, politics, law, and
art, took their fourth exam in history. (In Shanghai, Futan University was best known in these fields.)

Certain universities required applicants to take additional, special exams. Bourgeois students sometimes had an advantage at
these institutions. To take an extreme example, one entrance
requirement for the Architecture Faculty of T'ungchi University
was an ability to sketch well. This skill was not taught in most
middle schools, so the prerequisite discriminated against students
from poorer areas. In the classes entering this architecture faculty
between 1955 and 1957, only ten students (among an unknown
total) were of poor background and only one of these eventually
graduated. The failure rate was sometimes reported to be as high as
60 percent in special university exams required for matriculation at
such places. Poor-background students felt these extra procedures
were unfair.[31]

3. The test papers were read and graded on academic grounds by
committees of professors from relevant departments in local universities. The results, along with vouchers, school reports, testimonials, and other relevant documents were then assembled in the
city government's Education Bureau.

4. The most important stage of the university entrance process
was carried out by an admission committee (*chaosheng weiyüanhui*), which considered each applicant's exam results and other
documents. There was only one admission committee each year for
all university applicants taking their exams in Shanghai. Its mem-

31. Bruce McFarlane, "Visit to Shanghai" (Sydney, Australia: apparently at the
University of Sydney, 1968), mimeographed notes based on diary entry of April 19,
1968.

bership included distinguished representatives from many walks of life. (There was a single committee for Shanghai's senior middle school admissions, too.) The membership of the admission committee was chosen with considerable care. At least at the university level, it was apparently approved by the Ministry of Education in Peking.[32] Committee members usually had their primary jobs in other units. Some were seconded from Peking to do periodic "seasonal work" in the localities where selections were being made. These members provided "central leadership" for university admissions. In fact, the committee staff made most of the selections on the basis of the applicants' suitability in three main areas: grades on the entrance exams, social class backgrounds, and recommendations from secondary schools or employers. This information was supposed to be interpreted in the light of annual policy directives.

In some periods, exam grades were more important than social class. In other years, they were less important. Students from a wide variety of class backgrounds were regularly admitted before the Cultural Revolution. Especially after 1963, when some important reforms in both curricula and admissions were mandated from Peking, children from worker and peasant families were given some advantage in the selection process. Before 1963, the cultural advantage of bourgeois background students was generally more important than their political disadvantage. For example, only 18 percent of the 4,300 students at the East China College of Textiles in 1961 came from fully proletarian backgrounds and were regarded as politically reliable. Their admission was ascribed to their success on the entrance exams after attending factory spare-time schools.[33] Even after 1963 in Shanghai, where many of the applicants have always been from bourgeois backgrounds, a capitalist label would not of itself disqualify a good student, although admission to a well-known university might be more difficult to gain.

Nor was overwhelmingly great attention paid, in most periods in Shanghai, to candidates' social attitudes. Political reports on applicants' attitudes would have been more important in the admission process if their content had been less standard. Signs of political disloyalty or bad behavior could, of course, end a candidate's

32. Interview with an ex-university student from Shanghai in Hong Kong, December 1969.
33. NCNA, Shanghai, October 9, 1961.

chances for matriculation anywhere. The great majority of students had no such black mark against them and certainly were not eager to acquire any. The reports seldom distinguished one candidate from another. Positive credit for past activism was given where it applied; it was crucial only if current political campaigns made it so. In general, the academic test was a major hurdle especially before 1963.

5. The "student section" (*hsüehsheng k'o*) of each university decided, on the basis of the admission committees' reports and students' preference lists, which applicants to admit. At his or her main entrance exam, each student had received a form on which to indicate, in order of preference, the five or six universities he or she would like to attend. Shanghai students could always ask for Peking and Tsinghua universities, Harbin Polytechnical University, or *any* university in East China;[34] but provincial universities in other regions were ordinarily closed to them. This kind of geographical restriction, when it was enforced, probably caused more consternation among students of inland provinces than it did in Shanghai, where local applicants could specify some excellent universities.

In making its decision, a university's "student section" considered the number of places it had in various departments, and presumably it tended to accept the most highly qualified and recommended applicants on whose preferential lists its school name appeared. The extent to which the municipal admission committees made direct recommendations on the distribution of applicants to particular universities is unclear. Apparently, in most years, the universities' own offices made those choices, based on committee evaluations. The "student sections" were staffed by Education Bureau personnel similar to those on the admission committee secretariat. There were few policy options in this part of the procedure. The lists of various local schools were apparently coordinated at a higher level.

6. News of a student's admission was mailed home. Admission lists were publicly posted in some cases. Students who were not admitted to any school would receive no word, although they could

34. Interview with an ex-student of Shanghai's College of Law in Hong Kong, December 1969.

write to the admission committee and confirm their lack of success. A notice of admission from a university would include instructions on how to enroll and where to take a physical examination. Students paid for their travel to the university, but they could apply to their local education bureau for any assistance they needed. Tuition and maintenance costs were borne by the state.

A procedure similar to the one set forth above, with some variations according to campaigns, was used for all matriculations at least above junior middle school in the regular Shanghai education system through the decade 1955-1965. This general schema was as important for the students whom it did not promote as it was for those whom it advanced. A visitor to a junior middle school in Shanghai during the mid-1960s was told that usually only 15 to 20 percent of the graduates were accepted in general senior middle schools. A somewhat larger percentage could gain admission to specialized secondary schools. About 40 percent went straight to work in factories. The remaining graduates (presumably about 25 percent) were assigned to "communes and other organizations."[35]

These promotion rates may seem low, but they represented a major rise since the pre-1949 period in Shanghai. The general trend was for increasingly more graduates to remain in the educational system at each level, although there were some sharp wobbles from this trend. When labor requirement projections were low, the government may not have wanted such high promotion rates as had existed in years of major expansion, such as 1952. In the mid-1950s and early 1960s, the long-term advance in promotion rates was temporarily slowed.

POST-LEAP SCHOOLS AND STUDENTS

The post-Leap period was also characterized by great variety in the academic and vocational programs offered by different kinds of institutions. Gains in literacy during the preceding decade permitted more advanced programs than before in factory schools. By the end of 1961, 45 percent of Shanghai's regular workers had obtained junior middle school diplomas.[36] Although the factories continued most of their older full-time programs, some of the newer, academ-

---

35. Barry Richman, *Industrial Society*, pp. 143-145.
36. NCNA, Shanghai, January 8, 1962.

ically mediocre ones were dropped in 1961. Full-time programs tended to cause an unwanted expansion of labor staffs, because students had to be replaced on production lines. These programs were therefore largely succeeded by spare-time curricula. The Shanghai Plastics Factory, for example, had three kinds of schooling for its employees: a spare-time institute for regular workers, a "special" part-time training class for veteran workers who could spend some in-plant hours improving themselves, and another set of spare-time classes for graduates of the first two programs.[37] In a few factory schools where most students had considerable labor experience, however, the trend was to lengthen the academic study of worker-students, so as to enable them to "learn fundamental theories systematically."[38]

The main emphasis of factory-run programs during 1961 was on primary and vocational courses. Classes were increasingly taught by middle level technicians and foremen—the same men who were bosses on the job.[39] It is unclear how much the workers wanted to hear their managers lecture to them after hours, or how eager foremen were to disseminate their skills. Party organs were sometimes critical of the lack of ideological content in such courses, many of which reportedly had high registration but low attendance rates.[40]

The schools in the *minpan* system emphasized elementary and secondary education. *Minpan* enrollment at the primary level was as much as 17 percent of Shanghai's total.[41] The early 1960s saw a continued increase of *minpan* institutions. These schools still charged tuition; they often admitted candidates who had failed to enter the state-financed system; they sometimes had dormitories. The proportion of officially bourgeois students in 1961 *minpan* schools was probably large, although some students of proletarian background also attended. In theory, these schools were supervised

37. NCNA, Shanghai, June 9, 1961.
38. *KMJP*, October 5, 1961. "Theory" in this context referred to basic scientific knowledge.
39. NCNA, Shanghai, April 28, 1961. One ex-resident averred that "few of the foremen or workers were really interested in teaching or learning." This seems to be an overly negative report.
40. *KJJP*, May 14, 1961.
41. NCNA, Shanghai, April 9, 1960.

by municipal and district education officers.[42] Occasionally they received municipal subsidies, but in practice they were more independent than regular schools. *Minpan* schools could recruit teaching staff more freely than state institutions could, according to interview reports. The government was in no position, during 1961, to discourage any kind of organization that boded to reduce pressure on the labor market.

Because there were not enough places in regular full-time schools for all the students wishing to come, a movement began in 1961 to use radio to promote education more widely. The city's Sino-Soviet Friendship Association had sponsored Russian language classes over Radio Shanghai since Liberation, and these broadcasts had sometimes been coordinated with classes that met at night. In 1961, the Education Bureau and the radio station provided instructional facilities. Cadres of the Youth League and of the National Women's Federation were charged with mobilizing students to participate. By November, 310 "study groups" had been created. The pupils were "mostly youths and children who did not go on to middle school after graduation from primary school." These courses mainly provided vocational education. General subjects like history, geography, art, music, and physical education were not taught. The courses lasted three years before any certification.[43] A temporary advantage of this program, from the point of view of the government, was that it delayed the award of diplomas on which promotions and salary increases are partly based. At the same time, it trained students at a low cost and gave them a sense of advancement.

To serve similar needs at higher levels, Shanghai Television University (Shanghai Tienshih Tahsüeh) was also established in 1961. Its first office was a room on loan from Radio Shanghai.[44] Other TV colleges began at about the same time in Peking, Tientsin, Canton, and Harbin. The TV University had four departments: mathematics, physics, chemistry, and Chinese literature. Professors received no pay for their work, but the lecturers included quite a few distinguished academics from Futan University, from the pres-

42. Interview, Hong Kong, October 1969.
43. NCNA, Shanghai, November 7, 1961.
44. This and some of the other information below comes from an interview with a Shanghainese worker who studied in the Television University. A published source confirming much of the interview is *KMJP*, March 1, 1966.

tigious Chemical Engineering College, and especially from East China Teachers' University.[45] By participating in this new and publicly accessible institution, some of the professors may have hoped to avoid a "rightest" label during later political campaigns.

The Television University coordinated its broadcast programs with twenty-seven "supplementary tuition stations" (*futao chan*) that offered classes, laboratory sessions, movies, and examinations. Most of these centers were in the urban universities, which supplied professors and had extra laboratory and classroom space, especially on Sundays. County seats in the suburbs also enjoyed tutoring centers. The Television University was an important educational extension to these areas. Its programs, in coordination with correspondence courses, were also used to teach middle school math and science.[46]

The first year of the regular TV degree program was devoted to a preparatory course, in which applicants for televised higher education certificates could be, so to speak, screened. At least in the early years, most of the curriculum was not technical. The Chinese Literature Department awarded 35 percent of the degrees, whereas physics, math, and chemistry awarded only 26 percent, 22 percent, and 17 percent, respectively.

A television university presents special problems in maintaining academic quality. Shanghai students in most cases only had to watch the lectures, read their textbooks, and appear for exams. When scientific experiments were necessary, they were charged extra fees to cover costs. Among a group of shipyard workers who took the first preparatory class, 15 percent failed. Further attrition apparently occurred during the course. The academic intent of this program was at first very serious.[47]

Although the TV institution was called a "university," its diplomas were considered at best equivalent to those of a two-year college. By the end of the first year, 5,600 students were enrolled. Admission standards declined with the growing need, in the early 1960s, to use unemployed people's time. For this purpose, the main

45. The interview informant mentioned in particular professors Ch'en Chankuo, Li Jui-fu, and Chang K'ai-ying, although published references to them have not been found.

46. *KMJP*, October 28, 1961.

47. NCNA, Shanghai, April 15, 1961.

sector of higher education in Shanghai, the regular system, could not easily be used by manpower planners in the government. Only 74,000 students (2 percent of Shanghai's regular school enrollment) were in "higher education" during 1960. More than three-quarters of these people (56,000) were attending the 31 regular university-level institutions, and less than a quarter (18,000) were in spare-time colleges and universities. Even after 1963, when the need for labor in the city expanded somewhat, many workers were admitted to institutions of higher education. Few of them received diplomas. By the mid-1960s, enrollment at the large Television University, for example, was about 50,000, but only 12,000 had graduated since the beginning of that program in 1961.

POST-LEAP CURRICULA

By 1962, the general lack of economic resources was having severe effects throughout the regular educational system. The job supply remained stagnant because of industrial shortages. The govern-ment wanted to encourage active people without jobs to study so that they would be less inclined to have political complaints, but not all the schools could be kept open. At primary and secondary levels, many institutions closed.[48] At higher levels, there were changes in curriculum, postponed openings, and efforts to find new sources of funds.

The main official solution for this problem, even in the regular postsecondary system, was to stress vocational and political sub-jects for more worker students, whose expenses would be borne by the firms that employed them. Old universities like Futan, with a strong humanistic tradition, had admitted many workers. The local Party and Youth League set up ideological classes to supple-ment new work-oriented offerings for them. This vocational em-phasis was apparent among the 12,100 graduates of the summer of 1962, of whom 58 percent were in engineering, 24 percent in teachers' training, 11 percent in medicine, and 7 percent in science and agriculture.[49]

In the fall of 1962, further scrutiny of curricula and continuing

48. The closures were not announced in the press, and indications of them come from interviews rather than from documents or surveys.

49. *KMJP*, July 17, 1961, and calculations of percentages from absolute figures in NCNA, Shanghai, August 1, 1962.

economic difficulties probably explain the decision to postpone the opening dates of at least ten of China's universities. None of the postponed universities was in Shanghai, but several were attended by Shanghai students. By far the most distinguished university to be affected in this manner was Tsinghua. The opening date of the Sian branch of Shanghai's Chiaot'ung University was also postponed that September.

Institutions that survived this difficult period were the ones that had both some academic standards and some loyalist credentials (such as the Shanghai Municipal Part-Work Part-Study Industrial University) and those that had strong support from local factories and unions (such as the Shanghai Television University). Industrial sponsorship of new schools was increasingly crucial for their maintenance. A few welfare institutions (such as Shanghai's four special schools for deaf mutes, or its institutions for the blind) were also given resources from the general city budget, even during the period of shortages, because of their obvious humanitarian value.[50] Most schools, however, fared well only if they could persuade business cadres that their educational work had financial value for particular industries. Schools were eager to make all possible links with factories and commercial bureaus, so as to gain political justification by acquiring more explicit economic roles.

This commitment to specific local or regional constituencies became more general throughout the education system. Applicants to the Shanghai Teachers' College in 1963, for example, had to prove that they were local residents before they could be admitted; virtually all of them lived in the city or in nearby counties under its jurisdiction.[51] The Shanghai Electrical Machines Manufacturing School at Minhang, on the other hand, seems to have been under the authority of the Party's East China Bureau, and the percentages of East China residents and Youth League members admitted there rose after 1963.[52]

In general, the depressed state of Shanghai's economy during the

50. NCNA, Shanghai, April 27, 1962; see also the earlier report, *ibid.*, April 27, 1957.

51. Interview with a Shanghai person who studied at the Teachers' College, Huangp'u District, and reported on the period prior to 1964. URI, December 1963.

52. NCNA, Shanghai, October 12, 1963.

early 1960s weakened the educational incentives for approved careers. State control over the regular system became somewhat tighter at this time, especially as regards admission procedures. On the other hand, the factory and *minpan* school systems, which were responsible to more local authorities, became more important in Shanghai as a whole. Plant schools trained people for specific jobs; *minpan* schools trained those who had no jobs. A low level of urban prosperity corresponded with a fairly low effectiveness of educational incentives to socialist careers, because the state then had few resources to devote to occupational guidance.

POLITICAL EXPERIMENTATION AND REFORM, 1964 TO MID-1966

Because of the Socialist Education Movement's emphasis on politics and a leadership change in the Propaganda Department of the Shanghai Party Committee,[53] the mid-1960s was a period of intensive political indoctrination throughout Shanghai's educational system. Improved economic conditions freed more resources for schools, which were now required to serve more fully national economic goals. The central government continued to approve major heavy industrial investment for Shanghai and for only a few other Chinese cities. In return, Shanghai provided tax resources and skilled personnel to foster economic development inland, especially in rural areas. During 1963, central authorities mandated education reforms calling for students to do more manual work. Admission committees were ordered to favor more proletarian applicants, as noted above. Spare-time and *minpan* programs continued, but outside the regular system, part-work part-study schools were the order of the day.

SCHOOLS AND STUDENTS, 1964 TO MID-1966

In 1964, more than 350 half-work half-study (or half-farm half-study) schools were opened at primary levels in Shanghai. These

53. In the spring of 1963, Mayor K'o Ch'ing-shih appointed Chang Ch'un-ch'iao head of the Propaganda Department of the Shanghai Party Committee. Chang's previous career was as an editor-censor for the *CFJP* and as a radical organizer in ideological and cultural fields. He later became head of the Shanghai Revolutionary Committee, and by the late 1960s he was a major leftist figure in national politics.

supplemented the regular and *minpan* systems, and the percentage of students from peasant families who attended them was quite high. Some of the students were as old as fourteen. As one local newspaper explained it, "Although these students' educational standards are comparatively low, they will overcome this problem with hard work and with the help of the schools."[54]

In mid-1964, spare-time programs for school children were greatly expanded at the street committee level. "Extracurricular tutors' teams" (*hsiaowai futao yüan tuiwu*) were set up to help youths with their homework, to show educational movies, and to tell stories about the bitterness of pre-Liberation society.[55] Increasingly, schools were able to call on personnel from economic and military organizations to help take care of their charges in off hours. When the students of Woosung No. 3 Middle School took a "spring tour" (*ch'un yu*), PLA soldiers were invited to accompany them and tell them revolutionary stories.[56]

When the post-Leap recession ended, more funds were available to set up spare-time vocational centers at higher levels also. A local newspaper of mid-1964 reported that 130 new elementary and middle schools for workers had "recently" been built in the city. The government encouraged these "employees' spare-time schools" (*chihkung yehyü hsüehhsiao*) both because they were very popular and because it hoped to send political instructors into them, to encourage unemployed youths to make their life careers in rural areas rather than in the metropolis.

By mid-August 1964, three urban districts of Shanghai (Yangp'u, P'ut'o, and Chapei) and a number of suburban counties had established "agricultural vocation elementary schools" (*nung-yehch'uchi chihyeh hsüehhsiao*).[57] These institutions, administered at the very important rural county and urban district level, received major state subsidies. Graduation was synonymous with placement in permanent, high-level, *rural* jobs. Some additional

---

Since the beginning of that decade, he had had close ties to Chiang Ch'ing (Mme. Mao Tse-tung). He was the most important administrative figure (a potential premier of China) at the time of his arrest in the "gang of four" during early October 1976, one month after Mao's death.

54. *HMWP*, October 7, 1964.
55. *HMWP*, May 29, 1964.
56. *HMWP*, April 8, 1964.
57. *HMWP*, August 26, 1964.

new schools were established in the countryside to attract as many students as possible out of the city.

The most important and numerous of the 1964 half-work half-study schools were set up at low levels in the city itself, usually by factories. In a group of 50 such institutions, established by large enterprises by mid-1964, students generally paid for their own tuition, fees, books, supplies, and board. Under this plan, small bursaries were given to the offspring of poor families who were unable to pay such costs.[58]

As part of the effort in 1964 to reduce differences between mental and manual labor, no fewer than 30 small teachers' colleges were set up by local agencies to offer five-year courses for the training of instructors in mathematics, physics, radio, and mechanical engineering. Over this long period, the students were scheduled to spend 50 percent of their time in academic work, 40 percent in manual labor, and 10 percent on vacation.[59] They were responsible for finding their own campuses and arranging their own workshops. As was often the case for popularly initiated educational projects, the government felt little need to send many academic supervisors into these schools. Most officials who were sent down to such schools had political jobs, not academic ones. The masses' enthusiasm for education usually assured the establishment of some serious scholastic programs, even at low levels.

By late 1965, there were 1,051 part-work part-study schools in Shanghai, enrolling 118,000 people. At the middle school level, these institutions were educating only one-fifth as many students as the regular system, but they had important and increasing government support.[60] Within the regular school system also, full-time students were called upon to spend more and more hours at manual work and in political classes. Part-time university enrollment had remained fairly constant since the beginning of the decade and was 19,000 at the beginning of 1964.

CURRICULA AND TEACHING, 1964 TO MID-1966

In 1964, Shanghai schools emphasized technical and political subjects and Party officials did everything possible to ensure that

58. *HMWP*, July 3, 1964.
59. NCNA, Shanghai, November 2, 1964. The percentages were computed from numbers of weeks (131, 104, and 25) given in the source.
60. For example, see NCNA, September 5, 1964.

the mass movement for schooling would mobilize students along lines favorable to government policy. Politics was stressed at all levels, both during school hours and in students' spare time.

To strengthen political education in higher level schools, political advisers came from the PLA and lived at many Shanghai educational institutions, to help students "learn from the army."[61] These counselors, and others from the Youth League and Party, attended regular classes. They lived in the dormitories and held political discussions on all possible occasions. Students from proletarian backgrounds were asked to remember past bitterness and to contrast it with current sweetness. Those from the former exploiting classes were told to write about the bad influence of family history on their attitudes. Socialist education "work teams" directed similar exercises in Shanghai factories.

Despite these activities of the Socialist Education Movement, political values did not completely overwhelm academic ones. Work, including study, was still the best indication of faith at Shanghai's vocational schools. A graduate named Wang Lin-ho from the first class of the Shanghai University of Science and Technology received the undoubtedly magnificent title of "technical reform break-through general" (*chishu kohsin ch'uang-chiang*), but only after his thesis-project innovation in machine building had been presented for technical criticism at a public debate.[62] Matriculation and graduation at this university continued to be somewhat restrictive. Since the school's founding in 1960, only 479 "advanced workers" had been admitted. To be sure, all had been accepted on the basis of their "political soundness," but they also were required to have a cultural level "at least equivalent to that of a spare-time junior middle school." They were all under thirty years of age and had at least five years of work experience. Educational progress was made, although it was certainly slower than it would have been with a more academic admission policy.

When the worker-students encountered formidable difficulties in their course of studies, the authorities began to waver a little and tried to enroll more young workers with a higher cultural level. But after finding that these young workers were not much different from young students in gen-

61. *WHP*, January 18, 1965.
62. *HMWP*, February 27, 1965.

eral, they held to the original standard for enrollment.... Because of their older age and lower cultural level, it is difficult for worker-students to reach the standards of university graduation in four or five years. It usually takes eight or nine years. But although the worker-students have less book knowledge, they still possess a wealth of practical experience in production. They can, after some exertion, grasp cultural and scientific knowledge more satisfactorily.[63]

The Socialist Education Movement favored preferential access to education for proletarians. It did not abstractly oppose the values of expertise, even when its practical operation made such values difficult to achieve.

During 1964, the argument was not between those emphasizing "redness" and those emphasizing "expertise," but between leaders who thought these ideals could be unified in practice and others who wanted them specialized in different agencies, because of doubts that they could be merged permanently and effectively. In late 1964, for example, a Peking student wrote that both redness and expertise have their phases. He theorized that the chief task of the democratic revolution had been to fight. Although loyalty had been more important then for most people, "as the country now enters into a period of all-round socialist construction, the state needs large numbers of experts." Those involved in social work and politics obviously needed to be good ideologues, "but for technical people it is more important that they be expert." Political study was simply separate from academic study. "To my knowledge, no great scientist was versed in Marxism-Leninism. . . ."[64]

The opposite and more orthodox view was put forward by a doctor at the Shanghai First People's Hospital. He denied that "concentrating merely upon technology will serve the people." He pointed out that his professional colleagues liked to do research work "which will provide them with the 'capital' for winning fame and fortune; treating the sick becomes a losing proposition." In this view, expertise might be antidevelopmental. An emphasis on personal achievement above collective achievement can fail to serve the people. An emphasis on vocations can lead experts to "play the

63. *KMJP*, March 13, 1965; see the translation in *SCMP*, No. 3430, p. 7.
64. *CB*, No. 757, p. 6, translates the Peking article in *CKCNP*, December 24, 1964.

connoisseur" and to develop techniques that are too refined to be useful for economic practice.[65]

The seriousness with which the academic ethic was still taken can be measured by the fact that cadres wanted students to spend less time on academic subjects, and it was not easy for them to obtain student compliance. The principal of Yüts'ai Middle School called for more "all-round moral, intellectual, and physical development" among his students. He no doubt spoke for some proletarian students, who were outshone in class by former capitalists and their own brighter "class brothers." His views had sufficient high-level support in 1964 to command space in the important national youth magazine *Chungkuo ch'ingnien*.[66] A local newspaper reported that many educational administrators in Shanghai felt students had too much academic work.

Not long after the beginning of last term, the attention of the Education Bureau was attracted to the fact that students had too much school work. The Bureau organized specialists to study this problem. They discovered that students were busy all day long, doing homework and preparing for tests. In order to pass examinations, the students had memorized whole books. Schoolwork had weakened education in political thought and labor production. This was because teachers did not understand the Party's education policy.[67]

These administrators, however much they wanted politics to take command of Shanghai's schools, did not ever in this period entirely dismiss the purposes for which the educational system had been created. The value of "redness" was represented by bureaucratic generalists, while the value of "expertise" was mostly administered by teachers at the bottom of the hierarchy. No administrative level was completely immune to either interest. A certain balance between the two principles was in any case assured by the fact that different institutions had different kinds of sponsors.

The most important demand of some proletarian students in Shanghai during the Socialist Education Campaign was for more free time. Actual class hours were not cut in most of the regular

65. *CB*, No. 757, p. 22, quotes a Shanghai doctor's article from *CKCNP*, January 23, 1965.

66. *CKCN*, April 1, 1964. This school principal was criticized during the Cultural Revolution for stressing academics too much.

67. *HMWP*, April 7, 1964.

schools even during 1965. Surprisingly severe attacks were launched, however, in the autumn of that year against excessive homework, and above all against excessive, required extracurricular activities. The Communist Youth League was said to have interfered too readily in the students' lives outside school. League leaders even agreed to call for a reduction in the frequency of extracurricular meetings and events. Collective study was still encouraged during evening hours, especially for students who lived in the same neighborhood, but they were now supposed to organize it themselves, without League or Party guidance. Their morning or afternoon time off was to be left free from official demands of any kind. In one middle school, no less vital an enterprise than militia training was to be limited to one hour per week. No meetings whatever were to be held at school on Sundays. Extracurricular labor was reduced. Regular students were to be responsible for only about four hours of manual work per week. The children of the workers had to be able to control their time.[68]

This movement even encouraged official limits on the allowable amount of extracurricular political study. At Yüts'ai Middle School, the local Party branch in late 1965 directed that political classes were to be held only once each week—and then for not more than two hours.[69] Participation in recreational activities outside of class was decreed to be entirely voluntary. An official distinction was made between compulsory "primary activities" and optional "secondary activities." The only student groups in the school with official recognition were now the League, grade organizations, study organizations, and militia organizations for the senior-middle upperclassmen.

After these reforms were implemented, the rate of library use at Yüts'ai increased 34 percent, while the number of "absences because of sickness" dropped 22 percent in comparison with the same

68. *CKCNP*, September 7, 1965; article by the Youth League Committee of Shanghai's Yüts'ai Middle School. Canton *Yangch'eng wanpao* [Sheep City Evening News], August 29, 1965, translated in *SCMP*, No. 3539, p. 15, carries an even stronger statement to show that the proletarian youths' complaints there had been both acid and effective. In this context, it was demurely admitted that education cadres and teachers "had underestimated the ideological consciousness of the students."

69. *KMJP*, October 5, 1965.

period of the previous year. The students used the time to study harder.

In pedagogical terms, the main reform of the mid-1960s was the removal of student responsibility for knowing specific facts. Homework, ideally, was to be abolished; lessons were to be completed entirely during class hours. Examinations were not totally eliminated, but some institutions, like Chiaot'ung University, made extensive use of open-book tests.[70] This method was introduced in 19 different subjects, ranging from applied sciences to politics. Although the open-book system clearly had high-level political sponsorship, academic values still could not be excluded from grading. The criteria for success changed slightly, but some students still did better than others. This reform may have seemed more novel in China than it would have seemed in Western schools, because traditional Confucian teaching put a high premium on memorization.

The most basic effect of the reform lay in the new social uses of different kinds of ability. Access to books lessened the value of such abilities as memory. Slow or untimed testing lessened the value of rapid perception of formal analogies among new things. When students are allowed to consult with each other, then traits like personality and cooperativeness become vital.

A second major reform was in the area of student-teacher relations. Ideological education was easier to proclaim than to perform, because much of the teaching force had a bourgeois background. Cultural difficulties between students and teachers arose directly out of reforms launched during the Leap and post-Leap periods. An article in *Wenhui pao* by Ni Chi-kuang, Chinese language teacher at the Shanghai No. 60 Middle School, is worth quoting because it elucidates many problems that directives from educational bureaucrats could not solve before the Cultural Revolution:

I am the son of a revolutionary cadre. My family's influence has been comparatively good. When I attended a senior middle school, I used plain

70. NCNA, Shanghai, September 9, 1964. A dispatch of the same day from Ch'engtu suggests that Szechwan University and Chiaot'ung University were chosen jointly by national education cadres for the purpose of pioneering open-book examinations. In Ch'engtu, this method was used for final exams in about half of the courses.

language in writing—with relatively true and healthy feelings. However, my teacher always found my compositions emotionally dry and insipid. He thought my writing lacked the fun of life and was artistically untouching. I still remember he was full of praise for Li Ch'ing-chao's poem "Ju Meng Ling," saying that it vividly molded the image of a young woman confined to her boudoir. . . . In order to write well, to master the artistry highly recommended by my teacher, and to cultivate sentiments that would evoke my teacher's response, I began under his guidance to read avidly certain works of the "May 4" period that were full of petty bourgeois sentiments as well as foreign literary works of the eighteenth and nineteenth centuries. . . . I was no longer interested in collective life. My teacher, however, continued to praise me for having made appreciable progress.

It was with this idea that I went to my work post. Accordingly, in the course of teaching, I took over the "relay stick" passed on to me by my instructors. Deliberately or otherwise, I also passed it on to my pupils. Although my ideological understanding had been somewhat heightened in a series of political movements in the past under Party education and concern, I sometimes could not help spontaneously expressing my own thoughts and feelings.[71]

Conflicts between personal and collective goals must be dealt with generally and on a continuous basis in the school system, maybe more than in any other part of Chinese society. Teacher Ni adopted the existential notion that there was finally no way to reconcile his personal interests with the interests of the society he saw around him. With this logic, he had simply to decide on the priority of collective goals. This problem did not arise out of his personal or "class" background. It arose out of the post-Liberation Shanghai culture in which he had been brought up. It presented itself not in abstract terms but in practical ones. The problem was very wide in scope for a secondary teacher; his job was not just to find out *how* students should be taught, but also to help create or discover *what* they should be taught. He, like almost everyone else in the city, was willing to declare abstractly that China's collective problems and destiny were paramount, but it was more difficult to make them so in practice. In matters of organization and policy, personal refinement could simply be excluded as a goal, but in the daily practice of teaching, the personal pride and use of knowledge proved some-

71. *WHP*, April 20, 1965, as adapted from the original and from a translation that was generously made available from a file in the U.S. Consulate-General, Hong Kong.

what more difficult to exclude. Teacher Ni went about his job schizophrenically at first.

No wonder some students said: "At a class meeting our teacher conducted education about 'one red heart and two kinds of preparation' and urged us to cherish the ambitions of going to faraway places 'as fine sons and daughters do.' In the class for practicing writing, however, he promoted tender feelings between men and women."

Ni claimed that he had learned in practice from his pupils:

For instance, one student wrote, "I want to study Comrade P'eng Chia-mu [an official hero], his readiness to suffer personal losses for the sake of the revolutionary enterprise, and his Communist spirit of sacrificing himself and voluntarily becoming 'a piece of stone for road surfacing' for the cause of the Party. . . ." After reading this composition, I felt particularly touched and solidly moved. I found in it my greatest satisfaction since becoming a teacher.[72]

Instructors during 1965-1966 were increasingly held responsible for the political attitudes of their charges. Many teachers' forums were held at Luwan District Middle School, Chapei District Second Middle School, Shanghai First Girls' Middle School, and other places to discuss the extent to which teachers should be made accountable for students' ideological errors—and in practice, to conclude that they were indeed liable for blame in most bad cases.[73]

It was now official doctrine that teachers' preferences among their pupils reflected the instructors' class standpoints. During the Socialist Education Movement of 1962-1966, teachers were directed to change many of their old ideas: they were supposed to cease liking pupils who just studied hard, preferred "quiz games" and creative writing to work in Sinkiang, or were merely polite and obedient. It was asserted that there was no virtue in being obedient to an exploiter or polite to an imperialist. Above all, teachers were warned not to choose favorites whose tastes in music, sports, clothes, or literature resembled their own, because taste derived from class status and most Shanghai teachers were not proletarian.[74] If workers' children were late to school, or if they fell

72. *Ibid.*
73. *WHP*, March 20, 1965.
74. Issues taken from *WHP*, February 20, 1965. The Socialist Education Movement (*shehuichuyi chiaoyü yüntung*) was a particularly complex propaganda campaign, involving several distinct stages, which in many ways foreboded the

asleep in class, the causes might lie in their devotion to the collective labor of their households.[75] The city's teachers were told in no uncertain terms that their work should serve economic purposes and the preferred styles of the laboring class.

DIPLOMAS AND JOBS, 1964 TO MID-1966

Between 1958 and the mid-1960s, the number of technicians in Shanghai industries almost doubled.[76] During the same period, however, there were ten times more technical graduates than new technical posts.[77] At this high level of education, Shanghai was clearly supplying national rather than local manpower needs. To a lesser extent, this was also true of the middle schools. As a result of the lack of jobs in the city for people coming out of schools, the middle of the 1960s was a period of intense pressure on graduates to volunteer for *hsiafang*. Many of them could simply not be induced to leave Shanghai for long. Lower percentages of graduating middle school classes were promoted than had been the case during the Leap. Despite this, the widespread popular desire for education did not abate. The government therefore placed even more emphasis than before on urban work-study programs, but very few high-level graduates emerged from the spare-time system during the 1960s. In the first three years of that decade, all of the city's spare-time engineering colleges together trained only 2,000 certified technicians. In 1964, only 500 more were added to the manpower pool; so the rate of technicians graduating from these institutions actually declined.[78] Only 3,000 cadres, teachers and doctors had graduated from the spare-time system by 1964. Diplomas were awarded sparingly at the Television University also. Because of a

---

Cultural Revolution. Its rural aspects are well treated in Richard Baum and Frederick C. Teiwes, *Ssu-ch'ing: The Socialist Education Movement of 1962-1966* (Berkeley: Center for Chinese Studies, University of California, 1968).

75. *Chungkuo funü* [Chinese women], Peking, Nos. 1-2 (February 1, 1965), pp. 28-29, an article written by a teacher at Hsiangming Middle School in Shanghai.

76. NCNA, Shanghai, December 1, 1963, gives a figure of 82 percent from the end of 1958 to the end of 1963. Other articles cite figures in the same range for similar time-periods.

77. See my "Shanghai's Polity in Cultural Revolution," in John W. Lewis, ed., *The City in Communist China*, p. 350, which expands on this point and refers to statistics in *PR*, No. 41 (October 9, 1965), and NCNA, Shanghai, June 21, 1963.

78. Compare *HWJP*, September 19, 1963, NCNA, January 6, 1964, and *HWJP*, September 11, 1964.

persistent surplus of students over available posts during this period, more education was being dispensed than degrees.

Promotion politics in the mid-1960s were stringent, but the urban economy could at least provide some jobs for graduates. The medium and rising prosperity in Shanghai after 1963 made educational aspects of the career incentive system more powerful than they had been in either the more controlled 1958 economy or the depression of the early 1960s.

EDUCATION AND CAREERS AT THE BEGINNING OF THE CULTURAL REVOLUTION

Students from bourgeois backgrounds in Shanghai still had more hopes than jobs, because of the same partial stringency that made the state incentive system important for students from proletarian families. The frustrations of the first group of students contributed to the rise of Shanghai's Cultural Revolution. This book, however, is not mainly intended to explain that movement. The system of career incentives described here changed during the Cultural Revolution in many ways. During and after that time, reliance on the mostly material incentives that are described in this book gave way to an increased stress on the incentives of idealism. To some extent, the Cultural Revolution serves as a natural watershed and ending for the topic of this book. Some brief comments on the educational effects of the movement are nonetheless in order here, if only to show how many forms career control can take.

EDUCATIONAL IMPACT OF THE CULTURAL REVOLUTION

On June 17, 1966, Radio Peking announced a Central Committee decision to revamp China's school system. None of the recommendations was entirely novel. The Cultural Revolution at first only widened the application of reforms that were already being tried on an experimental basis in some schools. Chinese Communist practice, in this example and many others, was more continuous and less subject to quick changes than either radical or rightist accounts have usually depicted it. The reforms, when they were finally applied, were based on a mixture of values. The Cultural Revolution did not immediately alter the stated goals of the system. It reinforced them, communicated them to the public, and made everyone aware of the gap between official goals and actual achievements.

The reforms announced by Peking included many that were already underway in some Shanghai schools. The examination system was to be changed. Middle school students were to be sent out for work in farms and factories before graduation. Political values were to be considered along with academic ones in the admission process. The schools were to enroll loyal "revolutionaries." Half-work half-study programs were recommended. The purpose of the directive was largely to urge less talk and more action on previously proposed policies.

A minority of Shanghai's teachers were from true proletarian backgrounds, but they were important in the preliminary stages of the Cultural Revolution. At Hsiangming Middle School, most of the students were apparently of capitalist background. But a politics teacher, who was proletarian, organized the workers' children in a special nonofficial discussion group. His pupils reportedly increased their class consciousness and complained about various kinds of discrimination against the sons and daughters of laborers.[79] Groups of this sort were apparently the main academic recipients of Cultural Revolutionary directives that later began to call for "rebellion."

Dissatisfied students could now easily challenge school leaderships on a wide range of new issues. Already by 1965, the movement to combine education with labor had, in some schools, become a movement for "combining labor with rest," as the critics put it.[80] The pace of academic work slowed for both teachers and students. This change reportedly originated in proletarian demands, but it did not correspond with the belief of many leaders that China must develop furiously in order to develop fast. Some schools began to relax their educational programs more than a year before they were ordered to close for the Cultural Revolution. During the summer of 1966, students were organized into groups of red guards and revolutionary rebels. Many of them spent the late summer and fall traveling across the country, making contact with other students and visiting Peking in an attempt to see Chairman Mao. The

79. *KMJP*, February 5, 1965.
80. *Shanghai chiaoyü*, No. 7 (July 12, 1965); an example from Chingan District Third Primary School.

upheaval in national politics, combined with widespread student unrest and disputes over reforms in curricula, meant that most Shanghai schools remained closed in the autumn of 1966.

After the start of this movement, students found it possible to voice sharp criticisms of the content of academic courses. Some students felt their scholastic efforts were largely irrelevant to their career prospects, and they felt a need to castigate required courses in particular. At T'ungchi University, some radical students sometimes said their professors had a penchant for insipid platitudes. One of their mentors allegedly taught: "Architecture studies space and groupings of spaces. This is a new concept in architecture, without which you cannot design well." He also disclosed, "A door is a component of space. A door divides two neighboring spaces, to be both divided and unified at the same time."[81] Wisdom of this nature was said to have come from foreign models.[82] When a Shanghai engineering professor was asked to draw blueprints for a new bridge in Shanghai, he reportedly spent several months cribbing a French design of a bridge that had never been built in France. His student opponents claimed that 400,000 yüan were wasted in the construction of this span, which in any case could not be used for heavy loads.

How were these problems of Shanghai's schools to be corrected? Three specific reforms were proposed in local journals during early 1966. First, teachers were to do more manual work to overcome the "three separations" (from labor, from the masses, and from reality). Under the previous system, intellect had allegedly been valued for its own sake, and the removal of these barriers would make it properly instrumental. Second, less of the students' time was to be spent on homework than before. "Less but better" academic policies were to be adopted. More time was to be spent on organized extracurricular activities, especially physical education. Third, students would be encouraged to get rid of their "blind faith in books." Toward this end, they could do research of almost any sort that was not conducted in libraries.[83]

81. T'ungchi information is all from Bruce McFarlane, "Visit to Shanghai," entry of April 19, 1968.
82. See, *ibid.*, a reference to the copying of French and German journals. Compare with this the hilarious description of "German socialism" by Marx and Engels in *The Communist Manifesto*, Chapter III, Section I-c.
83. These three points are given more abstractly in *Shanghai chiaoyü*, No. 3 (March 12, 1966).

In vocational education, the "four-four system" arose in 1966. This was a plan to speed up the rate of rotation in part-work part-study schools.[84] Pupils were supposed to study four hours and work four hours each day. Some shop foremen reportedly complained about this system, saying that they had to spend too much time assigning unskilled students to jobs and finishing up tasks that were left incomplete. But the ideological worth of combining manual and mental activities in this way carried the day despite their complaints.

At the secondary level, the city of Peking supplied many models for emulation in Shanghai. General and liberal training was denounced in favor of training to develop social consciousness. Curricula were supposed to be devised collectively, and some programs called for as much as ten years of work-study in a single secondary school. Winter and summer vacations, and many other aspects of the previous schedule patterns, were criticized intensively. Schools were supposed to run more factories, and factories were supposed to run more schools. Open-book examinations were tolerated, but real purists felt that it was best to abolish exams altogether. Tests were said to "treat the students as enemies by carrying out surprise attacks on them." Some people suggested that diplomas should be awarded by student-faculty-worker-peasant-soldier "joint appraisal committees." Others advocated that people who were more advanced in ideology should "leap" grades. Lest any loyalist be forced out, a teacher was not allowed to flunk a student; such action required collective self-criticism and discussion in school revolutionary committees. Not all of these suggestions were adopted in Shanghai schools. By the time schools resumed serious teaching, many of these policies were thought to be "ultraleftist." Nevertheless, there is a close logical relationship between these reforms and the criticisms of previous years.

The Cultural Revolution did not lead to any basic change in the ultimate goals of the Chinese Communist educational system. It was instead a dispute over how, and how quickly, those goals could be implemented. Collective interests in the school system were reaffirmed; but because personal education can be used to help social development, its value was not completely denied. The Cultural Revolution, like the Great Leap Forward, was a period in

---

84. Cf. *Hsingtao jihpao* [Singapore daily], Hong Kong, May 25, 1966.

which the previous structure of material incentives for socialist careers nearly collapsed. These inducements were supplemented or supplanted by pure propaganda, persuasion, and politics to an extent that was unprecedented in earlier years.

CONCLUSION: PERSONAL AND SOCIAL GOALS IN A MODERNIZING SCHOOL SYSTEM

Because China's development requires citizens who are both capable and loyal, the Shanghai educational system has sought to raise general levels of mass literacy and technical skills, while imbuing the population with a commitment to personal self-sacrifice for national goals. From the individual student's point of view, however, schooling was also a prerequisite for career advancement in this Communist society. The public's demand for education, and the government's determination to direct it toward economic objectives, resulted during the 1950s and 1960s in a kind of compromise. The government made primary and junior middle level schooling almost universal, but it restricted access to the senior middle level and above. Sometimes a student's academic qualifications counted heavily in promotions to higher levels; at other times political qualifications were more important. To satisfy popular demands for education, factories and neighborhood committees developed semiautonomous spare-time and part-time schools for workers and unemployed Shanghai residents. These programs frequently required several years of study before certification, and their quality and usefulness in terms of career promotion remain uncertain, even though they eased the mass pressure for schooling.

Government controls over curricular content and access to education have sometimes proved to be effective in directing individual energies into the vocational areas desired by the state. In this sense, the regime's overall educational policy has been well attuned to national modernist goals and its ideological words "red" and "expert" are, in development terms, probably more complementary than contradictory. But there can be no doubt that the personal goals of individual citizens were often stifled in the effort to serve the interests of larger units. Personal freedom and collective development are consistent as ends, but the means of attaining them are often inconsistent. An individual's education can help social development, even though the citizen and the state can often conflict in their immediate interests. In a quickly changing country like China, the goals of educational and other institutions are often interpreted differently according to the different levels with which people particularly identify themselves. Shanghai data suggest that these tensions have been temporarily resolved, at various times, in response to changes in the city's general economic prosperity. To gather still more information about the mechanism by which this restrictive and developmental guidance system worked, it is necessary to look outside of the schools.

2

CITIZENSHIP INCENTIVES TO
SOCIALIST CAREERS

Anthropologists, studying various kinds of societies, have found that adolescents in many cultures must go through a "rite of passage" after completing their education as children. Some ritual test, often related to the youths' ability to support themselves or to found households, is a prerequisite to adult status. They do not become full citizens until they have passed this hurdle assigned to them by their community. Practices of this broad sort can be found both in complex societies and in less differentiated ones. In urban China, the "rustication" of youth is the most common rite at this career stage.

Ever since the Chinese Communist movement was pushed into the countryside from its urban bases in the late 1920s, its leaders have been proud of their ability to get along in rural environments. The task of teaching this adaptability to youths who have gone to school in cities is nothing new to them. It was an especially important part of the Communists' mobilization program during World War II, when many youths fled from Japanese-occupied cities to Communist base areas in rustic locations. After 1949, the Shanghai government attempted to make some residence outside the city a prerequisite for fully respectable and prosperous existence inside it.[1] This is a principle to which youths must adhere

1. Cf. Pi-chao Chen, "Over-urbanization, Rustication of Urban Educated

before their urban careers can gain official sanction. Rustication also serves many other purposes: It is a method of controlling urban population growth. It is supposed to diminish the differences between rural and urban areas and thus to improve youths morally by teaching them to work with their hands alongside the peasants. It is supposed to raise cultural and technological levels in the countryside. Most important for present purposes, this policy directs both rural and urban careers into socially useful channels.

HSIAFANG AND HSIAHSIANG

The Communist government has used many methods to reduce Shanghai's population. The most direct approach has been to organize groups of people and, by means of persuasion or material inducements, to cause them to move their residences to rural places. This method since the mid-1950s has been termed *hsiafang* (downward transfer). The policy nonetheless predates the term, which is used loosely in colloquial Chinese for a veritable grab-bag of assorted government measures.[2] By no accident, this same term has also been used to describe a different and more popular ideal in economic, military, and government organizations: the assignment of high status officials to do ordinary work alongside lower ranks, enabling them to understand the problems of their subordinates (without necessarily leaving Shanghai). *Hsiafang* therefore has positive connotations for most citizens when it is applied to bureaucrats, even if those same citizens sometimes resent the policy when it is applied to their own residences.

Hsiahsiang (going down to the countryside) is a more specific expression for the most extensively applied kind of *hsiafang,* even though it occurs less often in Chinese conversations. The word *hsiahsiang* also has some semantic inadequacies, because many people sent out of Shanghai have gone to smaller cities, rather than

---

Youths, and the Politics or Rural Transformation: The Case of China," *Comparative Politics* Vol. 4, No. 1 (April 1972), pp. 361-386, and D. Gordon White, "The Politics of *Hsia-hsiang* Youth," *China Quarterly,* No. 59 (July-September 1974), pp. 491-517.

2. See T. A. Hsia, *A Terminological Study of the Hsia-fang Movement* (Berkeley: University of California, Center for Chinese Studies, Chinese Communist Terminology Monograph No. 10, 1963), particularly on the multiple uses of the term *hsiafang.*

to the countryside, in order to do urban rather than rural work.

The diverse meanings of *hsiafang* may be somewhat confusing, but the best course will be to retain the term and use it selectively, because it is employed so often in multiple ways by the Chinese themselves. It helps to suggest how the Chinese relate many different policies to each other.

TECHNICAL HSIAFANG

A first distinction can be made between the technological and residential purposes of planned emigration from urban areas. Technical *hsiafang*, as the term will be used here, is emigration organized by factories or universities for specific economic purposes. Technical *hsiafang* frequently sends people to inland cities. One of the most important examples of this sort of movement was the establishment of a new branch of Chiaot'ung University in Sian by sending some faculty from the older Shanghai campus to live in the Shensi capital. Participants in this type of program are teachers, workers, foremen, or students—people with skills that are needed inland. Often not young, they perform relatively specialized jobs. Their sojourns away from Shanghai have sometimes been short. In the early years, the people who went out to rural places on this basis were not supposed to return, but by the mid-1950s this policy had changed, and their stays away from Shanghai usually did not exceed three to five years. Upon returning, their rewards were similar to or greater than what they would have received if they had not been sent down.

RESIDENTIAL HSIAFANG

A second type of send-down might be called residential *hsiafang*. This is commonly organized by street committees, labor recruiting stations, and middle schools. From Shanghai, some of the participants in the residential movement have gone as far away as Sinkiang in China's Northwest. Almost all of the volunteers are young, recruited in large campaigns after school graduations. They are supposed to remain at their new assignments permanently, or at least for a long time. Their work is often agricultural, although it may involve more mental labor, such as bookkeeping, than most peasants would do. The residential *hsiafang* movement could be further subdivided in many ways. In general, the new rural settlers from Shanghai help modernize the countryside by bringing to the farm their interests in doing new kinds of work there. Thus there is a broad, unspecific technological reason for this policy, too, even though participants are not selected because of their previous experience at particular urban jobs.

The technical kind of mobilization has a longer history than the residential kind. It is uncertain which type has had more economic importance for Shanghai, or for China as a whole. The dispatch of a small number of people with technical skills has helped new investment projects inland. The export of a large number of urban generalists has diffused some broadly modern culture and education out of cities. Both sorts of *hsiafang* have had a large impact on the careers of participants. Technical *hsiafang* is not necessarily a prerequisite for full citizenship, however, so this chapter will focus on residential *hsiafang* as a rite of passage for many youths, prior to their acceptance for careers in Communist Shanghai.

ATTITUDES TOWARD HSIAFANG

China's public has had an ambivalent reaction to government controls over education, place of residence, food, housing, and jobs. On one hand, the government has conducted a continuing campaign to make the Chinese people understand that such policies further egalitarian and national goals, which are widely popular. On the other, such policies—and particularly that of residential *hsiafang*—tend to restrict personal choices and drastically to affect individuals' life patterns.

The *hsiafang* campaign has never been attacked in Shanghai's public media, although during the Hundred Flowers period in 1956-1957 there was freedom to do so, and during the Cultural Revolution there were many criticisms of its administration. Instead, newspapers have emphasized collective support for the ideology behind such career policies, and they have dealt with the issue in a specific political language. Informants, on the other hand, often confess their personal reservations, using common speech. The existence of these different kinds of data does not necessarily imply the existence of direct conflicts in practice, for two ways of thought can often coexist in a single person. Many Chinese have frankly mixed feelings about the whole career system, and about rustication in particular. One informant, after reporting that "rightists" often regard *hsiafang* as punishment, went on to state:

Some cadres apply for *hsiafang* because they sincerely want to train themselves and to transform their nonproletarian thoughts and ideas. A few cadres of proletarian background, including some leading cadres, apply repeatedly for *hsiafang*. They request transfer to villages, to the frontiers, and to places of maximum hardship where the Party needs them most.[3]

The sincerity of this kind of idealism served to balance, at least for some people and for some time, the banality of the strains placed on them by the residence controls.

COMMUNITARIAN INCENTIVES BEFORE 1956

Urban patriotism has a history in wartime and postwar China. The political value of *hsiafang* was propagated in Shanghai even before Liberation. During the Japanese occupation, many students fled the city and went inland to Nationalist or Communist areas, where they worked to free their coastal home from foreign control. After the defeat of Japan, a few students continued to go to rural places— often for long periods—to teach peasants and to help the nation economically. In August 1947, for example, a group of students from Chiaot'ung University abandoned their annual examinations and went to teach village youths in southwestern China, where the Communist movement was not especially strong.[4]

INITIAL PATRIOTIC CAMPAIGNS FOR YOUTHS

The first effort to send down some Shanghai university graduates on a systematic basis involved the class of 1951.[5] Summer schools were set up to persuade graduates to rusticate. Jao Shu-shih, the most important political manager in East China at that time, and Shu T'ung, the local head of cultural affairs, delivered addresses at the inauguration of this program on July 23. For the first time, they called upon graduates to abide by decisions of the central government concerning the "unified allocation" (*t'ungyi fenp'ei*) of jobs for graduates. After one-month political courses, these youths with higher education were supposed to accept assignments anywhere in China, so as to help in national development.

3. Interview, Hong Kong, October 1969.
4. *Ch'ünchung*, No. 31 (August 28, 1947), p. 20. Also, Wu Shao-ch'üan, *Tao nungts'un ch'ü* (Shanghai: Shenghuo Shutien, 1947).
5. NCNA, Shanghai, July 26, 1951.

During the Korean War, the patriotic campaigns in universities and middle schools gave new impetus to *hsiafang* efforts. The momentum of this kind of movement was sustained fairly well in later years. In 1952, more than 6,000 Shanghai university graduates left the city to take up at least temporary work in other parts of the country, and 1,200 of them were given a grand send-off in the plaza of Shanghai Railroad Station when they departed for work in Northeast China, near the Korean front.[6]

Ethical education for *hsiafang* was temporarily cut back after the Korean truce agreement of 1953. When the first five-year plan (1953-1957) began to pump money into less developed inland regions, economic justifications and material incentives could be offered to induce educated persons to leave Shanghai. As a result, the moral campaign became somewhat less necessary. Summer field-training programs for university graduates were nevertheless maintained, and they now included underclassmen also.

In 1955, there was a concerted effort to extend this moral education to students from senior and even junior middle schools. In the early summer of that year, no less than 10,700 students began their "summer field work." Engineering departments cared for 8,300 of these, and many went as far as Anshan, Dairen, Changchun, and other industrial centers to see firsthand the virtues of residence in somewhat smaller cities. From Shanghai's teachers' colleges, 1,000 student-instructors went out to practice their pedagogical skills, although many stayed in the city for this purpose too.[7] From June 4 to 6, the Shanghai Student Alliance called a conference of representatives from *junior* middle schools, to discuss their career prospects after graduation. Pledges were given to "obey the state plan." A student representative promised, on behalf of his peers, that "those who can pursue further studies will do so, and those who cannot will happily take part in labor production. . . ."[8]

MORAL EDUCATION OF FAMILIES

It soon became evident that the intensified 1955 campaign would not achieve its goals if it were restricted to the school system. Ethical education for the parents—to urge them to agree to whatever

6. *HWJP*, September 13, 1952; NCNA, Shanghai, September 13, 1952.
7. NCNA, Shanghai, May 27, 1955.
8. NCNA, Shanghai, June 8, 1955.

assignments their children might be given—was at least as important as ethical education for youths. The local newspaper *Hsinwen jihpao* published a series of articles on this topic in July, in hopes of persuading a wide audience of parents. The Shanghai chapter of the National Women's Federation was particularly active in this campaign, because much of the assistance came from mothers. Meetings and discussions were organized to assure the parents of graduating junior middle school students that their "children have a bright future no matter whether they study by themselves, go on for further formal education, or join productive labor." Some forums were even held for the mothers of primary school graduates.[9] These students were of course still too young to go live in the distant province of Sinkiang, but they did not yet know whether they would be admitted to junior middle school. The Party clearly felt that no chance should be missed to obtain commitments years in advance from the mothers even of students who would be promoted in school.

Every year, some primary and junior middle school graduates obtained neither promotions nor jobs. During the mid-1950s, these children were organized into "independent study small groups" (*tzuhsüeh hsiaotsu*), which were under district-level education offices. The main purpose of these groups was to keep unemployed youths out of trouble and on call for any assignments that might crop up at times of low investment and poor labor opportunities in Shanghai. The "May 4 Independent Study Group" of Ch'angning District on most days spent the morning listening to "broadcast forums" (*kuangpo chiangtso*), run by Radio Shanghai and the Education Bureau to teach youth that they should accept state-assigned work.

From the viewpoint of the personnel cadres, it was of course important to place school graduates in jobs, but it was just as important to make sure that they remained calm and willing to accept any assignment until places could be found for them. Studies in social psychology have indicated that persons waiting for work, and uncertain whether they will have any, show just as much anxiety as those performing tasks under great tension. To relieve such strain, the Party emphasized the importance of students'

9. *HWJP,* July 2, 1955.

pledges. On June 16, 1955, all graduates of the Wuai Middle School wrote Mayor Ch'en Yi a letter saying that they would do anything the Party requested.

They guaranteed that they would respond to the call of the Party and of the government. They expressed their determination to obey the plan of the state, and to hold correct attitudes in dealing with future problems after graduation.[10]

The logical implication, which may have helped reassure the young graduates, was that the authorities accepted responsibility, too: they would eventually get around to allocating some legitimate and recognized jobs.

ECONOMIC REASONS AND MODEL CASES

The idealistic motives for compliance with this system must have been strengthened by the fact that a few people were given, and accepted, some very romantic hard work. In 1955, the first major campaign to send middle school graduates to the Northwest was initiated. This was a result of the 1955 Shanghai net disinvestment and stagnation in the supply of jobs, which in turn was caused by pressure on Shanghai's capitalists to make the transition to socialism. It had become clear, even before the placement-matriculation season of 1955, that Shanghai's new graduates would not find many local jobs. State plans were forcing the city's economy to operate with an even greater excess capacity in labor than in capital.

The Party therefore called a series of "young socialist construction activists' meetings" at district-run auditoriums. More than 40,000 unemployed youths were specially invited. The largest of these conclaves, held in the Workers' Culture Palace, was attended by Director of the Shanghai Peasants' Association Chang Yao-hsiang, by Director of the Women's Federation Chao Hsien-yeh, by Shanghai Youth League Secretary Li Ch'i-t'ao, and by many other notables who came "to express their warmest congratulations to the activists." Five young socialists at this large meeting read a joint pledge to find 95 peers and organize a wilderness volunteer team (*k'enhuang chihyüan tui*) to "go to the country's poorest part."[11] This campaign to send youths to the Northwest continued

10. *HWJP*, July 3 and 13, 1955.
11. *HWJP*, September 12, 1955.

through 1956. Within Shanghai, the program was as important for the economics of socialist transformation as it was for strengthening the Party's moral claim on urban people who were doing less self-sacrificial work. Shanghai experienced a sharp increase of technical *hsiafang* during the first quarter of the year, when 32,000 ordinary workers, more than 2,000 skilled workers, and 1,000 construction workers left Shanghai to take difficult jobs at Yümen Oilfield, on the Paokou-Chengtu Railway, on the Lanchow-Urumchi Railway, and on other projects in the Northwest. The number of intellectual youths who departed from Shanghai from January through March 1956 also exceeded the total who had left in 1954 and 1955 combined. According to one report, "most" of Shanghai's 12,000 junior and senior middle school graduates of that year were at least nominally pledged to join construction work "in the interior and frontier parts of the nation."[12] Many became teachers, and, at least in original intention, this kind of *hsiafang* was partly residential. Other educated youth went to help with oil prospecting and geological surveying in the T'ienshan Mountains of Sinkiang and in the Tsaidam Basin of Tsinghai. Some went to build new factories and farms in Kansu. A select few became soldiers on the Indian and Soviet frontiers. Others went much less far, some to build the Wuhan Bridge across the Yangtze. The inducements for people to comply with this campaign were partly restrictive, but they were also partly normative. Christopher Howe has described the controls on Shanghai's labor force in this period:

In 1955 the grip of the authorities was tightened further as a result of a detailed check on the work force, in which the work of the Labor Bureaus was actually merged with that of the Public Security organs.[13]

The reasons for job shortages and ration campaigns during these early years were explained in campaigns to persuade the people to make sacrifices for the common good. The quickly changing mixed economic situation was a concomitant of the first efforts to organize citizenship education systematically.

12. NCNA, Shanghai, April 1, 1956.
13. Christopher Howe, *Urban Employment and Economic Growth in Communist China, 1949-1957* (Cambridge, England: Cambridge University Press, 1971), pp. 114-115.

CARROT AND STICK TECHNIQUES, 1956-1959

During the years 1956-1959, the Shanghai government used a variety of methods to induce young people to accept *hsiafang*. Persuasion was the keynote of efforts during the Hundred Flowers period in 1956-1957. The antirightist movement after mid-1957, on the other hand, moved to discipline intellectuals by subjecting them to a combination of moral and labor education. In the enthusiasm of the Great Leap Forward, more people went down to rural areas than before, but these areas were more frequently close to Shanghai than they had been before. Also the assignments were more often temporary than permanent. Throughout these years, moral education and criticism meetings, the carrot and the stick in combination, proved effective tools to direct people toward selected careers. Shanghai's citizens also found ways to avoid some of these pressures and to lighten their *hsiafang* tours of duty.

PERSUASION AND ITS LIMITS
DURING THE HUNDRED FLOWERS

An important means of persuading young people to volunteer for rural work was to tell them of the good morale among contemporary rusticates. At first, selected Shanghai groups were sent to rural places where the *hsiafang* youths were already living. In 1956, for example, a drama and art team from Shanghai was sent to the Northwest, mostly to entertain workers at various construction sites but also to do some labor themselves.[14] This and other groups, sent to nearby Anhwei, Chekiang, and Kiangsu,[15] had one thing in common: their reports and letters-to-editors were intended to boost public tolerance for rustication.

Leading Party members within the city made ostentatious efforts to encourage the *hsiafang* campaign by giving assurances and honors to the families of sent-down students and workers. Deputy Mayor Sung Jih-ch'ang invited more than 2,000 of these family members to a public rally at the Shanghai People's Theater. He made a speech proclaiming, in general, that glory was inextricably connected with hardships. He criticized any regrets that these families might have had for sending their members off to distant

14. *CNP*, January 1, 1957.
15. *HWJP*, February 5, 1957.

areas. Shen Han, deputy head of the Shanghai General Federation of Trade Unions, then announced a list of special perquisites such families would enjoy. He said that trade unions should "give more attention to the work of caring for families whose members have been sent away." Specifically, he promised festive parties for them during the New Year season. He said that they would have the right to use workers' cultural palaces and clubs.[16] Meetings of this sort undoubtedly helped the *hsiafang* cause, even though—or perhaps because—everyone who attended them stayed in Shanghai.

Intellectuals also played a role in the persuasion process. Some Shanghai writers, who had been sent down during the Hundred Flowers period, published articles pointing out how well they should be treated for doing this public favor. Li Huai, a writer, expressed himself quite clearly in the main Shanghai literary journal of the time:

Young authors who are transferred to villages should not be treated in the way most cadres are, such that no attention is paid to them. Writers who are transferred to rural areas should be supported and cared for.[17]

Partially because of the liberal atmosphere in which such claims could be made, the March 1957 *hsiafang* campaign among Shanghai students brought some volunteers. The Party Committee of East China Teachers' University received 100 decision letters from groups of prospective graduates.[18] Important Shanghai leaders like K'o Ch'ing-shih, Wei Wen-po, Ts'ao Ti-ch'iu, Hsü Chien-kuo, Liu Chi-p'ing, Ch'en Lin-hu, and Li Ch'i-t'ao spoke at a "Representative Conference of the City's Graduates This Term." They emphasized that production work would not waste the graduates' talent. At this quasi-liberal time, however, there was strangely little insistence that the production had to be rural.[19]

Despite the liberal atmosphere, ordinary and obvious loiterers were not allowed to wander freely in Shanghai. The main purpose of liberalism in the city during this period was to mobilize the energies of the urban bourgeoisie. If directives did not specify which aspect of socialist construction youths should help promote,

16. *HWJP*, January 4, 1957.
17. *Mengya*, No. 12 (June 16, 1957), p. 31.
18. *HMPWK*, March 25, 1957.
19. *HWJP*, April 28, 1957.

the new graduates were nevertheless supposed to engage in something. No security bureau worth its salt missed a chance to make exemplary cases out of obvious miscreants. In one instance, a large group of "teddy boys and girls" (*nannu ahfei*) were rounded up by the Huangp'u District Public Security Subbureau for "treatment." Twenty-five girls were sent to a special reform school, and the boys were dispatched to a number of units—some of them economic— attached to the police system.[20]

Sometimes, in the effort to discourage malingering among prospective rusticates, the local newspapers reported very frankly about individuals who had refused to accept their assignments. For example, the Shanghai Power Machine School's Steam Turbine Specialized Class No. 308 had 44 graduates to place in early 1957. Forty-one of them accepted their assignments and went to work. The local placement secretary must have been a person of formidable principles, because he did not take the usual course of handing over his three stubborn cases to low-level Shanghai labor bureaus for eventual assignment to second-rate local jobs. Instead, he studied each of the three cases intensively. Investigators visited the brother of one reluctant student, who was from a family long resident in Shanghai. When they pressed him to accept rural placement, he said, "My mother will not let me go. Can you force me to go?" He was allowed to stay. A second student was also permitted to remain in Shanghai because he and his wife were involved in a divorce suit. "This could not be solved in a short time."

The third case was finally not excused. Investigators not only interviewed the dissident's parents but also went out to Ch'itung in Kiangsu to talk with his brother and sister-in-law. It was explained that the graduate's parents in Shanghai needed his care and would not allow him to leave the city. He was taken under the school placement secretary's wing and "educated several times." Finally he agreed to go, but he insisted on traveling by sleeping carriage. He also asked to be paid regular student stipends for the months during which his case had been pending. The school demurred, explaining that stipends were for enrolled students, that he would have received a wage had he accepted the job assigned him, and that he would

20. *HWJP*, November 19, 1956.

travel, like all sent-down graduates, on third-class "hard seats" (*ying hsi*).[21] No one ever seriously questioned the student's patriotism. He had, after all, volunteered.

Shanghai authorities based their appeal for *hsiafang* on moral principles in 1956-1957, but at the same time they reinforced it with implicit career lures. An example is a 1956 campaign to send 10,000 educated youths out of Shanghai "for various construction tasks of the state." The government made clear that these students' long-term careers would be affected by their response to the call. It also honored more than 1,000 compliant and activist students with official titles such as "three good," "superior level," or merely "good" (*san hao, yu teng,* or *lianghao*).[22]

Military conscription was also used to send able youths inland, where they engaged in nonmilitary work as well as national defense. Service in the People's Liberation Army has always been an honor in Communist China, and the military is able to recruit enough men without a draft. To increase the number of soldiers with special technical skills, however, conscription procedures were modified in 1956. The Shanghai Military Service Committee, the main local recruiting organization, ordered all male civilian residents of the city, aged eighteen or nineteen, to report for medical exams. Under a decision of the State Council in Peking, other Chinese localities also organized conscription at this time, but only eighteen-year-olds were involved, except in Shanghai, Tientsin, and Peking. The existence of modern skill pools in cities may be the reason why China bothered to have a conscription law at all. It was reported that most of the new urban inductees had qualified for admission to senior middle schools at least at the time they were drafted—an indication of their considerable talent.[23] Laws, honors, and education each played a role in directing youths' energies toward national ends.

Throughout this period, a combination of persuasion and coercion was necessary because the majority of people who participated

21. *CNP*, March 19, 1957.
22. *KMJP*, May 5, 1956.
23. *CFJP*, November 19, 1956; and *CFCP*, December 25, 1956. My colleague Gilbert Rozman has pointed out that the high educational level of Shanghai inductees is also partly a result of the fact that the pool of advanced students of that age group at Shanghai is greater than that in most parts of China.

in rustication were aware of both the collective benefits and the individual sacrifices involved in *hsiafang*. The ambivalence of popular attitudes toward the program is reasonably clear in press reports. Even the city cadres who administered rustication were happy to shift responsibility for rustication upward in the bureaucracy. When 18 prospective graduates from the Journalism Department of Futan University wrote a letter pledging to obey "unified distribution" in their career plans, they were encouraged to address it not to the placement secretary of their unit, nor even symbolically to Chairman Mao, but instead to the head of a ministry in Peking.[24]

RENEWED DISCIPLINE IN THE ANTIRIGHTIST CAMPAIGN

The antirightist movement, starting in the late spring of 1957, tightened administrative control over the *hsiafang* program and intensified the moral component of rustication propaganda. These changes affected the typical class backgrounds of rusticates and their tours of duty. After the antirightist movement was launched, the outward form of *hsiafang* meetings for school graduates did not change, but such meetings were less devoted than before to recruiting volunteers and more emphatic in justifying administrative assignments. The Shanghai Democratic Youth Union (an affiliate of the bourgeois parties allied with the Communist Party) held conferences to talk about decisions of the State Council concerning the placement of graduates in 1957. The purpose was as much to hand out information as to arouse enthusiasm.[25] The results of this businesslike approach were less ambiguous than those of previous *hsiafang* efforts. As Liao Shih-ch'eng, president of Shanghai Teachers' College, announced at a late graduation in August:

After practice in the antirightist struggle, this year's graduates tightened the reformation of their political outlook. We received an unremitting stream of decision letters requesting assignments to work in the most arduous places.[26]

Most of the graduates were Shanghai people, and a third of them had accepted jobs in distant places. This pattern was also apparent

24. *CNP*, March 19, 1957.
25. *HWJP*, July 25, 1957. See the index for romanizations of the Chinese names of the Democratic Youth Union and other organizations.
26. *HMPWK*, August 10, 1957.

at a conclave of the city's Higher Education Bureau on July 26, when graduate representatives from many Shanghai schools pledged on behalf of their peers to obey the Party's distribution of jobs.[27]

The rate of ostensible compliance was no less impressive at secondary schools. Ch'en Lin-hu, head of Shanghai's Education Bureau, convened a "General Meeting of This Term's Middle School Graduates"—or, in fact, of their representatives—at which all were urged to participate at least temporarily in agricultural production.[28] During the summer of 1957, no less than 30,000 middle school students went to voluntary labor in Shanghai's suburban fields.[29] Those who had already graduated were given responsible jobs in cooperatives; some became veterinarians, accountants, and tractor operators; others worked as ordinary field laborers.[30] The Shanghai Communist Youth League, whose members could look forward to longer and brighter careers than any other group in the city, held a meeting of its activists to stress that "individual interests should be subordinate to the interests of the Party."[31] The people who were asked to participate in the send-down apparently had ambiguous feelings about it, but the program in late 1957 was large enough that individuals could not convincingly claim unfair treatment.

Shanghai's government, Party, and mass organizations coordinated their efforts in directing various aspects of the *hsiafang* program. The municipal organs took administrative control of assignments. The Party focused on the moral education of volunteers, making claim on all important careers. The mass organizations served as recruitment channels. Explicit economic rationales for the *hsiafang* policy were now clearly overridden by moral ones. The send-down campaign sought to make people better by subjecting them to labor education. Students were no longer the only targets; older intellectuals were also sent to labor reform camps in 1957. The most important mass organization involved in *hsiafang* was still the Communist Youth League, but the municipal

27. *HWJP*, July 27, 1957.
28. *HWJP*, August 2, 1957.
29. *HWJP*, July 21, 1957.
30. *HWJP*, July 26, 1957.
31. *HWJP*, August 14, 1957.

branches of two other associations for bourgeois people, the Democratic Youth Union and the Students' United Youth League, were also active in this work under the guidance of the Youth League.[32]

Moral education and tightened administrative procedures were more effective at controlling careerists who wanted "white-collar" jobs than at controlling people who were willing to trade low status for urban residence. In practice, these techniques worked most effectively on the people for whom the Party had mainly designed them—those with capitalist backgrounds. In the first few months of 1957, for example, a patriotic campaign for *hsiafang* put many educated Shanghai youths into socially useful positions elsewhere. Nevertheless it is probable that some people who were repeatedly sent out of the city returned many times. The regime's incentives and career controls were apparently less effective with laborers, especially trade union members who held regular jobs in the city, than with most ex-capitalists. They also had less effect on peasants, who were willing to take hard, low-status urban work.

The city thus slowly became more proletarian. Shanghai absorbed many people with relatively few skills and then educated them. Statistics on the class composition of Shanghai's immigrant community since 1949 are not available. It is likely that many of those who managed to remain in Shanghai were of nonproletarian origin, but because of the differential effects of the career guidance system, the proportion of proletarians was probably rising. The city's population may also have become somewhat less prone to consume luxury goods than would otherwise have been the case. There may also have been a tendency for the urban work force, under potential pressure from the career system, to accept low wages.

Although *hsiafang* administration during the antirightist period became more effective in recruiting intellectuals and students, the conditions of service for rusticates were often less arduous than before. The first 1957 contingent of students who left the city for purely residential *hsiafang*, in late August, contained only 362 members.[33] The second group of students went only as far as the three suburban districts of Shanghai at that time (east, west, and

32. *HWJP*, November 18, 1957.
33. *LTP*, August 23, 1957.

north), and they were spread among 22 agricultural cooperatives. They probably had more contact with peasants than typical participants in any other *hsiafang* before the Cultural Revolution. Yet on weekends, or even in a single day, they could easily take a bus into the city and visit family and friends.[34] In December, a group of 1,000 graduates (mostly from Yimiao and Hsinch'eng urban districts) went to the suburbs for work in their school groups.[35] The 290 volunteers from Yimiao District could even hike to their agricultural producers' cooperatives in the East Suburban District, and 100 of the 271 from Hsinch'eng District went to a single cooperative in Hungch'iao Township, near the airport. These people were supposed to live permanently in their new, semirural settings, just as they might have lived in dormitories, if they had been assigned to factories or higher schools. No less painful form of *hsiafang* was ever developed. But the functionaries thought that this quasi-industrial, rural send-down had to have its propaganda meetings in the usual style, lest morale sag among the volunteers' families. At one such assembly, held in P'englai District, careful cadres followed precedents that had been set for gatherings of the parents of rusticates sent to Sinkiang in the extreme Northwest. It was convenient, as well as ironic, that the youths could now be invited to hop on a bus from their rural workplaces, in order to attend the meeting.

The increased emphasis on discipline and moral education during the antirightist period was also directed at various kinds of antisocial behavior. The *hsiafang* movement was sometimes used to control such activity. In dealing with many capitalist-class youths in urban Shanghai, the antirightist movement focused on a new, narrow conception of "law and order." Criticisms often dealt with simple police issues. Some persons who could not be promoted in school were sent out of the city so that the government might control them more easily. Others managed to remain. A harbinger of new disciplinary measures was a newspaper headline declaring, "Teddy Boys and Juvenile Delinquents Run Wild in Shanghai."[36] China's newspapers at this time were full of admoni-

34. *HWJP*, August 31, 1957. A third group of 196 students in this program set out from Shanghai on September 13; see *HWJP*, September 14, 1957.

35. *HWJP*, December 26, 1957.

36. *Chiaoshih pao*, June 25, 1957.

tions to fight the lures of capitalism and rightism, and to study hard at school so as to serve the people later. In June, the Shanghai Federation of Trade Unions called a forum for young workers. Mao's speech, "On the Correct Handling of Contradictions among the People," was discussed, but the distinctions made in this politically flexible discourse were reported to be for the most part beyond the youths' comprehension. Youths were officially supposed to conclude that because they were not very adept at thinking about politics, they had better follow orders:

All the young workers held that because they had little experience, they knew little about policy. They had been unable to distinguish clearly the right from the wrong, and they always made disturbances in the city. Their actions were therefore disadvantageous to the working class, to socialist construction, and to themselves.[37]

A young car repairman grumbled that hooligan gangs sometimes caused fracases on public buses. A prim salesgirl complained that some youths (following an old bourgeois custom) tried to bargain with shopkeepers when they bought things. A woman garment worker protested that rowdies "always follow the night-shift female employees." A young electrician asserted that "the teddy boys [*ahfei*] are created by capitalist thought."

Under this official line of the second half of 1957, any previous distinction disappeared between real rowdies, unemployed graduates, youths not registered in the city, and people who had returned without authorization from residential *hsiafang*. All were treated alike. All could redeem themselves by behaving like leftists.

In the autumn, when the "basic victory" of antirightist reeducation had strengthened the Party's control over the careers and aspirations of Shanghai's people, the government put forth a new set of rules for dispensing penalties in public security work.[38] These procedures emphasized sending people out to the country for moral reform. Shanghai shortly thereafter created a municipal Labor Education Committee. The committee made pronouncements justifying the need for ethical education, and it apparently

37. *HWJP*, June 22, 1957.
38. *HWJP*, October 27, 1957. Also: "Chunghua jenmin kunghokuo jenmin chingch'a t'iaolieh" [Regulations of the People's Police of the Chinese People's Republic] in *Chunghua jenmin kunghokuo yukuan kungan kungtso fakuei huip'ien* (Peking: Ch'ünchung Ch'upan She, 1957), pp. 94-98.

took considerable responsibility in guiding residential decisions during the next few months.

THE LEAP: IDEALISM AND DIVERSITY

The *hsiafang* movement continued during the Great Leap Forward, but the idealism of the Leap, when it combined with some decentralization of decision-making to provincial levels and some centralization in towns and communes, made for great diversity and different rustication programs.

The national government in Peking apparently did not send detailed orders to local education bureaus concerning rustication in the Leap. Shanghai does not seem to have had any large, nationally set quotas for personnel to be sent down during 1958. The result was a good deal of improvisation, many problems of coordination, and a tendency for youths to go to nearby provinces rather than to the borderlands. The participants were nonetheless numerous. Their tenures in rural areas were sometimes rather long. In August, for example, 600 teachers and students of Futan University's journalism and economics departments were sent to Anhwei and Kiangsu to work for one year.[39]

In Shanghai, after the first spring graduations during the Leap, plans to mobilize more youths were drawn up quickly. On April 18, 13,000 youths rallied on Culture Square to "state firmly that they want to go to Hupei and Anhwei."[40] On the following day, 11,175 of them actually applied to go. Hsinch'eng and Yimiao districts were cited in newspapers as having the most successful registration drives in this campaign.[41] Within the first four days, some 22,000 people signed up in those districts alone. A local paper noted, perhaps sheepishly, "The number of applicants that the two provinces expected was 12,000."[42] The effectiveness of middle-level mobilization apparently exceeded even the Party's expectations. On May 4, the first group of youngsters left Shanghai.[43] Five hundred Shanghai intellectual youths, destined for Hupei villages, had already arrived in Wuhan by May 8.[44] One news report said

39. *HWJP*, August 30, 1958.
40. *HWJP*, April 18, 1958.
41. *HWJP*, April 20, 1958.
42. *HWJP*, April 23, 1958.
43. *HWJP*, May 5, 1958.
44. *Ch'angchiang jihpao* [Yangtze daily] (Wuhan), May 8, 1958.

that 44,000 Shanghai intellectual youths had registered for rural send-down in early September 1958, although the provinces had not yet found places for so many.[45]

Educational institutions sometimes undertook to set up rural farms of their own. There they could control the terms of work while still remaining faithful to the national Great Leap movement. Thus school term schedules were often coordinated with agricultural cycles. Futan's philosophy department sent 120 teachers and students to a single commune at Haining in Chekiang, where they remained from March until the end of October.[46] They were on the farm from the planting of first-crop rice to the harvesting of the second crop.

The meaning of *"hsiafang"* was not at all standard at this time. Many alternative forms of service existed by which people and organizations could show their patriotism. A refugee informant said there was no regular system for these arrangements:

A school could send personnel of its own down to contact the peasants. Conditions always varied. Some of the communes would lend their land freely, and some would demand a certain percentage of the crop at harvest time. . . . We did not need the help of the peasants to work the land we borrowed. Sometimes, we would ask old peasants to come and give us lectures on how to plant the crops, however. This kind of farm was only for the purpose of education in labor, and *hsiafang* personnel would not stay in those places forever.[47]

This kind of nontechnical non-*hsiafang* was common both during the Leap and later. In practice, it reduced the claims on many intellectuals for more strenuous kinds of send-down. They could assert that on branch farms they were fulfilling their duty to the nation. In reports, they could deemphasize the relative painlessness of these schemes.

Many of the Shanghai students and teachers sent down to the countryside in 1958 did not become full-time field workers but served as rural instructors. Educational promotion was, in effect, offered to some youths only on condition that they go inland. Between the beginning of the Leap and October 1958, 40,000

45. *HWJP*, September 8, 1958.
46. *Hsüehshu yüehk'an*, No. 9 (September 1958), p. 37. The scholar-author of this article stayed at Haining for only 20 days.
47. Interview, Hong Kong, December 1969.

Shanghai youths were sent from Shanghai to inland provinces. Three-quarters of them worked on farms, but many were teachers there. The rest became students in "middle-level technical schools in Tsinghai, Sinkiang, Kansu, Kweichow, Anhwei, and Kiang-si."[48] Promise of further schooling was an effective bait for volunteers at a time when purely residential controls in the city were rather weak. This educational lure could be offered quite openly during the Leap. Propagandists could argue in this optimistic period that improvement of the country was naturally compatible with individuals' ambitions for personal improvement, especially when the education took place in undeveloped inland places.

Special efforts were made to maintain good Leap morale among students sent down to distant provinces. In November 1958, a forum of Shanghai students in Tsinghai Province was called at Sining. The 60 representatives were studying agriculture, forestry, hydro-electrics, geology, light industry, coal mining, public health, highway construction, nursing, telecommunications, finance and economics, machine building, petroleum industry, meteorology, railway engineering, and "culture and art" at 16 secondary technical and specialized schools. A deputy governor in the local province administration urged that the youths "discard worries, overcome defeat and difficulties constantly, and be good students in all respects, ... combining education with production."[49] He said that if they found weaknesses in the education they were receiving, they should "point them out directly to the school authorities and help the leadership improve that work." In Shanghai, these youths would probably not have been in school at all. The Party clearly wanted them to feel that in Tsinghai they would be bigger frogs even if in a smaller pond. Some of the volunteers in this period earned great distinction in their *hsiafang* posts. A nineteen-year-old Shanghai girl was reportedly elected by local peasants to be their deputy to the Yihsien County People's Congress in Anhwei, even though she had arrived only four months before the election.[50]

Many *hsiafang* tours of duty in the Leap consisted of short-term work in Shanghai's rural communes. The autumn of 1958 saw the

48. *HWJP*, October 12, 1958.
49. *Ch'inghai jihpao* [Tsinghai daily] (Sining), December 2, 1958, translated in *SCMP*, No. 1960, p. 14.
50. NCNA, Hofei, May 23, 1958.

recruitment of a "labor army" (*laotung tachün*), which became a seasonal institution to aid summer and autumn harvests. It continued in various forms long after the Leap had ended. This limited form of *hsiahsiang* had both educational and economic values. Urban units of many kinds formed teams and brigades to help bring in the harvests of Shanghai's suburbs. Because large groups of people worked as integral units for short periods only, their "voluntary" decisions to participate were made collectively rather than individually. In this period and some others, the main real "persons" of Shanghai's politics were collective groups.

The labor army was formed along the principle of "following the military pattern in organization, the combat pattern in action, and the collectivist pattern in living."[51] Rural harvesting was a work assignment like any other and was accomplished in urban occupational organizations. Labor brigades and smaller units were created in government offices, in factories, in student bodies, in faculties, in clubs, and even in regular army units. On just two days, October 18 and 19, no less than 120,000 people took up "their labor obligations" in all the counties of the greater Shanghai Municipality (as well as in Ch'uansha, Nanhui, and Ch'ingp'u counties of Kiangsu, which were soon to be added to the city's jurisdiction). Other volunteer groups soon followed. They performed "three autumn jobs," i.e., harvesting major crops, planting, and harvesting small crops.[52] They deep-plowed (*shenfan* or *shenkeng*) 13,000 acres of land, transported seed for more than 3,600 acres, and sowed more than 4,800 acres. They picked no less than 3,800 tons of cotton. This was nothing in comparison to the 720,000 tons of fertilizer that they transported to storage. They also did roadwork. On the lighter side, they selected some new species of grain to plant.[53] The work experience affected many people. It may have taken some romance out of the urbanites' view of agriculture, but it also gave some of them a bit of farm experience. For some, it may have laid a basis for more realistic assessments of the way the majority of Chinese people live.

51. NCNA, Shanghai, October 20, 1958.
52. *Sanch'iu laotung* divides into: *ch'iu shou, ch'iu chung, hsiao ch'iu tsowu ti chouhuo.*
53. *HWJP*, November 21, 1958. These figures, some of them fantastically high, have been converted from the original catties, piculs, and mou.

Nevertheless, city people often found it difficult to adjust to rural life. A labor training school for cadres at the "East Is Red" Commune of Paoshan County, Shanghai, reported "periods of high and low spirits" among people who were sent there for long spans of time. The same emotional sine-curve was noted among some office workers who were expected to go to the suburbs for long periods to do agricultural work. At this commune, the average urban participant put in 180 labor-days, but there was also a category of "cadres whose major job is not labor." These bureaucrats contributed only about 20 labor-days each. According to a Shanghai magazine article, the first low-spirit period ordinarily occurred at the beginning of an individual's *hsiafang*, particularly if he were assigned very hard work in the first few days. There was also a danger, especially after harvests and planting times, that functionaries would become "too satisfied with their work" and allegedly suffer another so-called "low-spirit period" because of their consequent low production then. It was frankly admitted that "many cadres use their [rural] social work as a pretext to avoid field labor. In some areas, 50 percent of the cadres were completely cut off from labor, and the rest were partially cut off from labor."[54] At "East Is Red" Commune, 228 *hsiafang* cadres from nearby Shanghai took up jobs as work-point recorders and procuring agents at different levels of the commune Party organization. Among these, 112 leading cadres were above the platoon chief (*p'aichang*) level. To keep these city cadres working on the farm, it was best to give them "social" work to do. In self-defense, officials pointed out that sometimes "villages need political struggle," and then "most of the *hsiafang* cadres take charge of lower-level affairs in the villages."[55] One reason for the enthusiasm of the Leap may be found in the fact that many cadres, recently sent to rural areas, would have had to do even more manual labor, if they had not instead spent their time mobilizing people for the great new national movement.

The idealism of the Leap, and the considerable if brief prosperity in 1958, certainly furthered citizenship education even while weakening its long-run material supports. The spirit of that time could be applied only unevenly.

54. *Futan*, No. 2 (February 1959), p. 14. An ex-resident of Shanghai, to whom I showed this quotation, replied that the situation it describes was "quite usual with *hsiafang* cadres."
55. *Ibid.*

THE PERIOD OF RETRENCHMENT, 1960-1963

Hsiafang during the Great Leap Forward had largely been administered by work places and was based on group voluntarism. The excesses of the Leap, and the resulting shortages of food and materials during the early 1960s, changed the motivations of volunteers. Moral education came to play a less important tole in inspiring the send-down. Fewer high cadres had to make examples of themselves by going to work in the fields; they had only to report enough participation by various unit members so that higher levels would be satisfied. One ex-cadre confessed that "the functionaries who joined *hsiafang* to lower levels were not high-placed, responsible personnel."[56]

Working people were selected for *hsiafang* by Party personnel departments and government organization departments in their offices, factories, and schools. The files kept by these organs assumed greater importance than they had in the Leap, because fewer jobholders were now chosen to go.

Students' *hsiafang* also became more selective in the post-Leap recession. By early 1961, Shanghai Teachers' College was sending its graduates to work in rural areas, and for this purpose it "investigated the graduates' thought and their specialized knowledge." These graduates had all entered college after the "educational revolution" beginning in 1957-1958 and had received a good deal of political instruction. Many "came to the Party with requests that they should be accorded the honor of spending their whole lives in the countryside as school teachers."[57]

To encourage this ambition, and to provide more central organization than the 1958 Leap had allowed, the local Education Bureau and Youth League jointly called summer conferences of middle school graduates' representatives. Parents, teachers, and previous rustication returnees spoke at these meetings. Ch'en Lin-hu, head of the Education Bureau, explained that "The fundamental goal of education is to develop social production." Graduates' plans therefore "had to mesh with the economic conditions of the country." He promised that "proper arrangements will be made for those who cannot go on for further study." This representative conference

---

56. All information in this paragraph is from an interview, Hong Kong, October 1969.
57. *KMJP*, May 6, 1961, dispatch from Shanghai.

wrote a letter to all middle school seniors that year, urging them to "keep a red heart and be ready for anything."[58] The next annual meeting in 1962 was thoroughly similar.[59] By 1963, these educational conferences had become routine, and they were extended to include representatives of university graduates in the city.[60]

PROPAGANDA AS A SUBSTITUTE FOR PROSPERITY

In the post-Leap recession especially, the Party did not use social coercion to encourage Shanghai students' *hsiafang*. Because of some urban discontent caused by the food shortage, the government felt easiest when it did not push people too hard. National propagandists for *hsiafang* saw a special need to highlight cases in which family members persuaded each other of the program's value. When a young university graduate was depressed about his assignment to a small factory in Shantung, his uncle (a major in the army) and his elder brother showed him the errors of his thinking. When a northerner went to work in Fukien, his parents and wife pestered officials with requests for his return home. The rusticate himself wrote letters to his family decrying their mistaken attitudes. Eventually, they accepted the Party's viewpoint, too.[61]

Some published descriptions of the opportunities available to school graduates sounded very permissive:

There are many outlets: some persons will join a higher school; some will go to the countryside; some, who cannot go to a higher school this year, will stay at home to make up their lessons so that they may sit for the entrance exams again or take up work next year; some will join the armed forces; and some will take up financial, commercial, or other kinds of work. All these arrangements are good.[62]

An ex-cadre informant described the propaganda for early 1960s *hsiafang* in more concrete but similar terms:

In middle schools and universities, there were many ideological meetings before each graduation day. Every student was told that he should have "one red heart and two kinds of preparation" (*yik'o hung hsin, liangchung*

58. *KMJP*, August 9, 1961, dispatch from Shanghai.
59. *KMJP*, June 12, 1962.
60. *HMWP*, June 9, 1963.
61. *KJJP*, December 13, 1962.
62. *Shihshih shouts'e* [Current events handbook], No. 11 (June 6, 1962), translated in *SCMM*, No. 325, p. 13. See also another article in *CKCNP*, August 14, 1962.

chunpei). This meant that if he passed an entrance exam, he would be promoted; if he did not, he would be transferred to the countryside. But there were many people who did not want to go to the countryside after graduation. In the short period following commencement, each school had to undertake the work of persuasion. Many students who failed the exams would go to the meetings, but not all the students in attendance wanted necessarily to go to the countryside. Even those who did not join such meetings could not easily escape being transferred, because the school would send people to visit their families. Teachers and activists [those who had decided to go to the country] would do the work of persuasion, and street cadres would join in, too. But as time passed on, and as the campaign faded, the school would not care about the transfers any more. They would leave the whole matter for the street committees to handle.[63]

An invitation to a farewell party for volunteering classmates put pressure on a student to volunteer for a later contingent. The ex-cadre refugee who provided information on this topic (a strong upholder of *hsiafang* policies) said, "Frankly, these farewell parties were formal arrangements" and were sometimes none too happy.

RELATIONS BETWEEN RUSTICATES AND PEASANTS

After sent-down youths arrived in their rural posts, they faced a great variety of experiences, depending on their ideals and the attitudes of local peasant or other leaders. Many of the Shanghai youths on state farms in Sinkiang had most of their contacts with people like themselves, and with retired or active army officers who were their *hsiafang* supervisors. Some youths, mostly the ones sent down to places in East China, had considerable contact with local people. League branches in such areas were often instructed to find useful and responsible roles for the rusticates.[64] University graduates assigned to places close to Shanghai in the early 1960s often did rural work that related to their previous studies. For at least one group of 600 university graduates who went to factories and farms in Shanghai proper, a rule was established that no more than one-quarter of their time was to be used for political and professional education. For most of the rest of the time, they were still not doing the ordinary jobs of workers and peasants. Trainees at a commune in Sungchiang County, for example, were given jobs teaching

63. Interview with an ex-cadre, Hong Kong, December 1969.
64. *CKCNP*, August 16, 1962.

school and writing daily "blackboard newspapers."[65] Often these highly educated youths were able to develop technical innovations, and one of them thought up a way to reduce the amount of coke used in a steel-making process. Trainees sent down to the Shanghai No. 2 Textile Mill and to the Holungsha State Farm in Ch'ung-ming County won prizes for their inventiveness and productivity.[66]

When Shanghai youths were too inventive, frictions sometimes developed between them and local cadres. Certain youths who were sent down to the Shanghai No. 2 Radio Factory used incorrect lengths of wire to make receivers. Their design had to be "improved" by older workers. This kind of difficulty also arose in agricultural units. A *hsiafang* volunteer from Hopei wrote that "the leadership comrades of some communes, brigades, and production teams have not shown sufficient concern for educated youths who were returned to the countryside to take part in agricultural production." He suggested that brigades should systematize agricultural education for city youths and that an old peasant should be assigned to teach each new arrival. Many youths reportedly had a sincere interest in learning farm techniques. A correspondent from Shansi claimed that 58 percent of urban sent-down students in an area there had enrolled in correspondence courses, because they needed to learn more about agriculture and accounting. Their aim was to complete senior middle school within four or five years and to obtain recognized degrees at the end of that period.[67]

Even agronomical expertise could not entirely wipe away the stain of urban cosmopolitanism, in the eyes of some peasants. An ex-student from Kwangtung reported that one of the main problems of sent-down youths in rural areas during the early 1960s was the animus that peasants then felt for city people in general. Urban students were lumped in peasants' minds with urban cadres. The *hsiafang* students found themselves closest in attitude on many issues to *hsiafang* bureaucrats from the cities. Peasants tended to blame cadres and students indiscriminately for any unpopular government policy. According to one informant, the farmers were hardest on them both during the post-Leap distributive failure,

65. *WHP,* June 29, 1964.
66. *Union Research Service* 36, No. 14 (July 1964), p. 217.
67. *JMJP,* December 22, 1962.

which the cadres' policies had indeed caused.[68] A student refugee who had done rural labor at two different places in South China, first in the difficult post-Leap period and then later in more prosperous years, reported:

> In 1961, after the failure of the people's communes, the peasants' life was hard. Therefore peasants deliberately gave all the difficult work to us, and they scolded students. . . . In 1965, life was easier and the peasants were not so tough. What I saw was not the difference in place but was the difference in time. The enmity of peasants toward transferred cadres also was most severe during the least prosperous times in the peasants' own lives.[69]

This situation may have been exacerbated by the tendency to send more graduates of landlord, rich peasant, and bourgeois backgrounds on rural *hsiafang* than graduates of other family backgrounds. The general policy, after all, was that people in the former upper classes were morally deficient, because they had no experience in working hard with their hands. For their own good, they were supposed to be the first to go to the farms.

Distinctions between social classes were not usually major sources of dissension among the students, especially when groups of them went together to work their own farms in frontier spots like Sinkiang.[70] During the early 1960s, material shortages were common to all classes, and even after the Socialist Education Movement was launched, bourgeois-background youths were often quite willing to believe in the importance of "class hatred," as long as it remained a rather abstract source of inspiration for all Chinese and did not hurt them personally. The rural peasants in China proper were often less forgetful of class distinctions, however. One refugee said, "Some of the peasants called the transferred students 'landlords.' "[71]

Some of the more enthusiastic peasants took their job of class education quite seriously. The acme of this practice was ritual

---

68. Interview, Hong Kong, October 1969.
69. *Ibid.*
70. Interview, Hong Kong, January 1970, with a middle-aged man who had not been to Sinkiang himself but knew others who had been.
71. Interview, Hong Kong, November 1969, with "Dai Hsiao-ai," a Swatow student of proletarian family background who made this statement generally, not especially about Shanghai. He said he thought it would apply in East China, which he visited in 1967.

hazing, to which educated urban youths were sometimes subjected for their edification. "Class congee" (*chiehchi chou*) was a cuisine consisting largely of twigs, grass, soil, and similar delicacies. It was concocted by peasant chefs in order to show *hsiafang* students how hard life had been under the old pre-Liberation regime, in which some of the students' parents had participated.[72] This was all no doubt marvelously integrative, and it had stylistic precedents in the practical jokes played on newlyweds at marriage ceremonies in some areas.

Chiehchi chou may have won more converts when it was offered as communion rather than imposed as hazing. A short story, "Aunt Liang's Dinner Party," describes an invitational feast that stirred some faith:

People wondered what delicious food Aunt Liang would offer to the new commune members. "She didn't go to the fair to buy any meat." Aunt Wu who lived next door was puzzled, "How can she cope with the dinner? . . ."

Aunt Liang ushered her guests into a large courtyard which contained three brand-new rooms. . . . And on the door was the editorial comment Chairman Mao wrote in 1955 on an article describing the experience of organizing agricultural cooperation: "All intellectuals who can work in the countryside should be happy to go there. Our countryside is vast and has plenty of room for them to develop their talents to the full. . . ."

. . . On one side were pinned up many notes and appreciations the family had written after studying Chairman Mao's works. . . .

Then the dinner was served—wild vegetable soup, steamed bran and husks! The students understood what this dinner meant at once. Aunt Liang looked around and said with deep emotion: "Children, take and eat. . . ." No sooner had she spoken than the tears raced into her eyes and streamed down her cheeks. With so many bitter grievances recalled to her mind, she began to tell of her sufferings in the old society.[73]

When these rituals were properly administered in the context of contemporary Chinese social beliefs, they were probably quite an

72. The author thanks Martin Whyte for prompting him to inquire about *chiehchi chou*. The report in this instance is South Chinese, but the same ritual is prominent in other parts of the country too, where the meal is sometimes called *yi k'u fan* (food for recalling the bitter past). An ex-resident of Shanghai said the practice was now very widespread.

73. Yu Jean, "Aunt Liang's Dinner Party," *Chinese Literature*, No. 12 (December 1968), quotations from pp. 83 and 86–87. This story is clearly set in North China (probably Honan); the student-guests were from Chengchow.

effective means of civic education. They could serve that purpose well, but only after the real impoverishment of the post-Leap period had ended.

RUSTICATION DURING THE SOCIALIST EDUCATION MOVEMENT, 1963-1965

Propaganda efforts to persuade youths to volunteer for *hsiafang* intensified during the Socialist Education Movement, with an emphasis on patriotic self-sacrifice and on the use of more symbolic, rather than material, incentives. A special characteristic of the period was an effort to send down more proletarian youths than before, instead of concentrating on students from bourgeois families. The increased proletarian *hsiafang* arose for two reasons. In the first place, a *huihsiang* (return to the homestead) campaign began, which sent urban people of all classes back to the particular villages from which their families had originally come to Shanghai. This movement affected workers' children as much as it affected bourgeois offspring. In the second place, more affirmative action for proletarians in school admission slowly created graduating classes that contained more workers' children, who were thus more often pressed into regular *hsiafang* service. Rustication propaganda was directed, even more than before, at senior-year students from middle schools. Many of the programs in 1963-1965 involved short stints in areas close to Shanghai, but there was also a campaign to increase the number of youths sent permanently to distant provinces—particularly Sinkiang. In this period of medium prosperity, Shanghai authorities were more successful than before in mobilizing volunteers to further the goals of the state economic plan.

REWARDS FOR RUSTICATION

The career incentives for youths leaving the city during this time remained fairly strong, even though most of the encouragement was symbolic rather than material. Many *hsiafang* volunteers, who had worked for long periods in communes near Shanghai, received the title "five-good youths" (*wuhao ch'ingnien*). This designation would inevitably help their future careers anywhere, even though its importance may have diminished as they grew older. To some extent, the movement to honor young workers came in waves. One of the high points occurred in October 1963, when 1,300 intellectuals became "five-good youths" all at once in Shanghai's Fenghsien County. They had served as teachers, work-point recorders, granary watchmen, militia members, and even production team leaders.[74]

The rewards for rusticates who went farther, or stayed longer, were correspondingly greater. A local Shanghai newspaper headlined "Happy News from Sinkiang" in reporting the successes of favorite sons and daughters sent there:

Since July, many youths from this city have gone to Sinkiang. . . . According to letters and cadre reports . . . , some Shanghai youths have been named "five-good workers" and "activists." Among the 1,300 youths from Huangp'u District who went to the Sinkiang Communist Youth League Farm, 256 [20 percent] of them are new "five-good workers" and 58 [4 percent] of them are "third-grade able hands for the summer harvest" (*hsiashou sanchi nengshou*). More than 1,000 youths from Hung-k'ou District went to the Sinkiang No. 9 Victory Farm, and now 142 of them have been named "young activists from Shanghai who help the frontier" (*Shanghai chihpien ch'ingnien chichifentzu*). From Luwan District, 700 youths went to the No. 18 Victory Farm, and 9 of them [1 percent] performed "acts of first grade merit" (*yi teng kung*), 35 received second grade merit, and 72 got the third grade. [All told, 17 percent did meritorious acts.] Among the 1,200 youths of Chingan District who went to Sinkiang, 94 [8 percent] have been awarded the title of "shock attack hands" (*t'uchi shou*). All this happy news makes parents realize that, in the past, when they did not let their children go to Sinkiang, they were wrong. It also encourages other lane youths to go to Sinkiang.[75]

Aside from what this tells about the relation between specific Shanghai districts and specific "victory farms" in Sinkiang, it also shows the importance of the award system and of escorters in the moral education program. More than 15 percent of all the Shanghai students who left for Sinkiang in 1963 had already been designated "five good" by the spring of the next year.[76] Of 200 educated youths who left Shanghai in 1958 for Hupei, 80 percent were either cadres or technicians on the farms six years later.

74. *HMWP*, October 25, 1963.
75. *HMWP*, November 1, 1963.
76. NCNA, Shanghai, May 3, 1964.

Political titles and medals, with fancy honorific names of the sort mentioned above, may seem to be more meaningful incentives to contemporary Chinese than to contemporary Westerners, because they are useful in directing and coordinating activities that are usually excluded from the political sphere in the West. The importance attached to awards is of course vital to their use in moral education. A brief excursion into the sociology of awards suggests the kinds of groups in which they are effective for motivation.

Gabriel Almond and Sidney Verba theorize that it is possible to rank the types of situations in which political socialization takes place. Such a list in ascending order of the degrees to which socialization is political, might be: family, school, job, voluntary association, polity.[77] The purpose of many Chinese Communist efforts at moral education is to apply at the primary-group end of this scale the work styles ordinarily used in state affairs, so as to organize the energy of primary groups for national goals. The award system and other efforts to reconcile families to the rustication of their offspring were means to this end.

The Chinese also strengthened moral education at basic levels in other ways. By late 1963, the city began to publish a special monthly magazine for youths who had been assigned to rural areas. It contained accounts of political events in China and abroad, information about agriculture and science, and a good deal of propaganda about *hsiafang* volunteer models.[78] This publication was edited and distributed by the Shanghai Education Press, with the support of the municipal Youth League, the Women's Federation, and the Education Bureau. On a national scale, an effort was made to equip the regular press to meet the interests of the rusticate readership. Peking called for a growth in rural circulations for both the youth magazine, *Chungkuo ch'ingnien*, and the youth newspaper, *Chungkuo ch'ingnien pao*.[79] By the middle of 1964, almost 70 percent more copies of the newspaper were being printed than in the previous year. The content of these publications was also meshed more closely with the *hsiafang* campaign.

77. Gabriel A. Almond and Sidney Verba, *The Civic Culture* (Princeton, N.J.: Princeton University Press, 1963), pp. 303-304.
78. NCNA, Shanghai, November 25, 1963.
79. NCNA, Peking, July 1, 1964.

Other continuing steps to cater to the rusticates are typified by some points in a report from Shantung. For example, county-level Youth League and Party organizations held regular meetings with the teachers of sent-down urban youth to learn about youth attitudes and to make educational policy. When sent-down volunteers graduated from their rural school programs, ideological training was arranged to convince them that they must not return to the city. Private tutoring was set up for youths who studied "subjects that could be taught in the countryside."[80]

NATION AS A SUBSTITUTE FOR LINEAGE

In 1964-1965, *hsiafang* morale-boosting efforts intensified. In particular, the Shanghai Party Committee strengthened its liaison with local youths who were already in the countryside or on the frontier. Above the impressive red seals of both the Party committee and the Municipal Council, "well-wishing letters" (*weiwen hsin*) were sent to inquire about the health of Shanghai volunteers in the field.[81] Letters from rusticates back to Shanghai were also important in support of the *hsiafang* program, when they could be arranged. Many such letters were published in both 1964 and 1965. A Shanghai graduate in Sinkiang wrote:

Perhaps mother has been worried. If only she will think of the past, then she will have no more anxieties. It is the Party, after all, that has fostered us to be university graduates.[82]

A group of letters, published together under the headline "We Love Sinkiang" included the following description of an oasis:

Is Sinkiang a desolate region? No. If you come to K'uerhle, where the headquarters of our Second Agricultural Division is located, you will see highways shaded by green trees and boundless stretches of "strip fields" (*t'iaot'ien*). Each of these has 100 mou of land. Around each strip field are planted tall poplar trees, and clear water flows in the irrigation ditches on all sides. The rice is luxuriant, and the corn grows tall in the fields. When a person comes to such a place, his mind is greatly broadened. How could one feel even slightly desolate?[83]

80. *KMJP*, May 10, 1964.
81. *HMWP*, February 12, 1964.
82. *WHP*, July 4, 1965.
83. *WHP*, May 26, 1965.

Wang K'o, head of the Shanghai Labor Bureau, told a general meeting of parents in Luwan District that sending youths to Sinkiang improves public morals and "changes the people's customs" (*yi feng yi su*). A group of propagandists, who had recently returned from there, also addressed the meeting to "tell their experiences, so that more youths will follow them."[84]

By the mid-1960s, *hsiafang* was advertised increasingly in terms of its value for individuals' self-development. The ethical values of *hsiafang* were taken to be at least as important as its contribution to economic development. China's political progress, the unification of all the nation's people under a single style of work, became more prominent in policy as post-Leap economic problems were solved. Individual self-sacrifices became rituals, replicating the misery of the exploited classes before Liberation. They were believed to have a value that was independent of the collective savings which they sometimes made possible.

Before the Spring Festival in most earlier years, people who had been sent down to central parts of China could occasionally receive permission to return to Shanghai to spend this most important Chinese feast day with their families. During 1965, however, newspapers published several letters in which young people wrote parents or spouses that they had decided to sacrifice the holiday trip for the good of the country. A model for emulation was Chang Hsiu-ying, a worker at the Fourth Northwest State Cotton Textile Mill in Sian, who wrote this reservedly filial letter to her Shanghai parents in late January:

I have decided to spend the New Year in my second hometown of Sian. I have missed you, as well as my brother and sister, during these nine years away. But I have more frequent thoughts of the Party that nourishes me. When I left you, I was still a child knowing nothing. Now, however, I can take charge of 32 automatic knitting machines.[85]

For the Party, this kind of dedication was probably at least as valuable as the technical ability to supervise machines, but it did not strengthen the fabric of family life.

84. *HMWP*, March 25, 1964.
85. *HMWP*, January 27, 1965.

MORE PROLETARIAN HSIAFANG
AMONG GRADUATING SENIORS

Hsiafang for students was originally a method of furthering the moral education of children from capitalist families. At first, the loyalty of proletarians was often taken for granted. For example, in the early years after Liberation, *hsiafang* for ethical education probably did not increase the numbers of political faithful among working class youths. After the education reforms of the late 1950s and 1963, however, the proportion of workers' children in middle schools increased. As the number of proletarian graduates scheduled for *hsiafang* rose, a new ethic, a new basis for propaganda, was needed to persuade them to go. New models were thus found. An adult worker-student at T'ungchi University, who had served as an apprentice before Liberation, was reported to have rejected the insult that "all students of worker-peasant origin are idiots." He pledged to make himself "an intellectual of the working class."[86] Such stories reminded graduates from all backgrounds of the social debt they owed the Party for their educations. Repayment was to be made in the form of *hsiafang*, for the sake of national development. Society's accounts were now better kept than before. Individuals' debts were billed as a matter of course.

Increasingly in later years, official "management committees" were established to help proletarian, as well as bourgeois, students "return" to the countryside. It was pointed out with embarrassing accuracy that the workers' children should do this because many of them had never worked in the fields with their hands. Some had never even worked in factories. A survey of one group reported that "most of them came from poor peasant families but had not yet experienced class struggle."[87]

The educational reform of 1963, which involved workers' children in *hsiafang* as they graduated from school, also tended to create a program that was (by its intention if not its behavior) increasingly residential in purpose—a population and labor force control. The Party could claim more support, and more sincere volunteers, from its class brothers than from its class enemies. Rusticates during the Socialist Education Movement came from a variety of educational as well as class backgrounds. By 1964, student

86. NCNA, June 11, 1963.
87. *KMJP*, April 7, 1964.

experts in technical fields were reportedly assigned to rural areas as frequently as those in the social sciences.[88]

Students graduating from middle school were the primary targets of *hsiafang* during the Socialist Education Movement. Power over educational promotions was power over careers, and it could be wielded to encourage the rite of passage to full citizenship. Especially during the Socialist Education Movement, the senior year in Shanghai middle schools was largely a political course. The Youth League was, on official instructions, supposed to be more prominent in organizing curricula for last-year students than for the lower grades.[89] News reports praised the 12,000 prospective university graduates of 1964 who had "warmly greeted the job assignments of the state," noting that "during the past year they have made much progress in moral education."[90] The high prestige of some universities was associated with a common desire there to accept state assignments. Chiaot'ung graduates were "very enthusiastic" about their new jobs, and graduates of the East China College of Textiles received 300 letters from their parents "supporting the children." One of the Chiaot'ung seniors exchanged letters with his wife to make sure it would be all right for him to accept a hardship post in the hinterland. The wife replied loyally that she did not want to prevent her husband from leading a revolutionary life, and her letter was printed in a newspaper to serve as a model for others.[91]

Some reports conceded that rustication did not always win total support from the families of graduating seniors. A graduate of Futan University wrote to her father, the head of a county hospital in Kiangsu, that she and several classmates had petitioned the Party to send them as a group to an exacting assignment. She was concerned that her mother might worry about this decision. On the other hand, she reflected that the Party had educated her and asked rhetorically how she could think of personal interests until her limitless debts to the Party had been repaid. Her father's reply (also published) praised her resolve but did not say whether her mother approved of her departure.[92]

88. Interview, Hong Kong, December 1969.
89. *HMWP*, June 15, 1964.
90. NCNA, Shanghai, June 26, 1964.
91. *WHP*, July 4, 1964.
92. *Ibid.* A negative model, on whom the author has been unable to collect further information, was Lin Yü-sheng.

RELATING TO THE PEASANTS:
LIAISON OR ISOLATION

Newspaper stories praising young people who worked successfully with peasants during *hsiafang* suggest that relations between rusticates and local people varied greatly in different places and were sometimes difficult. A hero of rustication, a model intellectual youth named Tung Chia-keng, was much advertised in 1964. His *hsiafang* in Kiangsu was not far from Shanghai, but his name was nevertheless praised in newspapers and on radio because he was especially good at learning humbly from old peasants about agricultural techniques.[93] In fact, many other rusticates did not have such extensive contacts with peasants. Some Shanghai youths who went to Chiahsing County in Chekiang were organized in units run by themselves, under only distant supervision by a county-level Party secretary. They were given their own housing and tools, as well as plots of land to work collectively.[94] Some peasants may have come to teach them how to use a hoe and when to plant, but most of their contacts were with other city people. In 1965, a group of 150 volunteers from Nanshih District, Shanghai, founded the Hsints'un (New Village) Brigade, in T'aochuang Commune of Chiashan County, Chekiang.[95] These youths ran their own unit on marginal land, apart from the main commune. A danger was that this kind of policy, despite its usefulness for reclamation, tended to separate educated youths from the peasants who were supposed to be teaching them. In rural East China, where many such bands of Shanghai intellectuals went to open up new fields in sparsely populated hilly areas, local League and Party committees made special efforts to promote contacts between them and old peasants.[96] Sent-down urban people were supposed to be given a more vivid sense of class struggle than they were likely to obtain in the city.

Student responses to such class education were not always positive. One graduate from a junior middle school called the people in the area to which he was sent "conceited," "selfish," and "unwill-

93. *JMJP*, March 20, 1964.
94. *JMJP*, February 16, 1964.
95. *KMJP*, May 10, 1965.
96. *JMJP*, editorial, February 28, 1964.

ing to accept new ideas."[97] When he wrote of his discontent to a magazine, he received a public reply to the effect that considerable tolerance should be shown even for the faults of the peasants, because they had played such a huge role in China's revolutionary movement. They had contributed so much to class struggle. The complaining *hsiafang* student was told that he would have to mingle better with the masses, if he really hoped to help them.

Senior middle school graduates sometimes fretted that the government wasted their educations by shipping them off to do agricultural work, that scientific experiments were impossible in the boondocks, and that sent-down talent was forgotten there. One particularly forward dissident said plainly that "graduates should work in government organs instead."[98] Such opinions were published to be criticized. The government clearly did not intend to hire youths for urban jobs, until they had gained experience working in rural places.

DESTINATIONS OF RUSTICATES:
SUBURBS, EAST CHINA, OR SINKIANG

During 1963-1965, most rusticates were sent to areas near Shanghai. In 1963, for example, large numbers of Shanghai university graduates and middle school students and graduates were sent to work in suburban locations, but their tours of duty usually lasted no more than six months.[99] By 1964, a Rural Reclamation Bureau (Nungts'un k'enhuang chü) was reportedly coordinating rustication efforts in Shanghai's immediate vicinity.[100] This agency organized a Shanghai Youth Agricultural Team (Ch'ingnien nungyeh chienshe tui) of 400 graduates, from levels at least as high as junior middle school. The team was sent to train with experienced cadres on the nearby Ch'anghsing Islands, a prime site for efforts to raise land out of water. The cadre heading the expedition, Chu Chü-

---

97. *CKCNP*, May 4, 1964.

98. *CKCNP*, April 11 and 21, 1964.

99. Interview, Hong Kong, December 1969. See also *JMJP*, October 21, 1963, dispatch from Shanghai.

100. *HMWP*, July 14, 1964. This bureau, called the Nung K'en Chü for short, is seldom referred to. Its main activities seem to be in suburban areas around Shanghai, not in the city or far afield. An ex-resident reported the continuing existence of this bureau into the 1970s and said it had jurisdiction over "all" the state farms in Shanghai's suburbs.

ying, had led a similar group to another island in 1962. The 1964 team was apparently an idealistic and well-motivated group. On July 12, several days before its departure, Wang K'o, head of the Shanghai Labor Bureau, officiated at its departure ceremony. Members of the team were clearly trusted not to defect back to the city, although some other groups sent to work on Yangtze River sandbars were in a different category.

The impulse to patriotic *hsiafang* was probably kept alive among some youths because their stints in the countryside were not long and because so many of their fellow students also went. For example, 170,000 Shanghai students from middle schools and universities went to the suburbs for "three autumn jobs" in 1964.[101] The exhortation assemblies and mass student decisions arranged by the Education Bureau were at least as important accomplishments of this particular *hsiafang* as was the farm work itself. The Shanghai students lived briefly with peasant families during harvest time.[102] Less than a month after they left the city, however, many were already back in their urban schools.[103] Ex-residents of the city indicate that the duration of autumn harvest work was usually three weeks, while the summer harvest lasted two weeks. This kind of *hsiafang* was undoubtedly the most popular kind among city residents, because it allowed them to help a bit in the national business of agriculture, without threatening their residential status in Shanghai.

"The three autumn jobs" during the Socialist Education Movement were designed to oppose bookishness by sending students out to the countryside for production. Indeed, nonpolitical and technical classes were eliminated from these programs (except for some lessons in agronomy), and the students were supposed to learn from and teach techniques to peasants, mostly in informal exchanges.[104] After returning to their schools, students and teachers "prepared to consolidate the gains of three autumn jobs" by summarizing their experiences and by political course work.[105] Ex-residents of Shanghai say that the immediate economic value of the program was

101. *HMWP*, October 14, 1964.
102. NCNA, Shanghai, November 12, 1964.
103. *HMWP*, November 12, 1964.
104. *Shanghai chiaoyü*, No. 11 (November 12, 1964).
105. *WHP*, November 13, 1964.

rather dubious. The main gains were clearly to be measured in numbers of loyalists rather than in catties of rice. Even so, such quick rustications were educationally superficial. Informants report that they achieved few conversions to long-term residential *hsiafang*.

During the "three autumn jobs" of 1965, some 160,000 students and teachers from Shanghai middle schools went to suburban communes, but for only two or three weeks. They were headquartered in the field by special education centers and went to Paoshan, Chiating, Ch'uansha, Ch'ungming, and Sungchiang counties (all within the municipality and easily accessible by bus or ferry from Shanghai).[106] The other Shanghai counties, Nanhui, Fenghsien, Chinshan, and Ch'ingp'u, apparently wanted or needed no special help in bringing in their harvests. Among older youths, the fall harvest campaigns were largely devoted to promoting the value of the "three togethers."[107] City folk were supposed to "eat, live, and labor" together with poor and lower middle peasants, but the latter were eager to give urbanites room and board only during the busiest agricultural seasons.

By 1965, this moral *hsiafang* of students had affected far more Shanghai people than long-term residential *hsiafang* had. It was even permissible to print this fact. The New China News Agency boasted that "the overwhelming majority [of 1965 university graduates in Shanghai] have participated in the Socialist Education Movement or in short-term labor in the countryside."[108] Fewer had been sent farther, for longer terms.

One distant province, Sinkiang, was nonetheless the focus of a *hsiafang* effort during the mid-1960s, and the organization of the 1964-1965 campaign to send people there sheds light on the whole rustication process. The basis for the campaign was laid in Party Secretary Ch'en P'ei-hsien's January 1964 report to the Shanghai Political Consultative Conference. Ch'en stressed that all the city's children should "plunge into fiery revolutionary struggles, into hard lives of labor, to carry out their systematic socialist educa-

---

106. *HMWP*, October 26, 1965.
107. See *Shanghai chiaoyü*, July 12, 1965, for an account of how a group from Shanghai's Kuangming Middle School were "three together" with the peasants.
108. NCNA, Shanghai, August 22, 1965. Italics added.

tions."[109] He urged them to read the works of Marx and Lenin, as well as of Chairman Mao, on the relation between manual and mental labor.

On April 22, 1964, Shanghai held an assembly of activists who had gone to East China villages near Shanghai. The purpose of the meeting was to persuade them to go still farther, especially to Sinkiang. Ch'en P'ei-hsien admitted that "Shanghai is an old industrial base; culture and science are better developed here."[110] For that very reason, he explained, Shanghai youths had a responsibility to develop other places. He urged them to "be ambitious and ready to go anywhere" and to be pioneers in frontier areas. Their material prospects were not unimportant, only secondary. In fact, their prospective host provinces and autonomous regions sent representatives to assure them of bright futures in their new homes.

The first large 1964 rustication rally was held on May Day at Culture Square in the middle of the city. No less than 10,000 youths were reported in attendance. The director of the Shanghai Labor Bureau presided, although few new jobs in Shanghai were available just then. Deputy mayors, women's officials, and student representatives all gave speeches. In a style that would have enchanted any evangelist, "many members of the Communist Youth League and other youths immediately handed in their decision papers (*chüehhsin shu*)."[111]

Low-level political figures—the elders and leaders of urban lanes—were also active in this mobilization. More than 100 "representatives of residents" in the Kiangsi North Street Committee area of Chap'u Road, Hungk'ou District, attended a meeting on April 23, 1964, to persuade youths to go to Sinkiang. Party, government, and mass organization leaders attended.[112] Retired workers and loyal army dependents also came along to hear the speeches and to encourage the oath-taking and the decisions to volunteer. The municipal Women's Federation held meetings for mothers of potential *hsiafang* youth, urging them to foster in their children ambitions beyond the city limits.[113]

109. *JMJP*, January 7, 1964.
110. *HMWP*, April 22, 1964.
111. *HMWP*, May 1, 1964.
112. *HMWP*, April 25, 1964.
113. *HMWP*, April 26, 1964.

Groups of youths going to Sinkiang from specific lanes would register together, would "receive permission" to go together, and apparently would often work together when they arrived at their destination on the frontier. In some areas, groups of this sort were the main units sent down. Often the bunches were not large. Eleven youths from the Second Committee of Meng Lane, Liyüan Road apparently remained a unit through the whole process from propaganda, to volunteering, to application, to acceptance, to Sinkiang —almost as if they constituted a single, indivisible person.[114]

A street committee would normally hold a lavish farewell party before any major departure of its local offspring. At a party given by the Fifth Lane Committee of K'unming Street, Yangp'u District, a woman seventy-three years old told stories to her departing grandchildren about the revolutionary deeds of their ancestors in Shanghai.[115] A "six-good" barber of East Ch'angchih Street, Hungk'ou District, vowed at another such party to teach his trade to a local youth who would then go to Sinkiang and practice it. Many evening celebrations of this sort were coordinated with larger daytime rallies in Culture Square, to which the volunteers were invited along with parents who had been unwilling to let their children go.[116]

Prominent Shanghai people were encouraged to announce publicly that their children wanted to go to Singkiang. On one day in May 1964, a Shanghai film actor, a deputy Party secretary of the Shanghai Civil Aviation Bureau, a hotel manager, the director of a hospital department, and some other local celebrities all proclaimed that they were sending their offspring to the frontier.[117]

In this context, members of local street committees who happened to be young could hardly avoid volunteering themselves. When newly Socialist-educated youths in Hsinkang Street of Hungk'ou District demanded to be sent-down, representatives Pao Ling-oh and Yü Mei-lan of the street's sixth and fourth lane

114. *HMWP*, May 15, 1964.
115. *HMWP*, May 17, 1964.
116. *Ibid.*, a different article, describes a rally in Culture Square called by the Shanghai People's Committee, at which representatives of the Labor, Education, and Culture bureaus, as well as of the Youth League, Youth Alliance, and Women's Federation, all gave speeches.
117. *HMWP*, May 11, 1964.

committees, respectively, thought it best to join in the program themselves.[118]

Persons going to Sinkiang were well cared for by the PLA Sinkiang Production and Construction Army Corps.[119] Any volunteers who joined this organization became loosely associated with the Chinese army, although they were not full members of it. Each volunteer was asked to bring documents (*chengchien*) "so as to prevent bad elements from filtering in" and so as to set up new household registrations.[120]

Partly because *hsiafang* involved matters of interprovincial policy, there was in the mid-1960s a good deal of high-level planning for it. Party Secretary Shih Hsi-min, who before the spring of 1963 was head of the city Party's Propaganda Department, had a special responsibility along with Ch'en P'ei-hsien for running the *hsiafang* campaign during 1964. On July 1, the Shanghai People's Committee heard a report on "the plan" to allocate jobs to primary and secondary school graduates that year.[121] It was publicly announced that "all the committee members" agreed to the quotas implicit in this plan, although the graduates did not yet know their roles in this scheme.

Good organization was necessary to make the program work at lower levels, especially during the period each year between school entrance exams and the acceptance of individual assignments. Some surveillance had to be kept over educated youths while the personnel departments were deciding how to use them. This kind of control was carried out effectively only at street and lane levels. At P'ingliang Road in Yangp'u District, for instance, the local neighborhood committee arranged a "summertime work plan" (*shuch'i kungtso chihua*) for local graduates. In addition, it set up "education work groups for youths and children" (*ch'ingshaonien chiaoyü kungtso tsu*). *Hsiafang* was so important that this "work group" consisted of the heads of most major local organizations:

118. *HMWP*, May 4, 1964.

119. The full title in Chinese is Chungkuo Jenmin Chiehfangchün Hsinchiang Shengch'an Chienshe Pingt'uan.

120. *Hsinchiang jihpao*, January 6, 1957. Also, *HMWP*, May 14, 1964. I have scanned available issues of the *Hsinchiang jihpao* for information about Shanghai sent-down youths after they arrived in their new posts and will report this research in an article.

121. *HMWP*, July 1, 1964.

the chief of the lane committee, the first secretary of the local Youth League branch, the director of the women's representative group, and officers from the people's police (*jenmin chingch'a*). These notables were often assisted by education cadres, by the principals of local schools, and by the director of the culture and education department of the neighborhood committee.[122]

These many efforts to organize *hsiafang* more tightly during 1963-1965 were generally effective. Partly because the recovery from post-Leap economic problems gave the government more urban jobs to distribute than had existed earlier, and partly because of the increasingly civilian role played by military cadres and values in Shanghai during this period, the officials were able to organize more training for sent-down among youths of all ages. The intensity of propaganda on this subject during these years can scarcely be stated. It was effective in persuading people to move out of Shanghai because officials now had more favors to bestow than they had had in the early 1960s.

RUSTICATION AT THE BEGINNING OF THE CULTURAL REVOLUTION

Long-term residential *hsiafang* was intensified during the 1965-1966 period, but the number of participants was still small in comparison to those in short-term educational programs. The Labor Bureau's district offices continued to form "Shanghai agricultural construction teams." Their personnel were recruited among youths of all classes, who were willing to rusticate permanently near the city. For example, Nanshih and Chingan districts sent a contingent in November 1965 to work on state farms in the suburbs.[123] An enthusiast from Hsinansha Farm on Ch'ungming Island reported that intensive agriculture on reclaimed land was now a science, demanding brains, and that educated youths from Shanghai should not think it a waste of their talent to become farmers. Considering the sophisticated methods by which crops were raised in some parts of Shanghai, this argument may have been valid even though it catered to the romantic urban idea that the toil of rural routine could quickly be eliminated.

122. *HMWP*, July 4, 1964.
123. *HMWP*, November 5, 1965.

Now agriculture is modernized. If we want to have greater output, we must know about soils, about crop breeding, about cultivation, and about biology. Such knowledge is not easy to obtain in ordinary cultural activities. Even geometry and trigonometry are useful in agriculture; they are needed in building irrigation schemes. . . . Youths should not imagine that they throw away their gifts by living in villages.[124]

In 1965, the advertised purposes of long-term residential *hsiafang* and short-term moral programs converged as never before. The intentions of the two campaigns, as stated in propaganda, became almost indistinguishable. Volunteers continued to have very different experiences, however, and awards for the relatively few who went to distant provinces did not differ much from those received by people who could stay near Shanghai. Almost all the volunteers going to Singkiang, and many going to central China, cleared fields where they worked separately from local peasants. They had contacts with each other, and with Party and Youth League cadres in their new homes, but sometimes scarcely at all with the local peasant populations.

Various *hsiafang* plans differed immensely with respect to their governmental organization. Party leaders in some areas of Central China had extensive, uncultivated tracts in mountainous areas and were eager to attract Shanghai graduates who could clear these lands and raise local production without conflicting with local peasants. A county-level Party committee in Ching County, Anhwei, developed relations with several districts in Shanghai, and it sent a detail of county cadres to escort volunteers from Chingan District to Ching County in mid-November 1965.[125] At Huangshan, a "South Anhwei [Wannan] Shanghai-Huanglin Tea Plantation" was established on unused land. A "youth brigade" (*ch'ingnien tui*) of 200 youngsters from Luwan District staffed the new farm.[126] Several other districts were scheduled to produce fixed quotas of recruits for this plantation, apparently under agreements between them and Huangshan, no doubt with the approval of province-level officials in Anhwei and Shanghai.

These important, rational planning procedures were based on an

124. *HMWP*, March 22, 1966.
125. *HMWP*, November 15, 1965. An ex-resident of Shanghai reported that Huangshan was a famous mountain. It has now, in effect, come under the jurisdiction of Shanghai, even though it is located in Anhwei.
126. *HMWP*, November 13, 1965.

ethic quite different from the general claim of patriotic obedience that was supposed to motivate a minority of selected young Shanghai volunteers. The Socialist Education Movement had tended to blur the way people were supposed to think about the distinctions between *hsiafang* to nearby places and *hsiafang* to distant ones, between *hsiafang* to mix with the peasants and *hsiafang* to set up new farms, between *hsiafang* to send out Shanghai techniques and *hsiafang* to do ordinary peasant work, between the moral and productive aspects of the program, and even between *hsiafang* of urban bourgeois and that of proletarian children. None of these categories actually disappeared. The selective program existed in all these forms until its temporary halt during the Cultural Revolution. *Hsiafang* was supposed to be a kind of social religion. It was justified as a communion, a means whereby each urban individual could help remedy the whole nation's problems. It was supposed to lay claim on what everyone would do and where everyone would live. The census and ration controls, the shortage of housing, the systems of placement in schools and jobs, and other related policies all still placed some external pressure on Shanghai citizens, telling them how they should live. So long as these pressures were separate, they could be resisted fairly well, but the cement holding them together was a communal ideology, which helped to keep the bricks of the more particular policies in place.

The difference between the ethics of enthusiastic rustication and the ethics of instrumental planning became obvious in the mid-1960s, when material incentives and controls were weakened by increasing urban prosperity. Rusticated youths returned to Shanghai in order to become Red Guards and to criticize the selective and nontotal way in which the policy had been previously administered. They pointed out, in effect, that the moral nature of the movement required universal *hsiafang* at least among graduates of senior middle schools and universities. By 1968, when rustication as a policy was restored, it was universal for these groups in principle. It had also become a new and much simpler phenomenon. It was now supported by fewer material career constraints than had existed in earlier periods, when there were local supply shortages. It resulted from a sharper organizational insistence on unified national purposes and on the guidance of personal talents to serve them.

3

JOB INCENTIVES TO
SOCIALIST CAREERS

Heads of households in modern Shanghai naturally seek jobs.
Their chances of success in this search depend mainly on two
factors: the total number of positions available in the city, and the
rules by which employment is distributed. Both of these variables
are deeply affected by politics. Government policies on apprenticeship programs, wages, welfare, credit, and proletarian propaganda have been used to direct careers along officially approved
channels. The Chinese Communists, like leaderships in other
developing nations, have had to mesh workers' desires in these areas
with the country's concrete development needs. A study of the
policies they have used toward this end will point to similarities of
the development process in Communist and non-Communist
states. It will also indicate how the job guidance system affected
citizens differently in various years, shifting along with political
emphases on different facets of the development process and along
with the state of the economy.

A FRAMEWORK FOR THE PROBLEM

It is common knowledge that industrialized, Western economies
undergo business cycles, in which the number of available jobs rises

and falls in response to changes in aggregate demand, capital, and technology. Any low-income modernizing city such as Shanghai—whether or not it is subject to a business cycle—typically has a long-standing, perennial and severe capital shortage relative to labor supplies. This situation deeply affects job opportunities and the structure of possible careers. It can also have some effect on the ways in which workers and unemployed people participate in urban politics.

One of the central theories on the subject is that of Karl Marx. He thought that the capitalist revolution, by using manpower in new and efficient ways, would inadvertently organize manufacturing workers for political action. He theorized that the urban industrial class, living together near factories in concentrated masses, would become unified by a common consciousness of exploitation. These technological and psychological processes are the bases of his class analysis. In Shanghai, the political importance of such divisions—even among different kinds of workers—has been largely determined by what Marx would have called "superstructural" decisions, i.e., government policies. On this basis, a very large "contract proletariat" (similar to Marx's *lumpenproletariat*) has developed to influence the city's political history.

The industrial sector of China, as of Japan and many other nations, has a "dual" economy. Because enterprises with different productivities and different amounts of capital per worker can afford to pay their employees at different rates, there are in terms of income many kinds of labor-capital relations. Divisions among levels of compensation are ultimately caused or eroded by economic factors that affect productivity rates. Such changes occur in the aggregate only over rather long periods of time. In China's cities, a fairly high degree of rigidity in the system of union memberships, wages, and privileges became institutionalized in the 1950s. It is therefore possible to make something like a class analysis of the parts of the urban proletariat that have sometimes become conscious of differential access to labor benefits in Communist Shanghai. The main reason for attempting such an analysis is that it will speak directly to the process by which capital development in this city has affected the structure of career opportunities the government can offer various kinds of workers.

A HISTORY OF STRATA AMONG SHANGHAI'S WORKERS

The roots of stratification in Shanghai's proletariat lie in the old practice of labor contracting, the purchase of workers' time for particular tasks. Labor contracts arise easily when industrial processes are specialized for efficiency. To take one example, a traditional industry in East China is silk-weaving. By the 1920s, power looms in Shanghai factories were competing with farm households that wove silk manually. Early urban silk factories often purchased inputs from contractors.[1] Steam-engine workers were hired and controlled by foremen called *laokuei* (literally, "old devils"), who might perform this service at several different plants, and who could be assisted at each of them by a subcontractor, an *erhkuei* ("second devil"). These contractors (*paokung*) supplied some inputs such as manpower, while the factory supplied other inputs such as coal and work space. Even labor for noncentralized industries, such as rickshaw transport, was often organized by agreements between workers and contractors who did not own capital.[2]

Workers in specific industries were often immigrants to Shanghai from specific places elsewhere in China. For example, most of the city's pedicab drivers have always been from northern Kiangsu. The first guilds (*kungso*) in Shanghai were just coprovincials' associations. In 1921, Shanghai had eight separate carpenters' guilds, representing various provinces and types of carpentry work. Shanghai's dyers were mostly Hunanese. The Small Sword Society organized many seamen and dockhands in East China.[3] Many regional associations refused membership to people who were not from their particular provinces. Secret societies and clubs of immigrants from particular places became pools of manpower for contract recruiting. The contractors were leaders in these associations.

Guilds of this sort were more like managements than unions. They decided wage rates and other terms of labor and apprenticeship. They often monitored the quality of materials and finished goods. They tried to keep trade secrets and set up many special rules for their members. For example, the Shanghai barbers' guild

1. The most exhaustive treatment of the awakening of Shanghai's proletariat is Jean Chesneaux, *The Chinese Labor Movement, 1919-1927*, trans. Hope Wright (Stanford, Calif.: Stanford University Press, 1968), passim. See pp. 89-94.
   2. *Ibid.*, pp. 54-57, 64, 89-94.
   3. The most accessible description is *ibid.*, pp. 113-118.

forbade its members to consume garlic, onions, or liquor. Periodic ceremonies had to be attended for the guild's "ancestral master" (*tsu shih*) spirits.

The contract institution, when it was organized in this way, encouraged many kinds of bribery and malpractice. Contract bosses often withheld parts of their employees' wages to guarantee obedience and good workmanship. Foremen would expect gifts and services from the workers, in addition to payments that they received from capitalists. Secret societies and coprovincials' associations caused a kind of division in Shanghai's proletariat that gradually gave way to more modern divisions, based more directly on different labor productivities.

TYPES OF WORKERS

For periods both before and after 1949, several categories of workers can increasingly be distinguished in terms of the amounts and kinds of capital supplied to increase their productivity. (1) "Fixed workers" (*kuting kungjen*) hold regular jobs. They tend to enjoy relatively high salaries and good job security because many of them have experience using relatively expensive capital tools. Since 1949, they have exercised some political influence through unions. Medical and social insurance for these workers has expanded beyond the programs offered by a few firms in pre-Liberation Shanghai. (2) "Contract workers" (*hot'ung kungjen*) have definite, long-term, relatively enforceable contracts. Apprentices and semiskilled workers who do not have fully regular jobs usually fall into this category. (3) "Temporary workers" (*linshih kungjen*) often have no contracts at all. Their work can be terminated by their employers, and they seldom enjoy any benefits beyond their salaries. (4) "Subcontract workers" (*waipao kungjen*) usually have no direct liaison with the organization for which they are ultimately working. When part of a production process can be done outside a main factory, the management can engage agricultural groups, street committees, or other organizations to do that task. The workers perform industrial jobs while remaining physically and politically in nonindustrial organizations.[4] Other categories of workers might certainly be added to

4. The list is from an interview, Hong Kong, October 1969.

these four, but all these terms will only be used heuristically, to find the extent to which they may apply to specific situations.

LABOR STRATIFICATION, INCOME, AND EXPENDITURES

Marx thought that the organizational processes of industry would generate a proletariat. In Shanghai, these processes have turned out to be more varied than he foresaw. There is no space here for a full history of Shanghai's economic development, but, in general, the structure of organized manufacturing and markets for Shanghai's products, as determined by factors such as the social and geographical distribution of wealth and the particular structure of available resources and technologies, combined at each time to encourage investments of widely varying productivities.[5] The result was a vast range of differences in the incomes that Shanghai's workers were able to earn for various tasks. The variation depended on social and resource conditions that could not easily be changed.

The stratification of labor productivity has a political aspect, because in the long run it affects incomes. It was exacerbated for Shanghai's proletariat because average real wages did not rise— even over very long periods of time. A careful Communist survey shows that the real expenditure of Shanghai workers' households in 1952 was 4 percent less than in 1929-1930. Average real incomes rose over this long period only by 0.24 percent.

Between 1952 and 1955, Shanghai workers' real incomes were reported to have gone up 13 percent, but their expenditures rose only 2 percent. Data on real income and real expenditure were also collected between 1953 and 1956-1957, but the newspaper article indicating this fact does not report the exact figures for these years, perhaps because the increases were embarrassingly low.[6]

5. Marxist economics holds that investments are determined by a somewhat different set of factors—the "relations of production" and the "forces of production." Together these constitute the whole "substructure" that generates classes. Before discussing stratification in a modern society, it is important to determine the market and material bases on which industries are established, no matter whether capitalist or Marxist words are used in the discussion.

6. *Hsüehshu yüehk'an* (April 1958), pp. 50-54. This survey has four bases: (a) data found in 1929-1930 files of the Social Bureau (Shehui Chü) of the Shanghai municipal government; (b) data collected by the city's Finance and Economy Committee (Ts'aicheng Weiyüanhui) in 1952; (c) 1955 data collected by the municipal government just before the national wage reform; and (d) data from the same source for the last half of 1957. The numbers of households in each sample were: (a)

The structure of Shanghai workers' expenditures changed after 1949, even if the amount did not substantially rise. The cost of rent, water, and electricity went down, and expenses increased for items like education (which had affected only a minority of workers' households before Liberation). A 1956 survey report confessed that Shanghai workers' average food consumption before 1949 was "slightly higher" than afterward.[7] Expenditure on fuel decreased, and that on clothing increased. In nonmonetary terms, it can be calculated from data on a sample of 529 Shanghai workers' households (population, 2,532) that in 1956 the proletariat bought about 16 new clocks per 1,000 people, 13 new watches, 3.8 bicycles, 1.4 private radios, 1.2 cameras, and 0.4 of a new record player. China is, after all, an underdeveloped country. In popular terms, a family's wealth is measured by the so-called four big things (*szu ta chien*), namely a watch, a radio, a bicycle, and a sewing machine. Anyone who possesses all four is considered rich. Even in the country's most prosperous cities, the workers have very limited real incomes (although many nonproletarians are better off). The Communists did not cause this longstanding concrete problem, but, because of their hopes and ideology, they certainly had to face it. Labor stratification and its effects on earnings have been persistent problems in Shanghai's development, and after 1949 they became significant political problems.

EMPLOYMENT IN THE EARLY 1950s

Soon after the Red Army came to Shanghai in May 1949, Chiang Kai-shek's navy blockaded the port against civilian shipping. Because much of the city's economy had been based on raw materials imports and foreign markets, unemployment was the natural result. Workers had also been laid off because many firms had gone bankrupt during the inflation and warfare of the previous few years. In addition, tens of thousands of unemployed peasants had

---

1,410; (b) 1,021; (c) 540; and (d) 529. Percentages above 3 percent, here as elsewhere in this book, are rounded. The samples of workers in the three periods were very similar.

7. *Ibid.* This fact was somewhat lamely attributed to a "change in the age structure of workers' families."

migrated into the city to escape the civil war's violence in rural areas.

The new Communist government immediately began to tackle this unemployment problem. Thousands of peasants were sent back to the countryside. Efforts were made to restore factory production as quickly as possible. During the economic recovery from 1950 to 1953, the number of factory production jobs in Shanghai increased by 29 percent, from 434,000 to 558,000.[8] An unemployment register was set up, and public works were launched. Employment control was less an aim of the government at this time than was employment expansion.

UNEMPLOYMENT REGISTRATION AND RELIEF

On July 4, 1950, Mayor Ch'en Yi presided at the founding of the Temporary Relief Committee for Unemployed Workers.[9] Later in the same year, a "mass food program" was carried out in various factories that had been closed down. Between May and September 1950, 90,000 workers and 133,000 dependents received rice or relief money. By the end of that time, more than 86,000 unemployed workers had been allowed to register with the 28 official unions of Shanghai. A few of these unemployed people already had membership, but the unions were instructed to admit no new members who did not already have jobs.[10] The municipal Labor Bureau, which had been taken over from the Kuomintang at Liberation, played some part in coordinating these efforts, but its level of administration was far removed from the local problems that concerned union branches and relief committees. Measures to reduce unemployment were funded very slowly. In 1952, a Ministry of Labor "Decision on the Problems of Employment" only slightly intensified the relief and registration that was already going on in Shanghai.

This "unified registration of the unemployed" became a continuous project of the city government. By late 1952, more than 5,000 registrars were actively trying to gather information about the

8. *CFJP* editorial, June 25, 1954.

9. Shihyeh Kungjen Linshih Chiuchi Weiyüanhui. *LTP,* July 4, 1950.

10. Liu Ch'ang-sheng, Chairman of the Shanghai Federation of Trade Unions, report on "Unemployment Relief in Shanghai," to the All-Circles' Conference of October 16, 1950, *China Monthly Review* (Shanghai), December 1950.

urban labor force and also about people who were in the city without any productive purpose. By that time, more than 100 teams of registrars had been established, and 27 lanes had been selected as "keypoints for gaining experience." This long campaign went through three prescribed stages in each neighborhood of the city. The first, preparatory stage emphasized propaganda work and the establishment of lane registration committees. The second, "assessment" stage gathered preliminary name lists and encouraged informants to ferret out all of the unemployed for registration. The third and final stage was given over to celebrations and to the issuance of registration cards.[11] In practice, though not in intent, unemployment registration largely became a form of residence control.

PUBLIC WORKS

Only about 10,000 of the registrants in 1950 were actually employed. They did unskilled work like planting trees, breaking stones, digging irrigation ditches, building roads, and acting as transportation coolies.[12] Study classes on politics, culture, land reform (and on unemployment relief-work) absorbed more than twice as many of the unemployed as were given jobs.

After the beginning of 1951, public improvement projects picked up momentum. In January, 76,000 square meters of roads in Shanghai were repaired, 42 kilometers of sewers were dredged, and work was begun on nine bridges and a tunnel.[13] By mid-year, when the Shanghai labor market began to tighten slightly, 1.5 million square meters of Shanghai's roadways had been patched up and a grid of waterpipes was being laid to supply public cisterns in Chapei and in other northern parts of the city that are filled with transport workers' slums.[14] By the middle of the next year, a large new park had been completed on Haining Road.[15] These plans

11. *CFJP*, Shanghai, November 13, 1952.

12. Liu Ch'ang-sheng, "Unemployment Relief in Shanghai."

13. *Shanghai News*, March 16, 1951.

14. NCNA, Shanghai, June 6, 1951. Christopher Howe, *Urban Employment and Economic Growth in Communist China*, emphasizes that the employment situation improved somewhat in mid-1951. Howe makes clear the severity of the unemployment situation in Shanghai throughout the period he discusses, although he also speaks of periodic fluctuations in the market, which seems for many categories of workers to have been minor relative to the large unemployment.

15. NCNA, Shanghai, May 26, 1952.

expanded so that by 1955 more than 30 new parks had been opened in Shanghai, including a "People's Park" on the site of the old race course and the huge "West Suburbs Park" containing more than 30,000 trees.[16] By this time, the underground sewage system was due to be lengthened by another 70 kilometers. Some of the most squalid canal-ditches were piped and covered by roads.[17].

Even during the height of this activity in 1954, only 35,400 of Shanghai's unemployed had obtained jobs after registration—far fewer than the total number of applicants for work. Temporary relief employment was found for 18,000 that year, but only 4,300 were given jobs in 137 official "self-help" factories.[18] The increase of new entrants to the Shanghai labor force meant that the local government could not provide jobs for everyone.[19] Labor service stations (*laotung fuwu chan*) were established to deal with the problem, but they could not fully solve it. These organizations recommended unemployed people for work. Most job-seekers in Shanghai did not depend on the official labor stations, because the bureaucracy did not have many jobs to offer. Throughout the early 1950s, it was possible to look freely for a position in Shanghai and to accept one if the private search succeeded.

GOVERNMENT'S POLICY TOWARD PRODUCTIVITY

Unemployment registration, relief, and public works were designed to improve the lot of Shanghai's unemployed. At the same time, however, officials began to limit the number of good factory jobs for broad demographic reasons. If the adult population of Shanghai could be reduced, in part through career control policies, then the long-range unemployment problem there would be lessened. Make-work projects were therefore supplemented by employment population policies.

Marxist Chinese demographers have theorized that the proper size of any city should depend on the "social production" there.

16. *China News Service*, June 22, 1955.
17. NCNA, April 19 and 21, 1954.
18. *CFJP*, January 9, 1955.
19. The total number of Chinese youths, ages five to twenty-four, increased in *millions* as follows: 1953, 225; 1958, 255; 1963, 300; 1968, 350. United Nations, Department of Economic and Social Affairs, *Future Population Estimates by Sex and Age: Report IV, The Population of Asia and the Far East, 1960-80*, No. 31 (ST/SOA/Series A), 1959, p. 31. Not all of these people were in Shanghai, but their number affected immigration to that city. The size of the statistics is noteworthy.

"Social production" in nonfarm areas is virtually equivalent to industrial output. This ideal norm for urban size can be refined, in the official theory, by factors for labor productivity, by the percentage of industrial workers in the population, and by the available food supply. The Chinese government has usually maintained that increases in the output of an enterprise should result from better labor productivity, not from hiring more workers, and some Chinese officials have insisted that the ratio of productive to nonproductive urban residents should constantly rise, or at least remain stable.[20] Thus, once factories had been restored to operation in the period of recovery, 1950-1953, the Shanghai government sought to maintain a balance between the growth of factory employment and rises in productivity. Efforts were made to restrain factory hiring and to send the unemployed to jobs outside of Shanghai.

In mid-1955, a group of deputies to the National People's Congress spent more than a fortnight in the city, inspecting enterprises to check the efficiency of restraints on hiring. They reported that "the census conditions in many districts were . . . very complicated."[21] They concluded that the government should take stronger measures. In September, at a meeting of the city's Political Consultative Conference, K'o Ch'ing-shih, who had been installed in the Shanghai Party apparatus only a few months before, spoke for a resolution "to overcome the conditions of overpopulated Shanghai and its excess labor."[22]

Initial efforts to control population focused on the unemployed. In early 1956, the Shanghai public security and civil administration departments launched a campaign to conscript "vagabonds" (*yumin*) for work both in and out of the city.[23] A few of these "vagabonds" were clearly well-educated, and some others were given technical education as accountants and scientific researchers. Some were placed in enterprises that had newly undergone the transition to socialism, but the great majority did ordinary labor.

20. See the important article from *KMJP*, October 7, 1963, in *JPRS*, No. 2245, pp. 50-61. Another translation of the same item is in *SCMP*, No. 3093. Travellers report that factories are proud of their employment growth, but ex-residents of the city confirm that doctrine stressed labor productivity.

21. NCNA, Shanghai, June 21, 1955.

22. *HWJP*, September 5, 1955. This is really ironic, because three years later K'o presided over the biggest immigration to Shanghai that has ever occurred.

23. *KMJP*, March 29, 1956.

PROCEDURES AND PERQUISITES OF EMPLOYMENT

A person's status as a jobholder or job-seeker was socially and economically important, but there was also major stratification according to different types of employed workers. Salaries and perquisites for regular, unionized employees were determined by two factors: job-rank (*chihpieh*) and level-rank (*chipieh*). Job-rank was dependent on the difficulty and specialization of each particular kind of work. A range of salaries was designated for each job, with a considerable overlap between different jobs. Level-rank, which indicates where within the range the worker's compensation fell, was determined by seniority, previous experience, education, and class background. This method of calculating salary has not been followed for all permanent jobs in Communist China or at all times, but it has been flexible enough to apply to most regular jobs, especially in state-owned organizations. A privileged employee with a regular job had many kinds of nonwage perquisites that were determined by his salary in combination with the size of his family as recorded in a "household registration book" (*huchi pu*).[24]

New entrants to the permanent labor force in many industries had to serve as apprentices before they could enjoy the benefits of regular-worker status. According to 1951 rules in Shanghai, any apprentice had to be more than fifteen years old; he also had to have a primary school certificate or the equivalent, good health, and "no undesirable hobbies." The first one-and-a-half months of apprenticeship were probationary. The content of training was decided entirely by the factory, which examined each apprentice after the end of his first year and each six months thereafter. The whole course was supposed to last less than three years. Compensation was low as a matter of policy.

In the middle of the training period, an allowance for clothing should be given; in the later stages [apprentices'] wages should allow them to be independent . . . [but] if the wages of apprentices become too high, the responsible staff of enterprises will be unwilling to employ them. Since we cannot afford to have many technical schools now, it would therefore be difficult to train workers.[25]

24. Interview, Hong Kong, November 1969.
25. Shanghai Shih Tsung Kunghui Tiaoch'a Yenchiu Shih, *Kunghui ch'ing-kung kungtso* (Shanghai: Laotung Ch'upan She, 1951), pp. 1-2 and 140-144.

There was some stratification also among employees who had cleared the apprenticeship hurdle and gained permanent jobs, even though trade unions strove to organize and amalgamate these workers. Long before the socialization of industry in 1956, unions were providing many assorted social services for their members. By 1954, Shanghai textile workers (in the city's largest union) had 100 recreation clubs, 200 libraries, and 400 dramatic, choral, dancing, and art societies. The textile union organized regular parties, dances, picnics, and free movies. Even at that early date, it subsidized 220 spare-time schools, enrolling 45,000 members.[26] In the five years after Liberation, Shanghai's total union membership increased by about two-thirds, from 800,000 to 1,330,000.[27] Some kinds of benefits were distributed among all the members—the textile union's clubs and schools were of this sort—but not all union members had access to certain other perquisites. By the middle of 1955, a total of only 1,700 Shanghai textile workers were retired on pensions.[28] Even by early 1955, only 400,000 of Shanghai's 1,330,000 regular unionized workers had any form of retirement insurance.[29] For example, Shanghai is one of the cigarette-packing centers of China, but only 300 of the tobacco workers who retired in the first half of 1956 received annuities. At the end of that year, the total number of Shanghai pensioners in this industry was 1,100.[30] These favored retirees received a generous 70 percent of their previous wages, but their small number suggests considerable elitism in the union system. From 1951 to 1955, a total of only 4,500 workers in Shanghai retired on old-age pensions.[31]

26. NCNA, April 5, 1954.

27. *CFJP*, February 2, 1955. See also NCNA, Shanghai, January 18, 1955.

28. NCNA, Shanghai, May 7, 1955. The main reason for this especially low statistic in the textile union is that at least 70 percent of Shanghai's textile workers are women. This is nevertheless only an extreme example. Few union members could qualify to maximize their benefits in other trades, too, as evidence in the text above shows.

29. NCNA, January 18, 1955, and *CFJP*, February 2, 1955. The percentage (30 percent) is not mentioned in the text because the simultaneity and rounding of the raw data are somewhat suspect. The qualitative conclusion still stands.

30. NCNA, Shanghai, April 18, 1956.

31. NCNA, January 10, 1956. China's traditional family system, under which children are supposed to care for their parents' old age, no doubt helped to make the reality behind these low statistics less severe than it would be in a Western industrial city. Noninsured retired workers' attitude toward favored workers (and toward the government) can hardly have been helped by that custom, however.

The government during this early period had not yet accumulated sufficient resources to establish comprehensive career controls and thus to guide the energies of most Shanghai citizens. The subsequent transition to socialism and the Leap which grew out of it provided essential economic bases for social guidance.

CHANGES IN EMPLOYMENT PRACTICES, 1956-1958

Shanghai's economic growth from 1956 to 1958, after socialist legitimacy had been established for most urban capital in the movement for joint enterprises, sustained somewhat more effective career guidance procedures. The transition to socialism, with its new investments and organizations, however, also led to a population influx that was further expanded by the heavy infiltration of people into Shanghai following natural calamities in many parts of Kiangsu, Anhwei, and Chekiang provinces. In May 1956, there were more than 6,020,000 permanent residents in Shanghai, and 60,000 more persons had legal status as temporary residents. By the end of November, the city's permanent-status population had risen above 6.2 million. Another 240,000 people had established temporary residence by legal procedures. The government officially estimated that a further 60,000 people were living in Shanghai without registrations (or rations), but this estimate may well be too low.[32]

EFFORTS TO CONTROL IMMIGRANT POPULATION

With the 1956 "transition to socialism," somewhat more capital was earmarked for economic expansion in Shanghai. This new money enabled the regular proletariat to coopt some contract laborers into its ranks. More than twice as many new apprentices entered the work force in 1956 as had been brought into it during the previous five years put together. In the last third of 1956, for example, Shanghai's textile and dyeing industries alone planned to hire 16,000 new employees.[33] Jobs in other industries also increased. According to calculations from one report, Shanghai people were

32. *CFJP,* December 26, 1956. The population figures in this paragraph refer to Shanghai's limited geographical jurisdiction in the mid-1950s. The area and population of the municipality were greatly expanded by the addition of new counties in 1958-1959.

33. *CFJP,* September 28, 1956, and *LTP,* August 6, 1956.

obtaining work at an average annual rate of 187,000 new jobs per year during the first three quarters of 1956.[34] Another report indicated that 140,000 workers were newly employed in regular jobs during that year.[35] The discrepancy between these two figures probably arises from different definitions of the term "worker," but both are evidence that Shanghai offered roughly 10 percent more jobs at the end of 1956 than at the beginning.

Even the newly socialized economic organization of the city, and a modicum of new capital to finance it, could not eliminate Shanghai's unemployment. The city government was candid enough in mid-1956 to make no pretense that Shanghai was fully employed. It announced that full employment would be a goal for achievement only at the end of the second five-year plan in 1962.[36] The urban economy's purpose was more to produce goods than to hire people.

When new jobs were created (e.g., for 2,800 new drivers in late 1956), most of the recruits were from lower productivity, good-status positions such as bus conductors and demobilized soldiers, not from the ranks of the unemployed.[37] Their previous positions were largely taken up by women recently recruited into the work force. Even semilegal "spontaneous enterprises" (*tzufa hu*), which "obtained labor through private influence and not through district and township governments,"[38] often employed peasants out of their rural jobs rather than hiring the urban unemployed. For example, 120 Sungpei Township farmers were engaged in Shanghai in July 1956, and they seem to have included some of the most active workers in that rural place—3 coop management committeemen, 3 production-team heads, 12 bookkeepers, 10 schoolteachers, and 14 health workers.

Because population in Shanghai was rising faster than available

34. Calculated from *JMJP*, Dcember 6, 1956, which gives a figure of 140,000 for January-September of that year.
35. From a speech by union leader Chung Min at a conference for young workers in December 1956. *HWJP*, December 14, 1956. The meeting was interestingly named Hsin Kungjen Ch'ingkung Huiyi (Conference of New Workers and Young Workmen).
36. NCNA, Shanghai, August 13, 1956.
37. *HMPWK*, December 25, 1956.
38. NCNA, Shanghai, August 14, 1956. This implies that urban *ch'ü* (districts) and rural *hsiang* (townships) were the main levels approving rural-urban job transfers to the Shanghai suburbs in 1956.

work at the beginning of 1957, the municipal People's Congress adopted resolutions that all new arrivals should be persuaded to return to their native places, that employees should be discouraged from bringing their dependents into the city, and that relief grants should be structured so as to encourage people to move away. The Congress further decided to reduce the number of workers in Shanghai by 30 percent.[39] Of course this could not be done by paper fiat. Efforts to restrict population growth by sending peasant immigrants back to the countryside continued throughout 1957, but the problem remained unsolved. According to one estimate, 670,000 people with household registrations in Shanghai were unemployed at the end of 1957. This was probably equivalent to more than one-quarter of the employed labor force.[40]

Some categories of applicants found jobs in Shanghai, but in the mid-1950s more of the unemployed were sent outside the city to find work than in the early 1950s.[41] Although statistics to prove this change have not been spotted, the following table shows the aggregate results of official employment efforts from Liberation to the antirightist campaign.

Labor bureaus continued to search for jobs that could reduce the number of idle urban residents. The employment they could offer was arduous: loading ships, collecting reuseable waste materials, and all kinds of contract work.[42] Many street-level cadres in labor

39. *HWJP*, January 17, 1957.
40. *Chanwang*, No. 33 (August 31, 1957), p. 20. Christopher Howe has made an excellent effort to estimate the unemployment rate for the end of 1957. See Howe, *Urban Employment and Economic Growth in Communist China*, pp. 38-40, and the complex tabular appendix, pp. 152-155. To make a long story short, Howe puts total Shanghai employment at 2,418,000 and total unemployment at 670,000. His quantitative assumptions are bold but are needed in order to make any economic analysis of this problem at all. One could ask if there is not extensive double counting in the emigration statistics, if 50 percent of persons returned to work in rural areas and their families had previously been in the urban work force, and if the number of women reaching age sixteen after 1949 who did not wish to work equalled the number over sixteen in 1949 who decided later to look for jobs. The calculation on these assumptions is very worthwhile, modestly presented and convincing.
41. The Shanghai Personnel Employment Committee by November 1956 had found jobs for a group of 6,000 well-qualified applicants. One of them had a Ph.D. in political economy from the University of Frankfurt. Of this group, 78 percent were finally employed in Shanghai, but more ordinary workers in 1956-1957 were sent farther afield. *HWJP*, November 30, 1956. The increased dispatch of personnel from Shanghai did not prevent the city's total population from rising at this time, both because of natural births and because of a net urban influx.
42. *HMPWK*, September 4, 1947.

TABLE 1.

Jobs Given to Unemployed Workers in Shanghai, Mid-1949 to Mid-1957

Job Category	Percentage	Number
Employed in state construction outside of Shanghai	25%	200,000
Employed inside Shanghai		
in industry and construction	57%	460,000
in commerce	9%	70,000
Not accounted for	9%	70,000
Total	100%	800,000

Source: Constructed from partial statistics in *China News Service,* Shanghai, August 17, 1957. This is a distribution of jobs, not workers; double-counting of workers is probable both within and between categories. Jobs found privately are not included.

stations were quite poor themselves and usually they received only 20 to 30 yüan per month. When street committees found loyal personnel for placement work, a major attempt was made to retain them by persuasion rather than by salaries. For example Wang Chih-fang, a Youth League branch secretary in Luwan District's First Street Committee, worked hard to improve the Party's relations with youth in that area. She apparently received no salary for her efforts and lived in a family of five that was supported only by her father's wage. The street office had no regular opening or closing time, and she kept long hours there. She helped many people through her labor bureau to land jobs that she would gladly have taken herself, if the other street committee cadres had not dissuaded her.[43]

When unemployed workers wanted jobs inside Shanghai but could not acquire them through the government, the usual recourse was to obtain them through illegal channels. Very few workers followed the intellectuals' example of May 1957 by making political complaints. An unknown number of workers in Shanghai were hired by "underground factories" (publicly called *tihsia kung-ch'ang*), whose importance in the city's whole economy was appar-

43. *CNP,* March 22, 1957.

ently not negligible. Some of these enterprises, such as the Chienta Leather Ball Factory in P'englai District, offered 50 percent more pay for night work than employees received on daytime jobs. Workers who were hired in both the regular and illegal systems had high rates of sick leaves, absences, and product rejects on their legal jobs.[44]

One of the ways to control workers in underground enterprises was to send them forcibly out of the city when they could be identified. "More than 1,000 unemployed workers," whom the Party apparently wished to deport, were sent to the Ch'anghsing Islands in the Yangtze estuary to take up "relief work," and "some of them were there permanently to perform agricultural jobs."[45] Another way of preventing the nonauthorized proletariat from finding jobs was to give state managers more flexibility in some areas. For example, in early 1957, the Shanghai Textile Bureau's factories were individually empowered to transfer workers among themselves without any higher approval. During the first two months that managers had this authority, they used it more than 5,000 times. This no doubt reduced the rate at which they needed to hire contract workers.

PRODUCTIVITY AND WAGE REFORMS IN 1956

Concern about maintaining a balance between the city's population and its jobs was matched by concern about raising worker productivity. In July 1956, during the most open period of recent Chinese politics, some members of a Shanghai Communist Party conference criticized the wage-lowering that had occurred at state enterprises in 1954. These changes had reduced Shanghai's salaries by aligning them with national levels.[46] Now the Party laid plans for more stratification of wages, to give workers more incentives in the hope that new capital invested in socialist enterprises might be used efficiently by careful labor. Trade unions called forums to "seek workers' opinions" about the allegedly fallacious, nefarious "principle of equality" that had restrained labor productivity in Shanghai before 1956.[47] Egalitarian salaries conflicted with social-

44. *CNP,* January 22, 1957.
45. *HWJP,* June 24, 1957.
46. NCNA, Shanghai, July 26, 1956.
47. NCNA, Shanghai, June 14, 1956.

ist development. A small conference called for more "democratic life" inside the Party. Lower functionaries, and even skilled workers, were urged to speak frankly about higher officials more often. Socialist development conflicted with egalitarian wages, but the need for select labor to ensure maximum productivity for new capital in some plants gave power to a few skilled workers.

The effect of the wage reforms was to raise the salaries of permanent workers, thereby enlarging the gap between the regular and the contract proletariats. By September 1956, the average compensation of permanent workers had increased 12 percent. A sectoral breakdown of the 1956 wage changes in Shanghai shows that capital construction pay was raised by an average of 89 percent, in commercial departments by 31 percent, in "people's organizations" by 27 percent, in government organs by 19 percent, and in cultural units by 15 percent.[48]

Officials clearly expected that the new incentive compensation structure would cause discontent in the lower proletariat. Welfare doles to a few unemployed workers were increased somewhat. One thousand cadres underwent training for a month, learning how to propagandize the new wage reform (*kungtzu kaiko*).[49] Local papers called for "putting work in the wage" in both nationalized and joint enterprises.

The reform began in state plants and in "old joint enterprises" (*lao hoying ch'iyeh*),[50] because pre-1956 capitalists had often given higher wages than state plant managements were allowed to pay. After the transition to socialism, there was still a differential to be erased between state wage scales and those of formerly private plants.

INSURANCE AND OTHER NONWAGE PERQUISITES

The nonwage perquisites of permanent workers also remained large. At the end of 1956, 800,000 Shanghai employees were covered

48. NCNA, Shanghai, December 17, 1956.
49. *LTP*, June 12, 1956. Also, Charles Hoffman, *Work Incentive Practices and Policies in the People's Republic of China, 1953-1965* (Albany: State University of New York Press, 1967), pp. 84 ff. For evidence that Mao never opposed material incentives in the socialist sector, see Jack Gray and Patrick Cavendish, *Chinese Communism in Crisis: Maoism and the Cultural Revolution* (New York: Praeger Publishers, 1968), p. 63.
50. *HWJP*, January 17, 1957.

by state retirement insurance—a healthy increase of 310,000 (63 percent) since the end of 1955. This was caused by the amalgamation of private enterprise insurance schemes into the state system and did not represent much expansion of coverage. Many workers, probably about two-thirds of them, were still not covered. Since most pre-1956 private enterprises had already subscribed to the government's "free" medical service on behalf of their core employees, the transition to socialism increased the medical coverage of Shanghai workers by only 3.6 percent.[51]

For heavy industries that were slated for expansion, the governing municipal bureaus announced "provisional regulations" to grant some basic recreational and major medical perquisites to workers who were not included under other insurance systems.[52] In spite of this program, many poor workers still criticized the wage reform. Factory cadres were ordered to explain to workers why the reform was necessary. A local newspaper said that "some plants care only about the welfare of workers and neglect their political education. . . . An investigation disclosed that most laborers with bad behavior are new workers (*hsin kungjen*) or apprentices (*yit'u* or *hsüeht'u*)."[53]

The recreational and other advantages of basic union membership were spread among an enlarged proportion of permanent workers, even though the lot of contract laborers was seldom helped. When full-fledged union members were in financial straits, their units were supposed to allot funds to relieve them. Unions and employers were expected to arrange any necessary personal loans. For example, in late 1956, 10 to 15 percent of all permanently employed dockers on the Whangpoo River held fixed-term or temporary loans from the Harbor Bureau on union guarantee.[54] Many of Shanghai's old private schools were set aside for union members. Efforts were also made to provide housing for permanent workers. The government built what housing it could afford, to supplement the projects begun in the early 1950s, but there was not

51. *Ibid.*
52. *CFJP*, November 6, 1956.
53. *HWJP*, November 25, 1956.
54. *HWJP*, December 14, 1956, and NCNA, Shanghai, August 26, 1956.

enough money to satisfy the space requirements even of all the skilled workers, much less those of the lower proletariat.[55]

Public health was an area in which official policy tried hard to fulfill requests from all workers, not just permanent ones. After the socialist transition period, great successes were achieved in industrial preventive medicine. To take just one example, Shanghai's twelve talc factories, which combined to form a single enterprise in February 1956, were instructed to eliminate new occurrences of talcum silicosis. By the end of the year they had done so, according to medical surveys run at that time.[56] On September 20, 1956, all Shanghai joint commercial enterprises began contributing 5.5 percent of their monthly wage bills to a common labor insurance fund from which medical care was provided.[57] In November, the government slashed fees at Shanghai's medical facilities, which had by then all been nationalized. It was decreed that costs for treatment of hospitalized patients would be reduced 60 percent, for lab tests 50 percent, for surgery 40 percent, for hospital room charges 26 percent, and for consultation 15 percent. Shanghai's medical system would then take in about 23 percent less revenue. Fees were not cut much on light illnesses, but they were slashed drastically in cases of both infectious disease (to encourage people to seek treatment) and serious illness.[58]

The socialization of 1956 greatly spurred the demand for medical services. The extent of the government's efforts was shown even better by the petitions it turned down than by those it granted. The Public Health Bureau was at pains to explain why it could not requite the "many letters" suggesting that hospital clinics should stay open on Sundays. "Now many doctors are already practicing twenty-four hours a day. They have to take care of outpatients,

55. NCNA, Shanghai, August 30, 1956, proudly announced the completion of new housing for 2,000 workers in the suburbs, but many projects of this size would not even have begun to solve the problem.

56. NCNA, Shanghai, November 14, 1956.

57. NCNA, Shanghai, September 21, 1956.

58. *HWJP*, October 20, 1956. Neither this article nor the similar NCNA, Shanghai, November 1, 1956, indicates where the medical system could find money to make good its deficit. Obviously, labor insurance funds played a role, but it seems that a bold policy decision was made to worry about this financial problem in detail later, after the plunge on medical prices had already been taken.

sickrooms, emergency wards, teaching, and servicing factories."
For these reasons, all outpatient departments had long since been
reduced to working only on an appointment system.[59] Since 1949,
Communist medicine in Shanghai had discouraged hospitaliza-
tion and emphasized outpatient facilities. The number of hospital
beds by mid-1957 had increased 70 percent, but the number of
outpatient clinics had increased 550 percent.[60] As for opening
Sundays, "this proposal was tried in the Third People's Hospital,
but labor insurance workers on Sunday duty expressed their opinion that it was awkward."[61] Too many patients showed up, and the
functionaries reported without much guile that they could not
handle the crush. Despite this work load, Shanghai sent doctors out
to other parts of the country.[62] In medicine, more than in any other
branch of Communist Shanghai's public service, administrative
headaches and efforts were immense. "Serving the people" was
indeed heroic, but it also meant appointments and queues for the
people and long hours for officials. Serving *all* the workers was a
project that Shanghai's government had the resources to try only in
limited fields, and then only with limited success. Serving only
some of them was unfortunately much more feasible.

EQUALITY VERSUS PRODUCTIVITY

The labor insurance system as a whole could not be extended to the
lower proletariat, because that might hurt production. After the
introduction of group insurance at the socialized Weihsin Stocking
Factory, for example, absenteeism rose to 14 percent, because many
workers found that they could live on their sick leave subsidies.
Temporary hands sometimes constituted as much as one-third of
the total work force when many regular employees were absent.[63]

59. *Yüyüeh chihtu.* The "appointment system" is one of the early symptoms to
warn of the onset of a modern medical delivery organization.
60. NCNA, Shanghai, August 12, 1957. The 1957 hospital bed total in Shanghai
was only 17,000. In comparing national levels of health, Bruce M. Russett et al.,
World Handbook of Political and Social Indicators (New Haven, Conn.: Yale
University Press, 1964), pp. 207-212, rely on the national indices for the number of
beds and for the number of physicians. Unfortunately, national definitions of these
categories vary enormously.
61. *HMPWK*, February 18, 1957.
62. *HWJP*, February 19, 1957.
63. *HWJP*, March 27, 1957.

Problems of this sort led the government to allow public expression of lower proletarian resentment against stratified work benefits. As early as November 1956, there was a blossoming of criticism against the "advanced producers' movement" *(hsienchin sheng-ch'anche yüntung)*, which awarded prizes and perquisites to highly productive workers. Some laborers were earning double the basic wage by doing overtime, and this practice was alleged somehow to "confuse the socialist principle of remuneration according to work."[64] Some managements, to correct these deviations and give the workers more pride and power, were "allowing laborers to set their own quotas." The practice was not widespread in this period, but lower proletariat complaints about the lack of democracy in quota setting recurred for the same reasons in the Cultural Revolution ten years later. Greed and materialism were condemned. Some workers in the Shanghai Machine Tools Factory (which was also a model in 1967) accused a Party branch committee member of hiding good machines and inputs for his own use, so that he could get more prizes for after-hours' work to which the competition was not supposed to apply. A Youth League member insisted on laboring in the repair shop, rather than at new construction, because his total output would then receive a higher count. A man in the refining shop hid useless rejects that he had made quickly, keeping the components so that he could later turn in good produce toward his competition total. A worker in the axle-case shop persuaded a less productive friend to take the responsibility for rejects, so that the first man could qualify to be an "advanced worker." People's Bank officers stationed in the factory said that prizes added too much to the wage bill and too little to savings. Above all, production pressure was blamed for hurting "discipline" among the workers. The stated reason showed why stratification in Shanghai's proletariat was politically explosive.

The factory's new workers this year were in the main previously non-industrial workers who had changed jobs. Among them, there are many who had belonged to the propertied class and to the unemployed. They are lazy at work but active at dances. Stealing, gambling, corruption, and quarrels are not infrequent with them. They even practice improper sexual

---

64. NCNA, Shanghai, November 26, 1956. An ex-resident indicated that over-time pay was abolished in many Shanghai enterprises in later years.

relationships and live a rotten life. But now there is a response in the Shanghai Machine Tools Factory. Senior cadres are urging political education to strengthen the thought of the workers.[65]

Advanced Communist producers and new workers from the dispossessed bourgeoisie were thus lumped together as an unclean caste. In effect, they were together accused of exploiting other workers for whom the government could afford few benefits.

The ideology behind these sentiments sprang mostly out of unskilled workers' resentments at being forced to produce more than they wished by the new managers who controlled enterprise capital. The sources of this very proletarian consciousness went beyond those that would be of interest to Marxist analysis. The lower proletariat sensed some Luddite problems, too, and their anger was directed against certain efficient techniques, not just against the men who controlled them. Shanghai light industries in 1956 made a survey of 500 "advanced experiences" for which worker-inventors had been given credit, and concluded that only 30 percent of them were really advanced. Many of these innovations were more labor-intensive than the systems they replaced (and because labor is cheap in China, they were indeed more economical), but these technical changes usually meant that the workers had to labor harder than before, with no increase in pay. Such changes were therefore criticized, usually on other grounds: "Some neglect safety measures. Other have proven to be injurious to the health of the workers, most of whom objected that they required too much physical effort."[66] Not only during the 1956 socialization but also later, technical innovation campaigns have been inextricable from general production pressure. The lower proletariat has generally resented them both.

When the Hundred Flowers movement peaked in May 1957, one of the many disparate complaints made in Shanghai was that the welfare system did not touch those who needed it. According to one critic:

Some units' managers and branch secretaries, in order to express their so-called understanding and caring for the people (*liaochieh jen, kuanhsin jen*) visited poor families on Sundays and gave them money. Some of these

65. *HWJP*, November 8, 1956.
66. *PKTKP*, October 27, 1956, based on a dispatch from Shanghai.

took the money. But they felt it was strange, because with the present restricted welfare payments there are people in real difficulties who get no help.[67]

The critics of the Hundred Flowers period were especially angry that unemployment was sometimes built into the economic plans. For example, 2,000 girls doing embroidery work in Shanghai lost their jobs when the wholesale department of a municipal company redirected their supply of floss to other purposes. No substitute materials were available, and the "Shanghai Association of United Art Shops" implied that bureaucratic heads should roll when plans failed to use current laborers.[68]

Nevertheless, these political complaints told more about the size of worker dissatisfaction over welfare and productivity problems than about the government's efforts to solve them. "Democratic management committees" (*minchu kuanli weiyüanhui*) had been set up in many "new joint [state-private] enterprises" (*hsin hoying ch'iyeh*) at the end of 1956 in an attempt to stop such complaints by decentralizing to shop and factory levels the responsibility for pressuring workers to produce.[69] District governments were ordered to inspect business cadres' treatment of their workers.[70] The Wuhua Umbrella Factory was made a model for success in "solving the welfare problem" by mobilizing its labor union to explain, in effect, why the proletariat needed strata as much as great expectations.[71]

The subsequent antirightist campaign saw a hail of abuse directed at the notion that the proletariat's lot as a whole was not improving quickly. It was easy for the Party to find favored workers to refute this idea, and endless testimonials about present benefits were printed in the newspapers. A woman: "In 1953, I was seriously ill, and the medical expenses were huge. My family of eight people still had a good life." A fifty-seven-year-old worker: "Before Liberation, I got half a portion of rice every day. Now I can't work, but I get 30 yüan every month from the labor insurance system. The

67. *HMPWK*, May 8, 1957.
68. *HWJP*, May 16, 1957.
69. See *HWJP*, November 21, 1956, concerning a conference for 13,000 Shanghai factory cadres that was called to instill such democracy in them.
70. *JWJP*, November 22, 1956.
71. *HWJP*, November 24, 1956.

government also chips in 10 yüan, and I need not pay my medical expenses." A sixty-six-year-old worker: "Before Liberation, I had no money to see a doctor. Now I have hurt my leg through carelessness, and they have given me a sick leave of 40 days. I get 2 yüan a day." A docker: "Before Liberation, we workers never went to the movies. Now many workers have bought their own home radios. In the past, very few were literate; but now, in our unloading district alone, we have 38 culture classes." A seventy-three-year-old coolie, who before Liberation could not afford to get married, was wedded to his sixty-six-year-old bride with great fanfare.[72] The Party emphasized that some of the proletariat were now better off, and on that ground it clearly hoped that all the proletariat would think itself so. About the new workers who had joined the proletariat when their capitalist class was disinherited in 1956, an instruments worker said in a benign fatherly way, "We give equal treatment to apprentices from the bourgeois class and teach them the skills we have."[73]

The unintended effect of some government welfare programs was probably to exacerbate temporary labor and unemployment problems in Shanghai more than any direct campaign helped solve them. Even after the wage reform, salaries in new joint enterprises often remained above those in fully nationalized plants. A complaint of 1957 summarizes this interrelated group of problems quite well:

After Liberation, state-operated companies absorbed in batches workers from private enterprises, but their wages and treatment still differed. Some of the labor insurance rules are not realistic. For example, the families of workers living in Shanghai have 50 percent of their medical fees subsidized, but those whose families live in the villages get nothing. Many employees try to transfer their families to Shanghai, and this contradicts the government's policy of mobilizing the peasants to return to the countryside.[74]

Some complaints of this nature brought forth new welfare programs that were designed to lessen the differences between various workers' compensations. When laborers felt that new product

72. These examples are from *HWJP*, June 24, 1957—a particularly rich day for this subject, for three long articles were devoted to praises of this nature. Almost any day that June will do, however.

73. *HWJP*, June 26, 1957.

74. *HMPWK*, May 8, 1957.

quality or quantity standards affected them too much, that cadres were too proud, that the perquisites of unskilled laborers were too few, or that hours were too long, worker representatives were sometimes invited to put forward proposals to improve these situations.[75] On September 1, 1957, no fewer than 110,000 workers in Shanghai's joint commercial enterprises were put under new coverage in the state's comprehensive labor insurance rules.[76] The Shanghai municipal government in late 1957 even reversed some aspects of the previous wage reform by adding four new regulations that slightly lessened favoritism in the workers' retirement system.[77]

This mobilization of wide proletarian support was, as always, limited by finances. When Chairman Mao visited the Shanghai state-owned First Textile Factory on September 18, 1957, he read the big-character posters put up there in connection with the anti-rightist campaign. The posters criticized Party work and cadres' arrogance, but it was reported with some emphasis that Mao also read "veteran workers'" counterattacks against new workers who complained about low wages. The official report of Mao's visit stated that the wall posters had been very critical, but "they were mostly correct and well intentioned."[78] The government knew that it had to strike a balance between rewarding industrial production and taking care of low-skill industrial workers.

EMPLOYMENT AND THE GREAT LEAP FORWARD

The only way to break out of the need for this compromising balance of good values was to raise productivity by means other than material rewards. In 1958, the road of mass mobilization was taken.

75. NCNA, Shanghai, August 12, 1957.
76. NCNA, Shanghai, September 1, 1957. This article mentions that the total proletariat enjoying labor insurance in China then numbered 8 million.
77. *HWJP*, December 11, 1957. This emphasizes that regular workers' unions should "discuss" the new regulations without giving any precise description of the rules' actual content. It says that Shanghai workers should "realize that in solving the problems of welfare and wages, all the people of the whole nation should be considered." The municipal People's Congress proposed to "encourage the masses to raise suggestions for the revision of these regulations."
78. *JMJP*, September 22, 1957.

IMMIGRATION AND UNEMPLOYMENT

To effect this mobilization, the Great Leap Forward promoted integration between Party and government bureaucracies at many levels. The reduction of residence controls was a natural corollary of the nationwide effort to mobilize labor through spirited propaganda, and under these circumstances Shanghai's population plan became a dead letter. The purpose of the Leap was more to maximize production and loyalty than to control them.

Checks on immigration to the city collapsed. By the end of 1958, the legal population of Shanghai's urbanized, built-up area alone exceeded 6 million.[79] Many peasants came to Shanghai in search of temporary work during the Great Leap. In late 1958, the city government took strong steps to organize a "labor army" (*laotung tachün*) to send some of the unemployed among them, as well as many students and cadres, out of the city for harvests. By the end of February 1959, nearly 500,000 people had been drafted for such work. Even in the slack winter season, they were given farm work storing fertilizers, selecting seeds, and repairing tools for their first major "battle"—spring planting.[80]

The rise in Shanghai's overall population was accompanied by a rise in jobs. By the end of 1958, Shanghai had 1,187,000 industrial employees, a rise of 135 percent over the 1949 figure. *Peking Review* could claim without too much distortion that unemployment in Shanghai had been "virtually eliminated."[81] In fact, the term "unemployment" was impossible to define in this temporary high turnover situation. In the low-skill slum area of Yaoshui Lane, a survey indicated that by 1960 people were working unless they were "without vocations." Of course, this was an exemplary lane, and it probably had a higher proportion of people employed than did other poor workers' areas in Shanghai.

79. P'an Hsüeh-min (member of the Shanghai Economic Planning Committee), "Shanghai's Industrial Development," *Tili chihshih* [Geographical knowledge], No. 7 (July 6, 1959), translated in *ECMM*, No. 182, p. 19. P'an noted that the urban area containing these people then had 192 square kilometers. This places the average population density at well over 30,000 people per square kilometer. The Economic Planning Committee is apparently successor to the earlier Finance and Economy Committee, mentioned in note 6.

80. *HWJP*, February 27, 1959.

81. Su Chih-cheng, "Shanghai's Industrial Progress," *PR*, No. 22 (June 9, 1959), pp. 10-12.

TABLE 2.

Reported Use of Labor Capacity, Yaoshui Lane, 1960

Employment Category	1949	1960
"Employed" (*chiuyeh*)	54%	75%
"Unemployed" (*shihyeh*)	17%	——
"Without vocations" (*wuyeh*)	29%	25%

Source: Shanghai Shehui K'ohsüeh Yüan, Chingchi Yenchiu So, Ch'engshih Chingchi Tsu [Urban Economy Group, Economic Research Institute, Shanghai Academy of Social Sciences], *Shanghai p'enghu ch'ü ti piench'ien* [The transformation of Shanghai's slum districts] (Shanghai: Shanghai Shehui K'ohsüeh Yüan, 1965), p. 65. The exact definition of the whole sample is not given. In other, more typical lanes, some people "without work" might be employed in illegal spontaneous factories. No figures were given for the "unemployed" category in 1960.

The size of Shanghai's contract proletariat soared during 1958-1959, even as the size of the regular proletariat was also increasing. Reliable statistics to prove this are no more available to Western scholars than they apparently were to the municipal government at that time, but many aspects of the situation give clues to what happened. There was a new attitude toward contract labor, which became better justified in theories that were put forward after 1958. Before the Great Leap, Shanghai's industrialization had been inhibited by the Marxist ideal that urban and rural work should be somehow similar. That doctrine, along with the guerrilla experiences of many leading cadres (and the example of Stalin's defensible economy in the Urals), had in the early 1950s led to more investment inland, and less in Shanghai, than would otherwise have been the case. After the Great Leap, however, Shanghai cadres were able to urge that the same Marxist theory could be used in support of investment in their city, too. The ideal of equality between urban and rural work could be used to plead for moving both capital and labor out of the city, but it could also legitimize contract labor and move investment into Shanghai. To be sure, contract labor is the kind of labor most easily subject to exploitation by managers (either capitalist or Communist), but it is also the kind which best insures that workers will have both industrial and agricultural skills. If workers go into rural production when the farms need them but come into factories during agricultural slack seasons, then the goals of urban capital accumulation and rural-urban work equivalence can both be fairly well fulfilled. The contract institution allocates manpower efficiently to seasonal needs, and it trains fully experienced proletarians, who are competent as either workers or peasants.

The difficulty with this useful interpretation of Marxist theory is that contract laborers in practice often refuse to return to the field after they have lived in the city. Moreover, while living in the city, they begin to wonder why they receive lower wages and have less job security than the noncontract, unionized, regular workers. One Marxist ideal (the equivalence of all labor) can be used to justify the contract institution, but if this notion is applied as it apparently was in Shanghai for the sake of increasing investment, another part of Marxist theory (the expectation of a unified proletariat) falls into abeyance.[82]

WAGES AND OTHER PERQUISITES

The need to mobilize the masses for the Leap suggested a partial solution to this problem—the extension to contract workers of some perquisites enjoyed by regular workers, and an egalitarian reform in the wage structure. For example, as early as March 1958, the hospital of the Shanghai Electricity Bureau, which had previously been reserved exclusively for workers in that organ, was thrown open to ordinary citizens.[83] Many local unions decided to widen the constituency to which their recreation facilities would cater.

The best evidence of progress in the status of the contract proletariat at this time was public criticism of piece-work wages. As a national publication said, "How is it that the piece-wage system has increasingly lost its positive aspect and shown its negative aspect?"[84] The magazine averred that, among contract workers,

---

82. An ex-cadre, interviewed in Hong Kong in November 1969, reported this Marxist justification for contract labor. See also the statement of Ts'ao Ti-ch'iu below.

83. *HWJP*, March 17, 1958.

84. Liu Ch'eng-jui et al., "Contradictions in the Piece-Wage System Enforced in Industrial Enterprises," and "A Discussion of the Problem of Piece-Wages," *Chiaohsüeh yü yenchiu* [Teaching and research], No. 9 (September 4, 1958), translated in *ECMM*, No. 153, pp. 10-18.

piece-rate systems generally result in larger wage packets than hour-rate systems. Many contract workers nevertheless strongly resent the pressure to produce that piece rates cause. The article complained that such salaries "destroy the unity of the workers." Under this system, it said, some workers are proud of their high wages and so look down on their hourly wage colleagues. On the other hand, they dare not be too obvious about raising their efficiency lest slower workers ridicule and resent them for working hard to get more money. Presumably this tension was most serious when an enterprise's total wage bill was limited by budget. Some hourly wage workers claimed that piece-rate workers "charged with bayonets" for better salaries. Old, unskilled contract workers, who moved slowly, were more opposed to piece-rate wages than young workers (in Shanghai, often of bourgeois background), who were relatively strong and fast. Cadres also objected that piece-work wages obstruct productive innovations, because a worker can increase his income without the community rewards that accompany technical ingenuity. For all these reasons, piece-rate systems were reduced in Shanghai during 1958. By October, it was claimed that 20,000 workers had already been switched to hourly wages, and the change was planned for 100,000 more.[85]

WORKER PROMOTIONS AND LEAP ADMINISTRATION

The extension of worker benefits and the movement away from piece-work wages were accompanied by new opportunities for upward mobility for both regular workers and contract labor. Since Liberation, an increasing percentage of factory technicians in Shanghai had been recruited from among workers. A May 1958 survey of four progressive Shanghai plants showed that 42 percent of their 1,000-odd technical and administrative personnel had been recruited from the work bench. Most of these were Communist Party or Youth League members.[86] At a conference that same month, Shanghai Education Bureau Deputy Director Ma Fei-hai promised that employees' spare-time schools (*chihkung yehyü hsüehhsiao*) would expand their activities and budgets.[87] Because

85. *HWJP*, October 19, 1958.
86. NCNA, Shanghai, May 26, 1958. A disaffected refugee informed the author that he thought only Party or League members could become "advanced workers" in practice. *If* this is true, it helps explain some resentment in factories against the Party during later years.
87. *HWJP*, May 13, 1958.

of efforts like this, especially at lower levels, the Great Leap offered new opportunities for many workers to obtain education and hope for promotion.

Apprentices were also recruited into the work force under better conditions than before. During 1958, no less than 130,000 apprentices were taken into the metal, machine, electric equipment, textile, food, transport, and construction industries in Shanghai. Although 80,000 of these were originally slated to take jobs outside the city, it is doubtful that all of them finally departed.[88] The Great Leap loosened many practical restrictions on the lower proletariat's mobility into temporary jobs, and some temporary workers were able to join the permanent labor force after apprenticeship. In a period of changing administrative control, it was generally not difficult to move from job to job.

Indeed, relaxed administrative control was one reason for heightened production during the early Leap in Shanghai. Great Leap policies largely succeeded *inside* the city, because they were vague enough to allow each kind of unit to work in its own way, without much control. At least for a while, imprecise directives were able to boost Shanghai's productivity higher than clear bureaucratic organization had done. The Shanghai Communist Party held conferences to urge its functionaries to "pay attention to the livelihood of the people" and to "unify with them."[89] It was never clear just what these phrases meant, but they gave mid-level cadres a free hand to use available resources and to gratify more of the workers under them.

PRODUCTIVITY AND INNOVATION

The initial success of Leap policies soon withered, however, largely because of failures outside the city that restricted agricultural supplies to Shanghai and encouraged a population influx that made urban authorities call for more controls. In January 1959, when Shanghai's newspapers were claiming an incredible 89 percent rise in the value of heavy industrial production over the same month of 1958, the Party called many factory meetings that resolved to increase production still further without employing any new

88. NCNA, Shanghai, April 9, 1959.

89. The largest of these meetings was the Shanghai CCP Congress of January 1959. See NCNA, Shanghai, January 19, 1959.

workers. This goal was to be accomplished not only by greater labor activism, but also by automation.[90] The "mass campaign for technical innovation and higher labor productivity" aimed to replace manual labor with machines. Automation had a prestige that made its implementation somewhat independent of economic cost.[91] New Great Leap machines increased labor productivity most notably on Shanghai's docks, in lathe factories, and in textile mills. A young worker in the Huatung Switch Factory was greatly honored for remodeling his grinding machine to make it operable by push buttons.[92] An important new device was popularized in 1960 to reset bobbins on spinning frames. This semiautomatic bobbin replacer had been applied to more than one-third of the city's spindles by the next year. Along with other new machines and work methods, this gadget no doubt had an important effect on both the productivity and the labor requirements of Shanghai's very large textile industry.[93]

In the first half of 1959, Shanghai workers put forward some 250,000 innovation suggestions. About half of these were reportedly applied.[94] The most significant ideas, such as the bobbin replacer, probably *decreased* labor intensity in production processes and so reduced the number of workers required per fixed amount of input. This kind of automation stirs Luddite worries in the contract proletariat, even though it is usually welcomed by regular workers who feel that their jobs are secure and may be made easier by automation. The most numerous innovations, however, set up systems that required employees to work harder out of political loyalty. These changes *increased* labor intensity in production processes and were subject to objections from all employed staff (both regular and temporary, but not the unemployed) who now had to put forth more effort to receive their old pay. Both kinds of innovation—labor-saving and labor-intensifying—were encouraged by means of a political campaign. Their political effects were

90. NCNA, Shanghai, February 3, 1959.

91. See, for example, the reverent and very noneconomic way in which automation (*tzutunghua*) is discussed in Ning T'ao et al., *Shanghai Wuching huakung-ch'ang ti tansheng* (Shanghai: Shanghai Jenmin Ch'upan She, 1965), pp. 60-61.

92. NCNA, Shanghai, March 24, 1959.

93. NCNA, Shanghai, November 26, 1961.

94. NCNA, Shanghai, August 7, 1959.

strong but of different kinds.[95] Labor-decreasing innovations serve the interests only of regular, unionized workers; they run counter to the interests of the contract proletariat, the unemployed, and (if the new gadgets are expensive to capitalize) management. Labor-increasing innovations, on the other hand, conflict with the interests of regular workers and often of contract workers, even though they may be popular among the unemployed and the business cadres.

THE PERIOD OF RETRENCHMENT, 1960-1963

Innovations in any case could not resolve the production bottle-necks caused by the Leap's huge demands on material resources. As it became apparent that Leap policies would not suffice to distribute China's agricultural produce, as bad weather took its toll, and as raw materials shortages affected Shanghai's industries, the urban Party had no choice but to reduce the pressure for production, to lay off excess workers, and to placate those whom it could. After mid-1959, Party organs gradually began to "unhorse"[96] many of the less successful industrial experiments and product lines that had been instituted in 1958. A formula of "adjusting, consolidating, strengthening, and raising" was adopted.[97] In this retrenchment, many laborers (even some who had worked in an enterprise

95. The Party's attitude toward automation has been beautifully expressed by one of its greatest managers of agricultural industry, Ch'en Yung-kuei, secretary of the CCP branch of the Tachai Production Brigade: "Some people think mechanization is aimed only at reducing labor intensity and providing more leisure. They do not understand that mechanization is the Party's fundamental line in the rural areas for adhering to socialism and defeating capitalism. Others regard mechanization as an ordinary measure to save labor and increase production. They fail to see it from a higher level as a measure to consolidate the worker-peasant alliance, promote socialist industrialization, and reduce the differences between the workers and the peasants. They fail to understand that unless we implement Chairman Mao's revolutionary line, mechanization will not necessarily bring about socialism and may even lead to capitalism." This clear statement contradicts Marx. The motive force of history here is basically described as hard work. "Capitalism" and "socialism" are generated wholly by superstructure, and the Marxist role of the former is now given to the latter. In fact, Ch'en Yung-kuei may know better than Marx what he is talking about. Quoted in *Eastern Horizon* 10, No. 5 (October 1971), p. 67.

96. An ex-cadre interviewee liked to use the colloquial expression *"hsia ma"* ("getting off the horse") to describe this.

97. *"T'iaocheng, kungku, ch'ungshih, t'ikao."*

for two years or more) were asked to go back to their native rural towns. They lost the opportunity for continued employment in Shanghai.[98]

Not only did the government lack sufficient resources, in this time of economic turndown, to offer significant job incentives (or to deny any new officially sanctioned careers) to labor market entrants, but it also lacked resources to sustain all the jobs of unionized labor, its main constituency in Shanghai. In some important plants, such as the Shanghai First Iron and Steel Factory at Woosung, there was open consternation when career advancement was held back by input shortages. The factory had to institute "heart-to-heart talks," not only with ordinary workers, but also with group leaders, foremen, and the chief foreman. "Rash attitudes" were condemned in the 30 political theory classes that the factory set up to occupy these workers' spare time.[99]

UNDEREMPLOYMENT, UNEMPLOYMENT, AND REDUCED CAREER GUIDANCE

With fewer materials to process, the work load slackened in many factories. Undercapacity use of capital and underemployed labor were both widespread in the city. Some favored workers were simply allowed to take off on vacations. As early as mid-1959, the Shanghai Federation of Trade Unions was sending small tour groups to its new resort beside the West Lake at Hangchow.[100] In the next few years, Shanghai travel agents continued to organize group trips to many parts of China.[101] This noneconomical method was hardly expected to solve the political problem of mass unemployment, but it certainly must have relieved the frustrations of a few favored workers during this depression.

At the beginning of 1960, offices were established at district levels to encourage more labor education for sectors of the urban population that were deemed to need it. At first, most of the jobs in this program were located in Shanghai. They were largely service jobs that required little material input. Eight city districts sent their

98. Interview with an ex-cadre, Hong Kong, December 1969.

99. *JMJP*, June 26, 1961. An ex-resident of Shanghai said that spare-time classes in periods of shortages were particularly prominent in the textile industry.

100. NCNA, Shanghai, July 17, 1959.

101. NCNA, Shanghai, January 28, 1962.

Party committee secretaries down to organize meetings and "personally to mobilize residents to seize this opportunity and unfold livelihood service work on a big scale."[102] These programs were difficult to administer in some parts of Shanghai where few cadres lived. This was a special problem in the shack districts of Shanghai's northwest sections, which were characterized in 1960 as "places occupied by ruffians and wicked people."[103] In these areas, there had long been efforts to foster official mediators and other liaison officers, so that the common people could be linked at least indirectly with their government. Such functionaries, as well as others in the school system, now provided information to supplement the house registration records, whose accuracy had deteriorated since the Leap. Only in this way was it possible to begin developing a selective "rustication" once again, so that newly immigrant peasants could be moved out of Shanghai.

Education was a major palliative for the unemployment problem. More than 120 graduates of Kunming Road Middle School in June 1962 could find neither a plant to employ them nor a higher school to admit them. The local Party branch, greatly concerned at the prospect of having so many dissatisfied youths on its hands and unwilling or unable to send them elsewhere, quickly organized a school of 11 "study groups." Each group met every morning in a fixed room to listen to tutorials on the radio.[104] This was career guidance of a sort, but it could not last long, and its effective social productivity was low.

To reduce net immigration from rural areas at this time, the government tried to reinforce its restrictions against indiscriminate hiring. There was a renewed official effort to strengthen the household registration system. In general, the policies of this period worked to reduce nonunion threats to the jobs of unionized workers. A national magazine urged enterprises to "reduce the waste of wage funds," "to block all kinds of loopholes," and "to lessen or eliminate acts that run counter to law and discipline" in the hiring of new employees.[105] The financial departments of all industrial

102. *CFJP*, January 13, 1960.
103. *HWJP*, August 21, 1957.
104. *JMJP*, June 5, 1962.
105. *Laotung* [Labor], No. 14 (August 18, 1962), translated in *SCMM*, No. 334, p. 15.

units were ordered to set up a definite limited wage fund and to make sure that the budget was not exceeded. This indirect supervision of the contract proletariat, administered through aggregate budgets, was less effective than more direct local government controls on careers had been in earlier times.

The year 1962 saw a revival of labor service stations, which had fallen into disuse during the Leap. These were now established in neighborhood offices, where it was hoped they would gain detailed knowledge of local situations. The new labor organs, dispatched by district governments, could coordinate their activities with the public security and ration systems, which by the 1960s had also been extended to lower levels. This approach to career guidance through the police system was necessitated by the dire economic situation of the time.

Because permanent jobs after the Great Leap were hard to find, the new generation of labor stations could in practice only arrange temporary work. These agencies essentially became labor contractors. For example, if a construction company needed a certain number of workers for a specific project, the station would undertake to provide them. Wages were negotiated between the company and the labor station. Temporary workers, in order to pick up their pay, had to show a testimonial letter from the labor station. The station deducted a "service fee" (*fuwu fei*) from each wage payment. Fees were levied progressively—that is, the station took a larger percentage of high wages than of low. Presumably this policy encouraged station cadres to negotiate seriously on behalf of job hunters, but the labor stations were definitely government offices rather than economic enterprises. They would not assist some kinds of people. Recent objectors to the rural send-down campaigns (especially if they had education and were of bourgeois family background) had to wait for long periods before they could get even temporary jobs by this official route.[106] Their incentive to approach the problem in less official ways was correspondingly increased.

By this time, the unemployed of Shanghai divided fairly clearly into two parts: immigrant peasants who dwelt in slum areas, and educated youths who refused to go to the countryside. Street cadres

---

106. Interview with refugee student (not from Shanghai) in Hong Kong, December 1969. Also, interview with ex-worker of Shenhsin Tool Factory, who obtained a job through a station of the Shanghai Labor Bureau in 1962; URI, April 1966.

and school officials would first attempt to persuade an unemployed person of either category to leave the city. If that effort failed, menial work might be found for him in Shanghai.

Although there were important differences within the contract proletariat, the group was treated as a unit by the labor service stations. The paucity of jobs in Shanghai provided a context for pressure on all kinds of contract proletarians to move out of the city. Enterprises were no longer supposed to advertise in newspapers for workers. Now, as one ex-cadre put it, "Everyone was supposed to go on recommendations made by the labor service stations." This caused "quarrels and confrontations" between the station cadres and unemployed people whom they were trying to guide.[107] Under such circumstances, propaganda for socialized job assignments combined less efficiently with the material incentives the government had to offer, and the effectiveness of the guidance system as a whole declined.

JOB DISTRIBUTION IN THE 1964-1966 PERIOD

The city government was not slow to realize that its policies for controlling urban employment and laying off excess workers implied augmentation of disadvantaged sections of the proletariat. Deputy Mayor Ts'ao Ti-ch'iu, at the first session of the Fifth Shanghai People's Congress in mid-1964, said bluntly that "factories and enterprises must employ fewer workers who are permanent. More workers should be temporary." He recommended that new employees should be "recruited from the peasants so that latent labor power can be tapped. The relation between town and country, and the worker-peasant alliance, can be further strengthened."[108] Under this formula, which was widespread in China at the time, employees were to be "both workers and peasants" (*"yi kung yi nung"*). Contracts, now legitimized by official policy even more than before, were used by management cadres with great alacrity. The employees under contracts usually had no compensation

107. Interview, Hong Kong, December 1969. This nationally minded ex-cadre, not from Shanghai, did not mention whether lane and street factories sometimes hired labor without recommendations, but his point is valid for permanent jobs in large enterprises.
108. *WHP*, September 26, 1964.

except salaries. They "had no seniority, and their contracts could be extended without any limit."[109] Workers could be dismissed from their posts arbitrarily, thus to join the ranks of the unemployed or to be given rural assignments. In the spring and summer of 1963, for example, the municipally run Hsienfeng Electric Factory in Chapei "sent down" 10 percent of its workers.[110] These employees were given "settling down fees" (*anchia fei*) to move to the countryside at least temporarily. An ex-resident informant noted that the explicit and public intent of this rustication was to send from Shanghai all factory hands "who did not work hard enough." *Hsiahsiang* provided the government with a peculiarly patriotic, justifiable kind of sanction, which could spur hard work in urban jobs.

Rustication also provided managements with an ideologically impeccable way to lay off workers. Better yet, it allowed managers to do this while maintaining some administrative connections with the rusticated workers, who might be brought back to urban production again, when the planned demand for products rose. Thus business cadres developed an economic interest in keeping a circulating supply of unemployed and contract laborers, who were willing to do hard jobs when necessary and who could disappear from payrolls at other times.

RUSTICATION UNEMPLOYMENT

By the mid-1960s, a revolutionary new form of unemployment had emerged in Shanghai. Traditionally, unemployment results either from a decrease in market volume (less consumer demand and/or a reduced supply of productive inputs) or from structural causes like the inability of unskilled workers to handle the available jobs. Part of Shanghai's unemployment between 1964 and 1966, however, was not caused by low market volume or inappropriate market struc-

---

109. See John Wilson Lewis, "Commerce, Education, and Political Development in Tangshan, 1956-69," in J. W. Lewis, ed., *The City in Communist China* (Stanford, Calif.: Stanford University Press, 1971), p. 163. This essay clearly implies divisions within the proletariat. In a smaller and economically less diversified city than Shanghai, these splits can be better understood in terms of changes in the structure of surrounding wholesale markets than in terms of technological and investment-opportunity factors.

110. Interview with an ex-worker of the Hsienfeng Electric Factory in Chapei, who reported on the 1956-1965 period. URI, February 1964.

ture. It resulted from political pressure brought against young workers who refused to go into agriculture. The urban economy could have absorbed them, and did absorb some of them in small "mass" factories (*ch'ü“nchung kungch'ang*) whose expansion was restricted. They could have done available work, but a larger social need was officially perceived in ethical terms, and their example upheld a temporary labor system that was economically inexpensive in terms of development. They could usually receive only temporary jobs in the city and permanent jobs only in the country.

The development of this "worker-peasant system" was gradual; it began almost as soon as the Great Leap ended. Many people in Shanghai were quite conscious of what was happening. An interview informant, who had been in the city's contract proletariat and had wanted to continue his education, indicates what people on the scene were thinking:

[After the Great Leap] enrollment became less and less each year. Many youth had no chance to receive higher education. Although the state hoped to send these youths to farms or to Sinkiang, many of them did not want to go. Shanghai workers were also supposed to be sent down to villages and were replaced by these youths. But the new salaries were much lower than what the sent-down workers had previously received. Of course, these youths were very discontented with their situation. To solve this problem, the state had to find some way to satisfy their desire to learn, to make up for their discontent on the job. For example, the Shanghai Television University was established to fulfill this kind of purpose.[111]

As long as managers had budgets, and as long as it was easier to press immigrant workers to return to their native places (mostly in East China) than it was to get bourgeois students to emigrate all the way to Sinkiang, there was a tendency for many of the jobless peasants to leave Shanghai and for many of the jobless students to stay. The students sometimes held temporary employment under the "worker-peasant system," but many of them never did put in any major stints as peasants. When city work was unavailable, they were simply unemployed. In this phase, they were known by the wonderfully ambiguous name "social youth" (*shehui ch'ingnien*).

Already by 1962, campaigns were being launched to strengthen

---

111. Interview with a Shanghai worker who studied in the Television University, reporting on the period 1958 to 1964. URI, 1964.

the political loyalty of these people. "Social youth study groups"[112] were set up to encourage the ex-student part of the temporary proletariat to join propaganda activities. By 1964, these campaigns had been regularized. The Communist Youth League of Fuk'ang Lane in Chingan District was made a model for its efforts in propagandizing social youths to perform the "eight musts" (*pa yao*).[113] Social youths were organized officially, as if they formed a functional club. Government-recognized leaders were chosen for them. Because these groups were constituted by their members' persistent refusal to go to the country, they were often invited to the farewell parties for rustication volunteers.

APPRENTICESHIP AND PROMOTION

Apprenticeship programs, the classic route into the regular proletariat, were now much reduced in Shanghai even though they were not completely eliminated. One source in 1964 remarked: "The old apprenticeship system has been discarded. Appointment to any situation is now done among graduates of at least junior middle schools."[114] The surviving apprenticeship programs were for trainees in enterprises that were not capital-intensive, such as shops, vegetable stands, market stalls, and handicraft stores. Some avowedly bourgeois enterprises also retained the apprenticeship system. In 1965, as many as 700 apprentice tailors finished a three-year course and all of them got jobs in this traditional Shanghai occupation, even though scarcely 175 were loyal enough for League membership.[115]

112. "*Shehui ch'ingnien hsüehhsi tsu*" or sometimes "*Shehui ch'ingnien hsüeh-hsi pan.*" *HMWP*, March 25, 1964.
113. *HMWP*, February 10, 1964. The "eight musts" are: (1) reading Chairman Mao and other revolutionary writers; (2) doing at least one thing a day that is beneficial to socialism; (3) taking active part in socialist culture and recreational programs; (4) propagandizing the slogan, "discuss science and eliminate superstition"; (5) following the policy of strict economy, hard work, plain living, and hygiene; (6) helping to do household work as an example for one's brothers and sisters; (7) respecting the old and loving the young and observing discipline to keep public order; and (8) raising revolutionary vigilance and helping lane public security cadres. These eight points were urged upon all youths in a lane-level urban campaign conducted by local Youth League branches.
114. *SHNL* of April 4, 1964, in *South China Morning Post*, April 11, 1964. This informative column was written, often with some courage, by a non-Communist Russian who had long resided in Shanghai.
115. *HMWP*, September 15, 1965. These tailors' jobs were all in Shanghai, either

In some occupations that retained the apprenticeship system, it did not operate very smoothly. By late 1964, some Shanghai Youth League secretaries in factories were complaining openly that veteran workers did not want to teach apprentices. Business cadres reportedly did not want League teachers in shops to rectify that situation.[116] Friction between masters and apprentices was openly admitted. Mutual respect between them was called for, but the cadres bemoaned their inability to counteract the "backwardness" of the older workers.

In general, spare- and part-time continuing education was the most effective means the government could find to allay frustration in the temporary proletariat. This method worked like an opiate in that it could aggravate in the long run the problem that it solved in the short run. Although temporary workers might be willing to receive low wages while they were still part-time students, they nevertheless expected promotions and permanent status once they had graduated. The school system and the labor economy were dependent on each other in policies both for employment and for unemployment.

Even youths who were able to continue their education on a full-time basis often had trouble finding jobs after graduation. There were some exceptions to these job placement problems, and they took the form of "escalator" arrangements between training and work. In a few special secondary schools that trained regular workers, commencement was synchronized with placement. For example, the Shanghai Communications School provided new jobs for its graduates along with their diplomas; all of them went to work immediately.[117]

At the level of higher education, which leads to greater career ambitions, the extensive spare-time enrollment of the Great Leap

under the Municipal Clothing Production Cooperative (Fuchuang Shengch'an Hotsoshe) or with various clothing cooperative factories (*fuchuang hotso kung-ch'ang*). Even by 1965, efforts to communize this famous Shanghai industry had not been notably successful, as the fragmented structure of the organizations shows.

An ex-resident said that the Cultural Revolution caused many students from closed middle schools to join factories and had thus effectively revived the apprenticeship system.

116. *CKCN*, No. 12 (September 16, 1964), article by a Youth League branch secretary in a Shanghai rubber factory.

117. *HMWP*, September 5, 1964. The school's name is Chiaot'ung Chihyeh Hsüehhsiao.

had been cut back sharply by 1964. It equalled only 40 percent of the full-time enrollment in Shanghai's regular system of universities and colleges.[118] The degree of stratification within the upper proletariat increased at this time. Shanghai had 70 percent more employed technicians at the end of the second five-year plan than at the end of the first one,[119] but it had also gained 700 percent more certified technical school graduates in this same period.[120] Half of these diplomas were held by persons of worker origin. Many of the new graduates nevertheless had to settle for ordinary jobs, because there was insufficient capital to justify hiring them more lucratively.

STRATIFICATION IN WAGES AND PERQUISITES

During this period, there were considerable differences in workers' wages both between industries and within factories. The permanent workers based in high-technology sectors of Shanghai's economy had developed their own class consciousness, because they were well organized into unions and especially because their compensation was relatively high and stable.

Some factories, such as the car repair plant of the Shanghai Public Utility Bureau, had a large percentage of old workers. Apprentices were few. In their first year, workers received only 40 to 60 yüan, and only about 5 percent of them had salaries of more than 70 yüan. Regular workers in the factory could expect occasional wage increases based on rises in their wages and level-rank.[121] In at least some factories at this time, the system of level-ranks became quite standardized. Eight such grades were distinguished by Ministry of Labor regulations. Apprentices were below the first grade, and their compensation was only pocket money when it was given at all. Technical personnel were above the eighth grade. Engineers

118. NCNA, Shanghai, September 5, 1964.
119. *PR*, No. 41 (October 9, 1964), article by Deputy Mayor Ts'ao Ti-ch'iu.
120. NCNA, Shanghai, June 21, 1963.
121. Interview with an ex-worker of the car repair plant of the Shanghai Public Utility Bureau, who reported the period 1963-1965; URI, March 1966. Cadres at this plant of about 100 workers received anywhere from 40 to 130 yüan. Medicine for permanent workers was free, and in time of sickness, wages could be received upon testimony of a doctor, although bonuses and overtime wages could not be allowed during the same pay period.

were paid according to a four-grade system that was separate from the scales for workers and technicians.[122]

Instructions from Peking may have been important in enhancing the general stratification of workers' wages, but they could not effectively restrict local control of who received how much. Shanghai's average industrial wage has long been the highest in China, and according to one survey of highly selected factories, it even approached 75 yüan per month.[123] The salary schedule handed down by the Ministry of Labor was not so much a directive as a list of options, and a wide list at that. The most important central controls came from political campaigns and from aggregate budgets, not from the details of the salary matrix.

In some places, such as the Shanghai 555 Clock Factory, most of the pre-Cultural Revolution real wage spread was to be found in piece-work bonuses rather than in basic rates.[124] The Shanghai branch of the People's Bank of China audited the bills of many Shanghai concerns, but as an executor of the wage laws, it seems not to have contravened local interests.[125] It apparently authorized "rewards for exceeding quotas" (*ch'aooh chiangli*) within fixed amounts whenever production was satisfactory. For example, at the car repair plant of the Shanghai Public Utility Bureau special bonuses were awarded in the fourth quarter of 1965: first prizes of 28 yüan to 35 men, second prizes of 20 yüan to 58 men, and third prizes of 12 yüan to 69 men. The plant had 385 employees, which means that 42 percent of them received prizes. For these workers, the bonuses constituted an average monthly salary increase of 21.5 yüan.[126] For an ordinary cadre, and for many workers, this bonus

122. Interview with an ex-cadre, not from Shanghai, who was well acquainted with the national system, Hong Kong, January 1970. See, also, the next note.

123. Barry Richman, *Industrial Society in Communist China*, pp. 686-687. Comparable figures for average industrial wages in other cities were: 71 yüan for Canton, 63-65 yüan for Peking, 60-62 yüan for Tientsin, 60 yüan for Nanking and Wuhan, 58 yüan for Soochow, and 50-55 yüan for Wusih and Hangchow. The factories were not typical, however. One ex-resident of Shanghai, when presented with Richman's 75 yüan average, replied, "It must be a figure from the early 1950s."

124. Bruce McFarlane, "Visit to Shanghai," diary entry of April 18, 1968. This clock factory, requiring 22 fairly skilled workers, then had a legal basic wage spread from 40 to 100 yüan. The average wage without bonus was 70 yüan. Average total compensation was more than that.

125. *Ibid.*, April 20, 1970.

126. This increment was computed by multiplying receipts and recipients in each category and then averaging. The salary percentage estimates are based on official wage norms for various grades of workers, but since the behavioral application of

would constitute a 10 to 15 percent raise or more. If was often paid in a lump sum as a year-end award (*nienchung chiangchin*). For a first-year, permanent worker, even this average prize might be equivalent to a raise of much more than 15 percent.

Often there were great differences among the various kinds of working staffs in Shanghai factories in the mid-1960s. Employees at the Shanghai No. 19 Cotton Textile Mill were 70 percent women, whereas those in the Shanghai No. 3 Steel Mill were only 8 percent female.[127] Some plants such as the Shanghai Truck Factory, relied much less than other enterprises on workers who had learned their skills at the bench. The truck factory recruited semiprofessional, bourgeois-background graduates out of specialized secondary schools.[128] Other enterprises, such as the Shanghai Weiming Battery Factory, relied on a veteran work force, old managers, old equipment, and practically no technical staff to produce export-quality goods.[129]

The rate of pay at this battery plant was relatively high, because many of the workers had long experience and because the average bonus for all employees was also a high 15 percent of salaries. Of the 563 staff, only 1 percent had higher education; only 2.5 percent had

these norms is questionable, the conclusions are stated in broad ranges. Basic data are from an interview with an ex-worker of the car repair plant of the Shanghai Public Utility Bureau; URI, March 1966.

127. Richman, *Industrial Society in Communist China*, Table 9-1, pp. 754-756. NCNA, Shanghai, March 4, 1965, claimed, however, that more than one-third of the technical staff in the Shanghai No. 1 Steel Mill and Shanghai Oil Refinery were female, and 50 percent of the researchers in the Municipal Insecticide Institute were also women. *HMWP*, October 8, 1964, has information on a woman technical worker in the Shanghai Yinghua Petroleum Plant who praised the Party for urging her to obtain a technical education. Recent interviews by radical scholars indicate that these cases were somewhat rare. Many more women in Shanghai were affected by the fact that the city's textile industry absorbed 20,000 young workers in 1964; NCNA, Shanghai, April 25, 1965.

128. Richman, *Industrial Society in Communist China*, pp. 150-151.

129. *Ibid.*, pp. 712, 734, 813, 837, 855, 869, and elsewhere as in the index. This battery factory, under the Shanghai Daily-Use Chemical Industries Corporation, was highly unusual in that it awarded larger bonuses to managers than to workers. It produced "White Elephant" brand batteries, which are prominent in Hong Kong and some other overseas markets. Very little new capital was added during the 1960s, but 1965 showed a 29 percent profit on costs. Summaries of Richman's data on various Shanghai plants can be compared with information in URI clipping and interview files, and in the reports of travellers such as McFarlane. The extensive statistics on job-ranks, level-ranks, and salary ranges in different industries would benefit from computer analysis.

any specialized secondary education; and there was a single engineer. Almost half of the staff was female. Some other plants, with relatively high percentages of male employees doing hard work, nonetheless paid wages that were not especially high. The Shanghai First Iron and Steel Factory, for example, expanded sharply after the Great Leap Forward, but in 1963, workers with three or four years of experience received only 40 to 50 yüan for very strenuous jobs.[130] At other post-Leap factories, such as the Shanghai Mining Machines Plant at Minhang, south of the city, the salary spread was definitely greater than normal. Beginning apprentices received a mere 12 yüan plus meals; this was only pocket money for them, not a real salary. Technical workers made only 25 to 30 yüan per month in their first year but could earn as much as 135 yüan per month by their seventh year. First-grade engineers could receive basic rates up to 335 yüan.[131]

Different shops of a single plant could also vary as to the types of workers who composed them. At the Shanghai Machine Tools Factory, the 200 workers in the Press Shop were described by an interviewee as "young" and "mostly from villages." The 80 men of the Assembly Shop, however, were largely "old workers with much experience who worked fast." The 30 members of the Electrical Shop were considered "experts" because of their jobs, and they got quite high salaries. The tasks of the Molding Shop were strenuous, and it was reportedly staffed by 300 "peasants."[132] This unevenness no doubt intensified politics in the Machine Tools Factory, which became an activist model during the Cultural Revolution.

Retirement benefits were also distributed unevenly among regular workers in the post-Leap period. As early as 1960, the number of pensioners in Shanghai had risen to 25,000.[133] This equalled only

130. Interview with ex-worker in the Shanghai No. 1 Steel Mill; URI, October 1963.

131. Interview with a Kansu man assigned in March 1966 to the Shanghai Mining Machines Plant; URI, October 1967. He had travelled to Kwangtung and then Macao in October 1967, disguised as a Red Guard. A Westerner who had travelled in China felt this salary spread was normal, but an ex-Shanghai resident tended to disbelieve the figures and at one point said, "Impossible." The trials of interview research.

132. Interview with an ex-worker of the Shanghai Machine Tools Factory reporting on the period 1960-63. *URI*, January 1964.

133. NCNA, Shanghai, March 21, 1960.

1 or 2 percent of the total urban labor force. It was an unknown but small percentage of retired workers. These people led the life that the Communist government wanted, but could not afford, for the rest of the retired workers. They received free medical care, pensions at 50 to 70 percent of their former wages, inexpensive housing provided by their factories, occasional organized pleasure trips, and all the club privileges they had enjoyed as regular employees. Many of them led training classes for novices and became "technical advisors" to their factories.

Medical care was not provided on an equal basis to all Shanghai residents. Most kinds of medical treatment still were not free in Shanghai except through work-place arrangements that protected employees and sometimes their families. The free supply system could not be extended to temporary workers, lest they flood into the city and abuse these privileges. Although Shanghai had the most sophisticated medical establishment in China, waste resulted when free benefits were spread too widely.

Some people make improper use of the drugs prescribed, because these cost no money. Some people go to see one doctor in the morning and another in the afternoon, without taking the medicines given to them by either. This shows that they are in a state of fear and that they lack revolutionary will-power.[134]

Partly to avoid receiving too many patients with minor ills, the municipal government emphasized preventive campaigns, by which it brought medicine to the people rather than encouraging them to bring diseases into clinics for treatment. The cost of medicine was increasingly included in the budgets of patients' work units.[135] An ex-resident of Shanghai reported that during the early 1960s a consultation fee—only 10 fen (.10 yüan), but enough to discourage egregious waste—was charged to state employees when they visited clinics.

A pattern of broad benefits but unequal access to them also characterized other perquisites in the mid-1960s. Comprehensive labor insurance schemes set forth in documents of the National Federation of Trade Unions were put into practice on a somewhat

134. *WHP*, November 25, 1964.
135. *WHP*, January 13, 1965.

wider scale than before.[136] Periodic campaigns against the "irrational welfare benefits" of the old society[137] were mostly forgotten during this era of the "welfare trade union" (*fuli kunghui*). For example, the food rations allowed to permanent workers in heavy jobs could at this time exceed average rations by 50 percent or more.[138] Free vacations were available to a few selected workers to escape hot Shanghai summers, although this left their less privileged colleagues to steam. For example, in 1964 the municipal Education Union organized fewer than 1,000 of Shanghai's many teachers to visit Hangchow, Tsingtao, and similar pleasant places for rest. Other teachers remaining in Shanghai were given tours of the Yangshup'u Power Plant, the Machine Tools Factory, the Rolled-Steel Plant, and other summer vacation spots inside the city.[139]

Regular workers enjoyed some privileges because they were better financial risks than temporary workers. When permanent employees of Shanghai's Nanyang Tobacco Factory requested time off through proper channels, they could receive 40 percent or more of their salaries, even if their reasons for asking were entirely personal. Sometimes they could request wages in advance.[140] At the Shanghai Mining Machines Plant in Minhang, every worker had to give 1 percent of his salary to a mutual aid fund. In case of a wedding, funeral, sickness, or pregnancy, the worker could ask for a loan that was limited to three times his monthly salary.[141] Members

136. See Hoffman, *Work Incentive Practices and Policies*, pp. 35-42, for a description of insurance coverage for death, sickness, injury, disability, and retirement. Hoffman shows the relation of these noncontributory plans to the Soviet models from which they were taken in the early 1950s. Benefits were in proportion to wages. When nonunion workers were covered at all, union members received higher payment.

137. James R. Townsend, *Political Participation in Communist China*, pp. 189-190 shows how this issue came up in 1957-1958, just as it later did during the Cultural Revolution.

138. According to an interview with an Overseas Chinese from Thailand who joined the Shanghai Shenhsin Tool Factory (URI, April 1966), favored employees in that plant's high-temperature workshops might be given rations of as much as 45 catties of grain per month.

139. *HMWP*, July 11, 1964.

140. Interview with an ex-worker of Shanghai Nanyang Tobacco Factory, who reports the period 1959-1965; URI, February 1966.

141. Interview with an ex-employee of the Shanghai Mining Machines Plant, URI, October 1967.

of the Shanghai Trolley Drivers' Union could obtain automatic loans of 15 yüan during the second half of any month, if they were short of money. When they had weddings or funerals in the family, they could easily obtain much larger loans. Their unions were taking no great risk, because repayment could be guaranteed from later wage checks, and the inherent value of permanent job status would insure against defaults.[142] Loans of this sort were common in many rural and urban Chinese traditional organizations. In a big modern city like Shanghai, though, the old kinds of material and symbolic collateral were scarce, and this customary credit could be extended only against mortgages of regular job status. The temporary proletariat had to live in the city on inconvenient modern terms; only permanent workers could arrange traditional credit facilities.

THE CULTURAL REVOLUTION

The initial phases of the Cultural Revolution stirred literary and academic circles, rather than workers. In June 1966, however, battling political factions became aware that divisions within the proletariat could be useful to them in the new movement. Communist Party memberships were given in that month alone to more than 20,000 permanent workers in Shanghai.[143] Although most factory workers did not enter the revolutionary fray until late 1966, the stratification among their groups shows why they reacted to this upheaval after it began outside their immediate sphere.

Contract workers may not at first have been passionately excited about the errors of historians, the ideologies of novelists, or the philosophies of musicians. They may have disliked some political leaders, however, and when men such as Mayor Ts'ao Ti-ch'iu were criticized for cultural policies, interest rose within the lower proletariat. The attack on "economism" is comprehensible only in terms of the fact that extra bonuses were usually given only to regular workers, not to temporary workers. As a notice from Peking warned at the end of the year:

142. Interview with an ex-employee of the Shanghai Communications Bureau, who reports the period from about 1955 to about 1965.
143. NCNA, Shanghai, June 30, 1966. Mrs. Jack Gray told me that she found a similar boost in workers' CCP memberships at the same time in Canton.

The Party Central Committee has ruled that in the Cultural Revolution no leaders of industrial and mining enterprises should strike at or retaliate against workers who have put forth criticisms and disclosed facts, nor are they allowed to reduce the wages of these workers or discharge these workers from their posts, or for the same reasons to discharge contract workers or temporary workers.[144]

The "contradictions between different kinds of workers that had been exacerbated by revisionist managers" were often cited quite bluntly as generators of the Cultural Revolution in Shanghai. Many of the issues of the movement bear clear relation to the contradictions that could be seen earlier. The distinction between veteran workers and young workers sometimes became an openly political one. The tensions between production workers, on one hand, and administrators, engineers, and maintenance men, on the other, became institutionalized in the form of conflict groups. In many factories, the employees in different shops formed factions against each other. Bonuses were criticized, reduced, and often eliminated. Certain kinds of pressure to innovate and to produce were abandoned, as were many piece-work systems.[145]

In the end, the Cultural Revolution had to solve these contradictions by trying to unify the proletariat. A broad political change could restructure the relations among different kinds of workers, so as to spread social benefits more evenly and thus reduce discontent. When wages were made more equal, when workers' militia teams were mobilized against the Red Guards of bourgeois background, and when workers' propaganda teams were used to reunite factions in many kinds of institutions, then the "proletariat" could be depicted in new colors as a great united clan. Political activism could break through the crusts of old career patterns. New emphases in old ideology were needed to reintegrate workingmen whom the practice of economic development had divided.

In Shanghai's economic substructure, there was no basis for this reintegration. On the contrary, it was all a great act of will, politics, and propaganda. That is how the revolution was really cultural. In the future, Marxist generators of class division among Shanghai's

144. *JMJP*, December 26, 1966, translated in *SCMP*, No. 3852, p. 1.

145. These issues are taken from an interview at the Shanghai Diesel Pumps and Engines Factory, conducted by Bruce McFarlane, "Visit to Shanghai," entry for April 21, 1968.

workers may again create some of the tensions that existed before 1967. If this occurs, there may be more desire to root out the causes of these problems before they become so severe.

DEVELOPMENT AND PROLETARIAN CAREER GUIDANCE

The needs of the development process for a mobile, inexpensive proletariat caused stratification in Shanghai's labor force, thereby undermining the ideal of the workers' fraternity. This economic process also frustrated the personal career ambitions of many low-paid workers. It did not, however, have these effects to the same degree in all periods.

In the early 1950s, job shortages concerned the government much more than possibilities for career guidance. Socialist orientations were supposed to be instilled in workers at this time mainly by trade union activities, not by job incentives. When the labor market tightened in some fields after the major socialization of industry in 1956, career guidance increased in importance until demographic and administrative changes during the Great Leap caused a sharp slackening in the market, and with it a temporary 1958 prosperity that made many jobs available without official sanction. In the early 1960s, Shanghai's government did not have enough political will to restrict its proletarian supporters' search for employment; the economic shortage restricted them in a way the Party could not direct. During the recovery of 1964-1966, jobs again became an important official resource. After that, the urban economy progressed still further, but its prosperity did not strengthen the career guidance system. The general state of Shanghai's economy clearly affected the government's use of scarce jobs to structure citizens' work lives. Generalizations about the mechanism that governs relations of this sort will be attempted in the last chapter of the book.

4

RESIDENTIAL INCENTIVES TO
SOCIALIST CAREERS

Shanghai's residential controls—household registration, food rationing, apartment allocations, urban transport, and birth control —may at first seem to be a scattered lot of topics. The purpose of this chapter is to show how they can be unified—indeed, how they can be considered alongside educational policies, *hsiafang* campaigns, and job supply in a single analysis of government efforts to guide the personal energies of men and women who want to live in Shanghai.

THE HOUSEHOLD REGISTRATION SYSTEM

Before the new Communist regime could develop and apply residential policies in support of national goals, it had to catalogue its citizens carefully. The previous KMT files were very incomplete. An adequate household registration system was an absolute prerequisite of any effort to ration scarce commodities—or to deny Shanghai ration coupons to persons whom the regime wanted to move out of the city.

RESIDENCE CARDS OF THE EARLY 1950s

Identity cards and household books, the most direct means of monitoring residence status, have a history in Shanghai that long predates the Communists. Even Chinese dynastic regimes tried to keep household records. The first really comprehensive effort, covering all parts of the city, was carried out under the wartime Japanese occupation. The collaborationist city government in Shanghai issued "citizen's cards" (*liangmin cheng*) so that its soldiers could check on people's movements. After the war, the Nationalists in Shanghai again issued "identity cards" (*shenfen cheng*). The Communists had excoriated this system vehemently before 1949, so they could hardly retain it after Liberation.[1] Nevertheless, for security, employment, and rationing reasons, they issued "resident's cards" (*chümin cheng*). These were not given to each person but to each head-of-household (variously called *huchang, huchu,* or *chiachang*). The document had to be shown when any member of the household applied for a regular job or made purchases at a state grain shop. In later years, when ration tickets were required to buy certain goods, the card was used to verify the identity of the buyer. The head of each household could obtain tickets only at a special office.[2]

The certificates issued before 1954 had two ostensible purposes. First, they helped to identify spies and persons wanted by the government. Second, they served as proof of legal residence for employment, or for unemployment registration. In the period immediately after Liberation, proof of identity had to be shown by anyone who wanted to buy a railroad ticket at the Shanghai North Station. A person who could not show legitimate Shanghai residence on the basis of old or new documents could only purchase a one-way ticket out of the city.[3]

By early May 1951, a more thorough migration control system

1. Interview, Hong Kong, December 1969. The government on Taiwan still issues *shenfen cheng*.

2. Interview, December 1969, with a Cantonese Overseas Chinese who lived in Shanghai for several years. He mentioned that Canton had maintained personal *shenfen cheng* even after 1949, although appropriately enough a red booklet was substituted for the KMT's white card.

3. Otto van der Sprenkel, with Robert Guillain and Michael Lindsay, eds., *New China: Three Views* (New York: John Day, 1951), p. 105. This restriction on ticket buying was apparently lessened after the mainland was unified militarily. After rations were introduced, however, travel was convenient only for people who had applied for special ration cards that could be used at restaurants and hotels throughout the country.

had been developed for Shanghai. New arrivals to the city were divided into three groups: those who had legally "moved in" (*ch'ienju*), those "from elsewhere" (*waich'iao*), and those "travelling" (*lühsing*). The new 1951 regulations were intended to prevent landlords and rich peasants from fleeing land reform struggle by hiding in the big city. Legally "moved in" people and temporary "travellers" were no problem in this regard. It was announced that:

Any new arrival, who for certain reasons has to stay with relatives or friends in Shanghai for more than one night but less than three months, must report his name, native place, sex, original address, reason for sojourn, and period of stay to the local public security subbureau. The head-of-household where such a person lives is responsible to see that this is done. People who plan to stay more than three months will be treated as immigrants.[4]

New arrivals were required to report within three days if they came from within China, and within five days if they came from abroad.

Household registration in Shanghai was recorded by local officials in police wards. Births were supposed to be reported to the police within a few days after they had occurred. Coffin makers and cemetery keepers could legally offer their services only after being shown death registration papers. At first, the household identification forms differed considerably from one place to another inside China. In July 1951, the Ministry of Public Security issued regulations to standardize the procedures for all cities, but the uniform system was not fully applied in Shanghai until June 1955, well after rationing had begun.[5]

THE 1953 CENSUS AND
THE ISSUANCE OF HOUSEHOLD BOOKS

In 1953, a nationwide census was taken in China.[6] Shanghai's household registration procedures were more advanced than those in most other parts of the country, but the city's census further

---

4. *Shanghai kungshang tzuliao* 2, No. 36 (May 5, 1951), p. 1303.

5. *HWJP*, June 5, 1955, cited in John F. Aird, "Population Growth," in Alexander Eckstein, Walter Galenson, and Ta-chung Liu, eds., *Economic Trends in Communist China* (Chicago: Aldine, 1968), pp. 220-221.

6. See Leo A. Orleans, *Every Fifth Child: The Population of China* (Stanford, Calif.: Stanford University Press, 1972), especially pp. 13-19.

developed its registration system and reviewed the records thoroughly. The ostensible main purpose of the census was to prepare for elections, which were held the next year.

In the spring of 1953, Shanghai census cadres began to study previous registration records to prepare for their survey.[7] Over a period of several months, more than 3,900 registration stations were set up in the city under district level supervision; on November 23, 1953, enumeration began. Famous Shanghai residents such as Soong Ching-ling, T'an Chen-lin and Ch'en Yi went with fanfare to their local registrars to popularize the census and to urge that everyone participate in it. Registration forms were distributed in both functional and residential groups through the lowest-level government committees. Spot checks verified the completeness of the census, but because this enrollment was associated mainly with upcoming elections, and because the implications of the census for food rationing were not yet obvious enough to encourage compliance, some residents not connected with any major work place may have been missed.[8] Shanghai residents away for less than six months at the time of the census were registered as permanent in Shanghai. Those absent for more than six months were supposed to register elsewhere, although note could be made of their status in the Shanghai household to which they planned to return.[9] The 1953 census was no doubt incomplete in details, but it was far more impressive than any previous inventory of people in Shanghai. It laid the basis for a more thorough check on population than most cities have.

After the census, household registration books (*huchi pu*) were issued in many parts of China, including Shanghai, to replace the earlier, simpler forms. More information was included. One page was devoted to each member of the household; blank pages were

7. *JMJP*, June 10, 1953.

8. See the long article, NCNA, Shanghai, November 28, 1953, where the census procedures are outlined in some detail and the possibility of systematic flaws in them can be readily seen. The speed of the campaign was one of its most spectacular features. About 280 stations in populous P'ut'o District estimated that they had registered more than half the district's population in only three days. P'ut'o has factories, slums, and workers' housing. In such a situation, the possibilities of intentional and unintentional doublecounting and not counting are quite large.

9. NCNA, Peking, July 8, 1953.

supplied for any later additions. Each page contained entries for a person's name, any alias (*piehming*), year of birth, occupation, place of work, usually the family background (*chiat'ing ch'ushen*), individual status (*kojen ch'engfen*), cultural standard (*wenhua ch'engtu*), marriage status, religion, and ancestral place of origin (*chikuan*). The registered family was responsible for keeping the book up-to-date. All births or deaths had to be reported to the local police station, which kept copies of the household books for its ward.[10]

Even short visits to Shanghai fell under the purview of this system. It was legally necessary to "report a temporary resident" (*paokao linshih huk'ou*), even someone staying for a single night, to security officers of the local residents' committee. In Shanghai, this requirement was often honored in the breach unless current campaigns especially enforced it.[11]

The typical police station (*p'aich'u so*) had 10 or 15 functionaries taking care of files, job applications, household matters, and so forth, in a jurisdiction containing about an equal number of residence areas. Some police stations were larger, although the municipal government tried to eliminate this situation by setting up new stations. There was at least one part-time civilian security officer in each residence area. Regular policemen were instructed to make all possible friendly contacts with local households. For this purpose they celebrated periodic "love-the-people months" (*aimin yueh*) to encourage popular cooperation with security goals. Urban police were usually not armed. At the low level of the station, regulations set definite limits even on the amount of interrogation to which they could subject citizens.[12] A great deal of effort was devoted to increasing the popularity of basic-level public security officials, because the thoroughness of the information they obtain from residents determines the effectiveness of many urban controls.

LATER DEVELOPMENT OF THE REGISTRATION SYSTEM

The enforcement and meaning of the household registration system has varied greatly over time. Some national campaigns, such as

10. Robert Tung, "People's Policemen," *Far Eastern Economic Review* 53 (August 18, 1966), pp. 319-321; and interview, Hong Kong, December 1969.

11. The interview cited in note 10.

12. Robert Tung, "People's Policemen."

the completion of the civil war, land reform, the Korean War, many agricultural collectivization movements that affected grain purchasing, and the Socialist Education Movement, induced a tightening of urban controls. Others, such as the Great Leap Forward and the Cultural Revolution, had the opposite effect.

People could, of course, change their legal residence in China even when restrictions were tightest. The procedures for this were not simple, and they varied somewhat over time. The core procedures of residence control, as described below at their most mature stage in the mid-1960s, are a model by which to understand the less elaborated forms that developed in the late 1950s and early 1960s. The carrot of the system can be found in rations and jobs; the stick was people's fear of lacking them.

Whenever a family wanted to move to another place, it could report this desire to the local police station. If a household planned to move from Shanghai to a smaller city or rural place, the application was normally granted after the police had checked that no household members owed money in the city, and after approval had been obtained from the Shanghai work places of employed family members. The local police station would then report to its district level public security subbureau and would request a "moving certificate" (*ch'ienyi cheng*). This document was necessary before any physical facilities for household moving could become available, and especially before legal facilities for establishing residence at a new location in China could be arranged.[13]

When only a single member of a household moved, for example to join the army, attend school, or transfer to an inland farm, the procedure was simpler. The person set up a formal "temporary household" (*linshih huk'ou*) in the new jurisidiction. Before moving he had to go to his local police station and show letters from the new institution. His name was then "cancelled" (*paoch'u*) from his family's household registration book, and he obtained rationing

13. Interview, Hong Kong, November 1969. The information for this paragraph and the next about "temporary households" came mostly from an ex-student whose family moved out of Amoy to a more rural place, and who later established a "temporary household" at a school dormitory. He (and two other informants separately) said that interjurisdictional public security matters such as household moving had highly standardized procedures throughout China. One Shanghainese informant had lived there for an extended period; the other two had been to Shanghai.

and other documents from the Shanghai police station to give to the security section at his new residence. Military units, universities, boarding schools, bureaucratic offices, companies, and other institutions running dormitories have collective household registrations (*chit'i huchi*) to which names can be added in this manner.

THE RATION SYSTEM

A government can establish tight, permanent rationing effectively only if it gains control over both consumer demand and commodity supplies. The household registration system helped Shanghai authorities to reduce demands. The government also moved during the 1950s to assert control over the city's supply of food and cloth.

EFFORTS TO MONITOR SUPPLY IN THE EARLY 1950s

Before rationing began, agricultural taxes and free-market supply restrictions had been the main methods by which government could restrain the urban use of staples. "Unified purchase and distribution" (*t'ungkou t'unghsiao*) of grains was first introduced in some areas during September 1953. Its stated purposes were to cut consumption, stabilize prices, prevent black markets, and support industrialization. As Ch'en Yün, vice-chairman of the Central Committee and vice-premier, later explained to a National People's Congress, this rationed and centralized system of wholesale supply was "only a temporary measure" that would be cancelled as soon as production in each region could meet demand. Ch'en made a momentous understatement in adding that cancellation would "not come very soon."[14] Many crops, even those harvested as late as December 1953, were taxed at fixed rates on the volumes of produce expected in a normal year from specific kinds of acreage. Production above these amounts was not taxed.[15] This was the beginning of agricultural quotas for the later collectives. It was also the basis of the ration-cum-market arrangements that followed.[16]

14. NCNA, Peking, September 23, 1954.
15. NCNA, Peking, January 14, 1954.
16. After a collective pays its taxes and delivers to the state its mandatory sales at fixed prices, the surplus grain can be sold to other units. Pricing arrangements for these transactions have varied according to time and place, but in recent years the government has made an effort to keep prices high and taxes and mandatory sales amounts low, so that the surplus can serve as an incentive to production.

By March 1, 1954, Shanghai's grain market was under state control and capitalism was officially restricted to nonstaples.[17] The new State Food Company authorized 1,498 rice shops in Shanghai to act as its sales agents. On the twenty-fifth day of every month, each shop submitted a "distribution plan." After bureaucratic approval, grain was issued to fill it. The company promised to pay a handling fee "approximately equal" to the profits that these shops could have made if they had set their own retail prices. For the first few months while this system was being prepared and used experimentally, the total state grain allotments to Shanghai increased markedly.[18] Uniform prices for various grains were instituted all over the city, and the government advertised that the new prices would be slightly less than they had averaged in private rice stores before the change. The ration systems for grain, cooking oil, meats, and cloth were all instituted in this manner.

RATION PROCEDURES

Rationing based on household registration books did not achieve its full form until the mid-1960s. During its most developed period, this system allowed the government to exert pressure on Shanghai citizens to conserve food. This pressure, as subsequent sections will show, diminished in periods of great supply or shortage and increased in times of partial shortage.

The "household registration section" or "household registration group" (*huchi k'o* or *huchi tsu*) of each police station in theory had charge of all residence and ration matters in its ward. In many places, it issued tickets monthly (or for some commodities less often) under the names of the commercial companies that governed supplies. In practice, the wards were quite large and inefficiencies developed. People complained that they had to wait too long at police stations when they came for routine registration matters.[19] Ration tickets were therefore increasingly issued by the commodity companies directly, on the basis of public security documents shown to them.

17. NCNA, Shanghai, March 1, 1954.
18. *Ibid.* says that the amount of grain shipped to Shanghai from November 1953 to January 1954 was 62 percent more than in the corresponding period in 1952-1953.
19. *HWJP*, June 5, 1955, and *LTP*, October 5, 1956.

The amount of paperwork involved in these systems was staggering. During shortages, tickets for some foods had to be handed out two or three times each month to each household, as supplies came into the city and their amounts were known. When commodity companies took over the ticket distribution, they also took over the management of some very long lines. To halt congestion, work units began acting as the agents of their employees, whether they lived at home or in company dormitories. The guard sections (*paowei k'o*) of production units then distributed the tickets to heads-of-household who lived elsewhere, and also to the cooks who bought food for dormitory canteens. The guard sections were discouraged from performing this service for employees who lived far away, and who might illegally obtain double rations by enrolling in two different urban districts.

Neighborhood committee security officials also sometimes obtained ration tickets for people living in their jurisdictions. The system of the mid-1950s was further complicated by the fact that public security stations, or their agents at whatever level, were only allowed to handle tickets. Commodity companies still distributed the goods. These state enterprises were supposed to follow plans by allocating the full scheduled amounts of their products to the ration system and by allowing no leaks even at the lowest retail levels. Such rules could not always be enforced.

Some services and privileges were rationed by other kinds of special cards. Unlike the household registration books, these cards were usually assigned to individuals rather than to collective households; they could be used to prove identity for some purposes. Anyone who had rights to clinical care under a range of schemes was issued a "medical card" (*yiliao cheng*). A person working for a government organization at any level owned a "state organ work personnel card" (*kuochia chikuan kungtso jenyüan cheng*). Many other kinds of employers also issued work identification cards. A few qualified people received "Overseas Chinese remittance cards" (*ch'iao hui cheng*). Soldiers had certificates issued by the People's Liberation Army: an "officer's card" (*chünkuan cheng*), a "military service card" (*pingyi cheng*), or a "People's Liberation Army disabled veteran's card" (*Jenmin Chiehfang Chün ts'anfei chünjen cheng*). Political parties, commercial-industrial managers' organizations, and many other voluntary associations also issued membership cards.[20]

In the 1960s, coupons continued to be issued under the general surveillance of commodity companies and public security organs. There were many kinds of ration tickets, but in prosperous times, supplies or prices were high enough to make many of them unnecessary. The procedures varied for different goods. Ration cards for grain, and often for other edibles, were generally issued by street "food management stations" (*liangshih kuanli so*). Cards for other commodities, especially those such as cloth for which the coupons came less often than monthly, were issued by the retail outlets of the companies concerned (not, as in the early 1950s, by local police stations). They were distributed on the basis of current household records supplied by the public security system. Often the food companies would "serve the people" by having messengers deliver the ration cards directly to households. If no one was home who could sign for the cards, instructions would be left to go to the company office and pick them up later. Food tickets of this sort were only usable at stores and restaurants in Shanghai, the jurisdiction where they were obtained.

In most parts of the city, there were fewer retailers of grain staples than of nonstaple foods like sugar, beans, or cooking oil. In some times only a few special stores, attached directly to food stations, were authorized to sell grain. Substantial towns in rural areas might have only one such store, although a large city like Shanghai had many. Large grain stores and food management stations were officially separate from each other. In fact, their offices often adjoined physically, and their personnel overlapped.

Food management stations were the procuring agents for retail grain stores. They were also the only wholesale sources of supply

20. Interview, Hong Kong, October 1969. Local governments of border areas issue additional kinds of identity cards, some of them compulsory and personal. Even in Canton City, an "urban resident's certificate" (*ch'engshih chümin cheng*) has sometimes been required. In coastal areas, a "frontier defense district resident's certificate" (*pienfang ch'ü chümin cheng*) is needed. Travel into some border districts is legal only for holders of "border defense pass cards" (*pienfang ch'ü t'unghsing cheng*), which are valid for specific areas. Boat households are issued proof of their status. When they are registered with the militia coast guard for passage from Hong Kong or Macau, they are given special passes.

for many other local stores selling nongrain foods. The stations ordinarily issued all food ration tickets for a specific area. In the mid-1960s, many kinds of coupons were included in a single "food book" (*liangshih pu*), supplied by the station. The name of the purchaser was not written on ordinary ration tickets when those were used. At times when food books were used, the purchaser's name was indicated, and retailers were supposed to check the name and tear out the tickets whenever purchases were made. Food books affected the black market, because they encouraged illegal trade in kind rather than in tickets.

The possible kinds of ration tickets are legion. In prosperous times, supplies or prices are high enough to make many of them unnecessary; in poor periods, they have not commanded large quantities of goods. The most important coupons are generically called "grain tickets" (*liang p'iao*). These monthly chits usually are valid for a specific amount of a grain (rice or wheat). Conversion into other starches is possible according to fixed rates at official stores. Other monthly rations are available in exchange for meat tickets (*jou p'iao*), which are commonly specialized for pork, fish, beef, lamb, and sometimes other meats; these are also usually convertible at rates determined by supply. Tickets have sometimes been necessary to buy sugar (*t'ang piao*) and edible cooking oil (*shihyu p'iao*). Cakes and many kinds of specialties have been rationed by nonstaples tickets (*fushihp'in p'iao*). Coupons issued by local food stations change from time to time, and they symbolize one of the most frequent interactions between Shanghai people and their government.

Local companies under the Ministry of Textiles make only annual distributions of cloth tickets (*pu p'iao*). Fuels are rationed by coupons like kerosene tickets (*shuiyu p'iao*). Tobacco and other luxuries have sometimes been sold only against chits such as cigarette-purchasing tickets (*hsiangyen koumai p'iao*). A wide range of items—bicycles, radios, and other light manufactures—are distributed in times of shortage by industrial commodity tickets (*kungyehp'in p'iao*).

From the end of 1957 to July 1966, some people could obtain Overseas Chinese purchasing tickets (*Huach'iao koumai p'iao*). These coupons were made available whenever relatives abroad remitted money into China. The concentration of Overseas Chinese dependents in some places, such as Shanghai, Amoy, and Canton, reduced residence control somewhat, because it increased the general level of local consumption. Hard currency paid into certain banks outside China could be remitted to the Shanghai branch of the People's Bank. An Overseas Chinese recipient in the city would collect Chinese money at the Bank according to fixed exchange rates, along with special ration tickets in proportion to the amount of foreign money changed. These certificates could be used only at special Overseas Chinese stores (*Huach'iao shangtien*) in the area where they were issued. The range of goods available in these stores, which served Overseas Chinese only, was better and wider than the selection in ordinary shops. Prices at the Overseas Chinese stores were generally lower, when comparisons could be made. The special ration certificates provided fixed proportions, for example, of pork tickets (*chujou p'iao*), rice tickets (*mi p'iao*), nonstaples tickets, edible oil tickets, cloth tickets and light industrial commodity tickets (*ch'ingkungyehp'in p'iao*). These coupons were convertible to some extent. The number of fixed sets of chits depended on the size of the remittance, rounded downward for uneven amounts. Because Overseas Chinese sometimes did not need all the commodities they bought, their excess goods appeared on black markets.[21] At least in some times and places, these extra commodities may have diluted the residential effects of supply controls under the household system.

PRESSURES FOR AUSTERITY, 1955-1957

Rationing institutions, first established in 1954, were consolidated for more than a year before the government began to make use of them to encourage austerity. By March 1955, the national grain shortage, and a quickening of the "transition to socialism," oriented the Shanghai ration system toward savings.[22] The immediate reason for the 1955 campaign was simple: there had been severe

21. Four interviews in Hong Kong on the ration system in November and December 1969, January 1970, and February 1972. Rationing practices in rural areas differ from those in Shanghai.

22. For excellent background on this, see Thomas P. Bernstein, "Cadre and Peasant Behavior under Conditions of Insecurity and Deprivation: The Grain Supply Crisis of the Spring of 1955," in A. Doak Barnett, ed., *Chinese Communist Politics in Action* (Seattle: University of Washington Press, 1969), pp. 365-399.

floods the previous year in East China, especially in northern Kiangsu, and the city's rice supply was short.[23]

The most pressing problem in Shanghai was to distribute a reduced food supply democratically. On March 24, the municipal Party Committee adopted resolutions for austerity in factories, better market control, and tighter storage procedures.[24] By mid-May, district Party committees were training "large numbers of temporary political reporters" to lead "economy meetings" for workers in every kind of urban organization. More than 10,000 collective units in Shanghai drew up "consumption plans" and submitted them to the State Food Company.[25] An inspection team of 18 national people's deputies went to alleys, factories, warehouses, flour mills, rice processing plants, restaurants, canning assembly lines, and grain stores to encourage adoption of the food plans. The team proposed that "catering units that are inclined to pad their plans should be educated, inspected, and supervised."[26]

There were still many ways in a large city to evade the regulations. In late June, the Shanghai Public Security Bureau arrested a gang of 53 entrepreneurs who had organized a "Taoist" secret society to transport grain illegally from counties in Kiangsu to Shanghai. Among the arrested criminals were the manager of the joint Huatung Switch Factory, some official grain salesmen, many boat people who were also engaged in legal transport, and retail agents in legal enterprises far removed from the food business, such as embroidery stores and tailor shops.[27] A Shanghai functionary of this organization was caught with 56 different counterfeit chops, both public and private, with which he had manufactured more than 100 fake household registrations to obtain extra rations. He was also prepared to turn out orders and invoices for interprovincial grain shipments, as well as many other sophisticated government documents.

By July 1, the shortage was severe enough for local committees to institute "family grain consumption plans" (*chiat'ing yungliang chihua*). In Hsinch'eng District, the first 22,900 households were

23. *HWJP*, July 10, 1955.
24. NCNA, Shanghai, March 26, 1955.
25. NCNA, Shanghai, May 17, 1955.
26. NCNA, Shanghai, June 13, 1955.
27. *JMJP*, June 28, 1955.

called to residents' meetings for instructions on calculating (i.e., minimizing) their family food consumption. By July 5, the second group of households in the district had already begun this process.[28]

Reductions in family grain use seem to have been distributed almost on a quota system among many units in Shanghai. For example, the Shanghai branch of the Revolutionary Committee of the Kuomintang called on all its members to estimate their household food consumption carefully, and exact accounts were kept of the members' grain savings. The basic levels of this organization called meetings to criticize wrong notions, such as "generous estimation and economical use" (*k'uanta chaiyung*) and "allowing a fudge factor" (*mao kuku*). Members reported in public meetings about their detailed calculations. In cases of "inaccurate" mathematics, other members stood ready to help resolve the problem. Newspapers did not say that each group had received a quota, but they did announce, "Now, when good discussions are held in basic level organizations, a fixed (*yiting ti*) result has been achieved."[29]

The seriousness of this planning program was underlined by major criminal charges against people who violated the plan. In a clearly exemplary verdict, the P'englai District People's Court sentenced Ho Wen-yao, hawker-owner of the Sanhsingch'i Dumpling Stall, to a seven-year prison term for having inflated the amount of ingredients he needed to make dumplings and for having sold the excess on black markets.[30]

Broad and specific social pressures, which the government applied over the city in many different kinds of units, effectively reduced Shanghai's gross grain consumption. Between May and July 1955, more than 1.2 million households and 10,000 collective provision units (*chit'i huoshih tanwei*) submitted food plans. Grain consumption in May was only 10 million catties less than in April, but "the residents in compiling their first consumption plans had made overestimations." To correct this sloppiness, the Shanghai Party Committee called on the Federation of Trade Unions, the Women's Federation, and on all democratic parties, districts, and street committees to hold another round of meetings

28. *HWJP*, July 5, 1955.
29. *Ibid.*, another article.
30. *HWJP*, July 11, 1955.

and to obtain lower estimates.[31] As a result of these efforts, the city's grain use in June was 24 million catties less than in May.

By August 1955, after the first harvest had been delivered from double- and triple-crop fields in East China, the worst of the crisis was over. The campaign abated somewhat, but the institutional structure for encouraging low rations and high savings was not abandoned. The government, however, announced that residents could now use their ration cards to buy food from suburban cooperatives, as well as from official food stores.[32] Despite the continuing shortage of rice, during the Autumn Festival Shanghai's bakers were allowed 32 percent more grain products than in 1954 to make the traditional mooncakes.[33]

Under a nationwide plan for urban consumption, the grain-use standard was supposed to be calculated according to the physical energy requirements of each recipient's job. Employment information was therefore entered in household books.[34] More than 10,000 cadres surveyed 260,000 people for this purpose during the autumn of 1955. To no one's surprise, they often found that rations were higher than the jobs really required. One team visited 20 plants, including the Kiangnan Shipyard, The Shanghai No. 15 Cotton Mill, and the Shanghai Agricultural Machinery Works, only to conclude that the 38,000 workers in these factories could get along quite well with one catty of grain less per month than they had previously been allowed.[35]

Some new rationing regulations came into force on October 16, 1955. The city's "total consumption" in the second half of that month was therefore 4.2 percent less than in the first half.[36] Many residents reportedly refrained from buying the full amount of grain due to them. The change was instituted during the second harvest on double- and triple-crop rice fields (and during the only harvest in late single-crop fields), perhaps because the regime knew there

31. *HWJP,* July 6, 1955.
32. *HWJP,* August 28, 1955. These official stores were then usually called *liangshih taihsiao tien.*
33. *HWJP,* September 1, 1955.
34. *JMJP,* September 5, 1955.
35. NCNA, Shanghai, September 27, 1955.
36. NCNA, Shanghai, November 7, 1955.

would in any case be some extralegal grain available as a safety valve for extreme discontent.[37]

Supply restrictions of nonstaple foods were less important than rations of rice for the purpose of residence control. The fall of 1955 saw the introduction of Shanghai's first "purchase cards" (*koumai cheng*) for nonstaples. Beginning on September 1, cards were necessary to obtain some dishes at restaurants and stalls. Shops were somehow persuaded that these changes, administered by district-level food supply stations, would provide them with both adequate supplies and "regular customers, so that their trade will be ensured."[38] This change, along with the new quarterly estimation and payment of profit taxes (which also began on September 1, 1955), created the basis for socialization in these stores.

During 1956, municipal authorities were concerned that the somewhat greater availability of food after the severe shortage would cause people to think rations could be raised. The Food Bureau allowed some "ration adjustments" (*t'iaocheng tingliang*), but it also set up an investigation to make sure they did not get out of hand. In November, each district-level subsection of the Food Bureau was instructed to establish its own group of 200 cadres to reexplore "the relation between the amount of provisions supplied to retailers and the amount used by residents."[39] Even New Year's cakes and long noodles were now to be covered by ration regulations.

The rules governing meat in January 1957 exemplify the complications of the system. Because that month began with a holiday, special "New Year meat tickets" (*yüantan joup'iao*) were issued. This kind of ticket could only be used between December 30 and January 1, to purchase four taels of pork. Three other ordinary meat tickets were to be used during the first, middle, and last ten days of January. The first chit could be cashed only between the second and tenth of the month. The next two tickets were issued during the same three-day period as the special New Year coupons, but the exact kind and amount of meat for which these future chits would be valid could not be specified until one day before each ration

37. Victor Carl Falkenheim, "Provincial Administration in Fukien, 1949-1966" (Ph.D. diss., Columbia University, 1971), p. 280.

38. *HWJP*, September 1, 1955.

39. *HWJP*, November 18, 1956.

period began (i.e., on January 9 and 19). Anyone wishing to buy less meat than the ticket allowed could do so, but the ticket was always collected at time of purchase. Some less desirable cuts, mainly pork tripe and pork brains, could be bought without tickets. In addition, certain parts of the hog required more certificates than others. For example, two "taels" of meat ticket could buy one pig's leg, and four "taels" of meat ticket could buy three pigsfeet or 1.5 catties of ribs. Pork rations could be converted into beef and lamb at regularly posted rates. An entirely separate local ration subsystem was devoted to Shanghai's Muslim minority.

Additional complicated provisions applied to any changes in a household's membership during that January. Babies born in the first half of the month meant another half portion of meat tickets. New mothers could also obtain a one-time bonus of three whole "catties" of meat tickets. Special arrangements were available in cases of marriage, miscarriage, or death. Patients having tuberculosis, cancer, or diabetes could ask for additional meat rations, but only at district-level offices. All such applications had to be properly documented, stamped, and filed within a certain period.[40]

The procedures changed quite often. Their complexity may have reduced consumption by discouraging some Shanghai people from trying to obtain their full rations.

By the first few months of 1957, the grain shortage had been alleviated because of careful distribution and improved production. There was still a shortage of nonstaple foods and "daily use products" (*jihyungp'in*), for reasons that are not clear. The shortages of some nonperishable commodities may have been caused by inventory depletions in 1954-1956, when many Shanghai industries were under financial and supply pressure to make the transition to socialism. The official explanation no doubt also has some merit: wage reforms had increased total purchasing power in Shanghai. Some of the short commodities could be bought without tickets, and money rationed the black market. In any case, 1957 saw the only kind of inflation that can occur with fixed prices on unrationed goods: the supply of them was exhausted.[41] One apologetic article

40. *HWJP*, December 30, 1956.
41. A speech by Deputy Mayor Sung Jih-ch'ang is reported in *CNP*, January 11, 1957, giving the official explanation for these problems. Many available 1955 and 1956 data are difficult to interpret because they should be seen in the light of other,

pointed out that *if* Shanghai's total provisions of supplementary foods had been divided among all its citizens equally during the previous year, each person would have received 19 catties of pork, 44 eggs, more than 2 catties of chicken or duck, more than 17 catties of fresh fish, and 211 catties of vegetables.[42] Clearly, the distribution had not been even; the most cogent argument for the ration system was that it should be.

Propaganda about saving grain did not cease when shortages of other products arose. In early 1957, a local Shanghai newspaper reported:

Even though China had serious natural disasters last year, agricultural cooperativization caused the production of grain to increase by 20 billion catties over 1955. . . . But this output must be divided for food, seed, fodder, rural subsidiary industries, handicrafts, and other industrial inputs. The supply is therefore still tight. Now that the population has increased, the labor force is greater, fodder animals are more numerous, and cultivated land has been expanded; there is more pressure for all these uses. Due to circumstances such as these, there is enough food to share but the supply is not abundant. To solve this problem, strict economy must be practiced.[43]

Specific kinds of waste, such as feeding chickens with rice and leftovers after canteen meals, were criticized with special vehemence.

---

unavailable statistics. Total grain supply in Shanghai went up 9 percent. Pig carcasses rose from 1,130,000 to 1,450,000 between these years (but it is unclear whether any of this pork was tinned for consumption elsewhere). Cloth supplies rose by 41 percent, and "other daily necessities" increased by 15 percent. Purchasing power rose even faster. The city's total wage bill (apparently only for unionized workers) rose 132 million yüan. Labor insurance and welfare expenses increased by 18 million yüan. Fees taken out of these emoluments dropped by 15 million yüan; property taxes brought in 4 million yüan less; and medical fees took 2 million yüan less. On these bases, purchasing power reportedly rose by 3,230,000,000 yüan. The result of high-spending fiscal policies to finance the transition to socialism—just as for other public works in other countries—had been inflationary during 1956. In China, rations and price controls were needed to dampen this effect. Residence control, rations, expensive organizational reforms, and ideological education were all related to each other.

42. *HWJP*, December 30, 1956. For this calculation, Shanghai had 6,280,000 citizens. In 1956, Shanghai received 190 million catties of pork, 18 million catties of chickens and ducks, 34.9 million catties of fresh eggs, and more fish and vegetables than could be traced accurately.

43. *CNP*, March 8, 1957. The article specified that potatoes were converted into grain equivalents at the rate of one to four.

To judge the effect of the government's insistence on continued frugality in 1957, it is necessary to look at long-term changes in the per capita use of various commodities. The average real consumption of *all* goods and services by Shanghai's workers in the 30 years before 1957 did not increase sharply, despite a sharp rise in the consumption of food and cloth. According to a survey, the real purchases per person in Shanghai of the following goods increased by the following percentages between 1929-1930 and 1956: eggs, 279 percent; poultry, 255 percent; fish, 170 percent; pork, 66 percent; vegetables, 21 percent; rice, 13 percent; and cotton cloth, 118 percent. The consumption of some less necessary commodities and services decreased between the two survey times.[44] Basic goods were rationed in the mid-1950s, but they comprised a more important part of Shanghai's consumables than ever before. The social incentive effects of the ration system were all the greater for this reason.

Early 1957 saw a further intensification of the austerity campaign. In February, the Shanghai Federation of Trade Unions' paper proudly announced that the city had some 7,200 lunch groups of at least 25 people each. No less than 60 percent of these groups delivered unused foods to the state on a regular monthly basis. Total savings amounted to 3.2 million catties of vegetables and grain during three winter months of 1956-1957. Standard-form accounting had also begun in 80 percent of the lunch groups.[45]

The new "five austerity" (*wu chieh*) movement was a responsibility of street committees in Shanghai. For example, four house-

44. Figures for consumption increase are presented in Chapter 3 on employment. The percentages above have been computed from absolute figures given in Nai-ruenn Chen, ed., *Chinese Economic Statistics: A Handbook for Mainland China* (Chicago: Aldine, 1967), p. 440, which is based on the same 1957 Chinese source. The 1956 figures in kilograms were as follows: rice, 135.37; pork, 8.10; poultry, 135; fishery products, 13.70; vegetables, 96.75; and 84.23 eggs per year per Shanghai worker. The figure for cotton cloth was 14 meters. Statistics for sugar and edible vegetable and animal oils are also given. If a dietician could calculate protein and caloric consumption from these figures, it would be interesting to compare urban and rural consumption. The figures clearly show a long-term rise in protein consumption (especially eggs and chickens). Consumption of high-protein products is a relatively inefficient way of obtaining calories. During any future shortage, at least some of the grain that hens now eat could be consumed by people, with less heat loss. Protein consumption is a buffer against famine.

45. *LTP*, February 4, 1957.

wives of East Peking Road, Huangp'u District, called a general street meeting to encourage the use of less coal, cloth, water, electricity, and rice.[46] This movement was carried out in alternating waves of propaganda meetings and estimation meetings. The submission of one set of austere family grain plans would be praised; then the importance of further frugality would be stressed in all media. This was followed by a call for another "revision of the consumption plans for grain" (*ch'unghsin chihting yungliang chihua*). The policy of recurrent movements was explained quite frankly in newspapers; government cadres felt that cyclically returning campaigns were necessary to prevent backsliding and luxurious consumption.[47]

At the same time, grain agencies launched a movement against the "four pests" (*szu hai*). This was to assure that food would be spoiled by no worms, no mold, no mice or sparrows, and no accidents (*wu ch'ung, wu mei, wu shu ch'üeh, wu shihku*).[48] At one meeting on March 5, 1957, to honor "four-pest activists," awards were given to 382 "superior units" (*yuhsiu tanwei*) and to 723 individuals in Shanghai.

No stone was left unturned to find models for this movement. The Shanghai Zoo cut rations at the specific request of its suppliers. A local paper gleefully bannered that "The Elephants, the Lions, the Bears, and the Monkeys Have Been More Frugal in Food Consumption." The story went on to say that, "Due to the efforts of zookeepers and food companies, the animals now use cheaper feeds." Decadent, unproletarian habits nevertheless prevailed in some quarters, even among undoubted patriots. One doleful sentence later in the article complained that "The pandas still cannot economize in food consumption."[49]

The government consistently explained that rationing was needed because demand had risen, not because supply had dropped. Most of the time, this was true, and savings were an increasingly important component of demand. The bureaucracy was eager to avoid price fluctuations, even if a considerable oscillation in rationing policy was the only way to do so. For example, sugar tickets

46. *CNP*, February 26, 1957.
47. *HMPWK*, February 19, 1957.
48. *HMPWK*, March 5, 1957, p. 4; also another article on p. 1.
49. *HMPWK*, March 7, 1957.

were withdrawn and called unnecessary in Shanghai during the last
half of 1956, but they were reintroduced in April 1957:

This is not because the production of sugar in our country has decreased.
Our country is one of the few nations in the world that can produce both
sugar cane and beet root. . . . Although the number of refineries and the
production of sugar have both increased, nevertheless the rise of the
people's standard of living has caused demand to soar. The consumption
of sugar in Shanghai rises every year. If the amount consumed in 1953 was
100, in 1954 it was 110.81, in 1955 it was 115.39, and last year it was 142.08.
An index only for sugar consumed in industry, based on the same year,
would by 1956 amount to 261.56. Production cannot meet this growing
demand. In the second half of last year, when rationing was withdrawn, the
country had to import about 130,000 tons. This year, in order to save
foreign exchange, this measure must be reintroduced.[50]

In early 1957, the government granted Shanghai residents tickets
for five taels of sugar but allowed rural and suburban residents only
three taels. An extra tael of sugar coupons was also available to
people who bought 30 catties of powdered milk; and four additional taels of sugar coupons were awarded with each sale of one
catty of whipping cream. In May, the sugar ration was raised to six
taels in the city, and to four in the neighboring countryside.[51]
Sensitivity and flexibility are the hallmarks of a just ration system,
but the same virtues also make it complicated and difficult to
enforce.

Legal free markets also hampered the enforcement of ration
procedures and reduced their residence control effect by making
money, rather than legal household status, an important source of
livelihood within the city. Shanghai's legal free market in pork
lasted until September 10, 1957. When it was closed by decree of the
State Council, Shanghai buyers were forbidden to visit rural villages to purchase either pork or living hogs. Transportation companies were prevented from carrying pork for peasants or individual merchants. The rationalization for this rule was that all
meat should be checked by the city's Public Health Bureau before it
was sold. The main cause, however, lay in the need to hold down
rural slaughtering and urban deliveries, lest partial exceptions
make the food management system as a whole unenforceable.[52]

50. *HWJP*, March 31, 1957.
51. *HWJP*, March 31, 1957, and April 25, 1957.
52. *HWJP*, August 28, 1957.

The city's Food Bureau extended its austerity procedures in 1957 to include industries that use grain for raw material, as well as individuals who consume it directly. Communal eating groups were also ordered to follow their consumption plans more strictly. Most important, local food stations were instructed to check the real sizes of households in their neighborhoods, and not to leave that continuing inspection job entirely to the public security system.[53] Purchasing branches in the countryside instituted the "five guarantees" movement. The weight, color, taste, purity, and nourishment value of all grain were to be protected by warehousemen so as to assure smooth and standard sales, and thus remove an obvious basis for criticism of the ration system.[54]

RELAXATION OF RATIONING DURING THE LEAP

By 1958, bureaucratic simplification and send-down movements had hampered the enforcement of rationing and population controls in Shanghai's urban area. Changes in the investment pattern also created many low-paying, temporary, contract jobs, and rural people could move quite freely into the city. Police stations did not have enough personnel or resources to check the economic merits of local factory managements' decisions to hire more employees. In practice, they honored factories' requests that household registrations be transferred from rural areas to cities.

Many new economic units were formed, and the ration system had to be extended to them. It was not easy to keep household records accurate, in a time of considerable labor recruitment and population turnover. Sometimes workers were criticized for moving, but they received permission to do so anyway. As one ex-cadre admitted rather sadly,

By the second half of 1958, during the high tide of the Great Leap Forward, the drifting population in Shanghai and other big cities had become very large. All of us cadres were busy purchasing industrial construction materials, manufacturing steel on a large scale, and setting up satellite fields. Some people were blinded by the false surface, and they slackened

53. *HWJP*, October 8, 1957.
54. *HMPWK*, March 9, 1957. These "five guarantees" (*wu pao*) will interest those who collect number slogans like exotic stamps: *ch'ungliang, sehtse, k'ouwei, tuntu,* and *yinyang.*

their public security work, so that for a short while the applications for households and the management of registrations became lax. In some streets, newcomers had only to notify an activist or the residents' group leader by word of mouth, and that would be counted as the legal procedure for establishing residence. Peasants from near the city blindly flooded into it and later became "black subjects and black households," creating a social problem. The Party later set up "acceptance stations" for these people and ordered them to go back to their original places of registration.[55]

Residence control was so weakened by the breakdown of the household system—and by the abundant harvests of 1958—that immigration to Shanghai was nearly unrestricted during the Great Leap period.

The main dikes against this flood were still institutional, both in the countryside and the city. The latter part of the Great Leap laid the foundations for the more political and more thorough kinds of population control that flourished later. The lives of Shanghai's people increasingly centered around their workplaces. In no area was this change more pervasive or visible than in the mundane matter of obtaining one's daily bread.

By mid-1958, two kinds of communal dining halls had been widely established in Shanghai. One kind supplied only rice, to be eaten with condiments that each individual brought for himself; the other kind supplied both dishes and rice, as in a restaurant. Economic units or bureaucratic offices might provide either or both services. Such matters were commonly regulated by a "mess-hall management committee" (*shiht'ang kuanli weiyüanhui*). Local newspapers admitted that different kinds of residents responded differently to these new eating arrangements. The degree of variation was particularly large in the suburban countryside, where peasants often had relatively direct access to their rations. In one village near Shanghai, three kinds of peasants were distinguished: those who took all of their rations in the dining hall, those who set aside only half of their food quota for use there, and those who gave none of their ration rights to the common mess hall.[56]

55. Another interview, Hong Kong, October 1969. The "acceptance stations" (*shoujung chan*) were for "black subjects and black households" (*heijen heihu*). "Blind flooding into the cities" (*mangmu liuju ch'engshih*) was a frequently expressed bureaucratic fear. The "satellite fields" were *weihsing t'ien*.

56. *Hsüehshu yüehk'an*, July 1958, p. 58.

Work places became more important in regulating and integrating the lives of many people in the urban area. During the late Leap, for example, the Shanghai Bicycle Plant built two dormitories for 1,100 workers (800 men and 300 women). Together they constituted a single huge collective household. The dining hall could serve all of them at once. Food was rationed by price, rather than by ticket, within the unit. Workers could choose four-tael, six-tael, or eight-tael boxes of steamed rice at any meal as they pleased, and they could choose other courses at 10 fen, 15 fen, or 20 fen, just as if they were in a restaurant. They paid at the end of the meal. A single official took care of both security and personnel affairs and also arranged ration rights for the whole collective. No less than 20 watchmen and clerks helped him in this work. The dormitory contained about 73 percent of the factory's work force, and some additional married workers' housing was also paid for by the plant.[57]

LIMITED RATIONING DURING POST-LEAP YEARS

When food shortages first became evident in mid-1959, the rationing system was revitalized out of necessity. Structural changes made in the system at that time formed the basis for a more complete household control during the early 1960s. Inadequate residence records in 1959 did not allow cadres to construct a rationing system of the sort required by the sudden shortages of the time. Some pre-Leap holes in the regulations were nevertheless now closed. Previously, some important kinds of food, especially for children, had been obtainable without ration cards. In late 1959, there was no surplus to allow these exceptions.

By 1960, a lack of agricultural inputs for industry had also caused unemployment in the city: laid-off workers no longer ate in their factory canteens. Shanghai restaurants became extremely crowded with people who had recently lived under institutional auspices. Long queues often formed for tables at public eating houses. The municipal government estimated that more than a million people

---

57. Interview with an Indonesian Overseas Chinese who after failing to enter a university in Shanghai had become an odd-jobber in the Shanghai Bicycle Plant. URI, February 1964. Other sources indicate that at some plants mess hall chits were all bought at the beginning of each month.

in the city were looking regularly for food in restaurants during late 1960.[58]

It became necessary to enforce the distinction between permanent residents and unregistered people, so that food preparation services could be rationed, as well as food itself. The government issued "go to eat coupons" (*chiu ts'an ch'üan*) to registered householders, allowing them to obtain restaurant tables without much waiting in line. Each such ticket was for eight taels of prepared rice, redeemable at any canteen in Shanghai. Permanent residents who needed further coupons for eating in public places could arrange with local grain stations to have their monthly rice rations converted into this form. A simultaneous shortage of fuel for home cooking also gave the restaurants an unusual appeal in 1960.

By the following year, the supply of food had become so low that the government had inadequate supplies for permanent residents who had registered and cooperated with these procedures. It was difficult, under such circumstances, to expect compliance with the household registration rules. A May 1, 1961, announcement said that, until further notice, there would be no more meat for sale in Shanghai. During the fall harvest of that year, monthly rations in the city were as follows: a usually sufficient allotment of 25 catties of rice, an insignificant quantity of vegetables, six or less taels of poor oil (but in the suburban country, only two taels), four to eight taels of sugar, one-and-a-half cakes of brown laundry soap, some soy sauce, and small amounts of fish and pastry. Milk, fruit, butter, margarine, sausage, potatoes, and good vegetables had not been on sale for some time. Illegal black market facilities could supply chickens, ducks, and eggs at high prices. Fuel was extremely tight, and Shanghai residents wishing to cook for themselves had to make do with two catties of kindling and 50 catties of coal balls each month. Beriberi and cirrhosis of the liver were rather widespread.[59]

58. "Interview with a translator from Shanghai," *Current Scene* 1, No. 6 (July 10, 1961), p. 3.

59. Letter written in the fall of 1961 by a German businessman resident in Shanghai, sent to Santa Cruz, California, printed in the San Francisco *Chronicle*, and reprinted in the *China Mail*, Hong Kong, March 28, 1962. Edgar Snow, *The Other Side of the River: Red China Today* (New York: Random House, 1961), p. 538, reports that a doctor in Peking had told him in 1960 that beriberi and pellagra existed at that time in Shanghai. Snow saw blackened teeth, presumably caused by calcium deficiency, among children playing on the Bund. It should be emphasized that these reliable reports are of malnutrition in Shanghai, not of starvation there.

There is no evidence of starvation in Shanghai at this time, but refugees say that the rice ration might have seemed almost enough if there had been something else to eat along with it.

Certain reports, of dubious credibility except that many appeared together at this time, suggest a minor revival of prostitution and illegal dealing in gold and foreign currencies during the height of the food crisis in 1961-1962. Prostitutes reportedly accepted commodities and ration tickets as well as money in exchange for their services, and they plied their trade near amusement halls, parks, and special stores for foreigners and Overseas Chinese. The clientele consisted mainly of seamen, who could obtain goods in ports abroad, and privileged persons whose jobs gave them extra rations. Some people were even able to emigrate during the food shortage. Bourgeois emigrants, seeking to convert their savings of Chinese money into more transferable forms, sometimes risked heavy punishments for unauthorized dealings in gold and foreign currencies. In 1962, they reportedly got only one-eighth of the official exchange rate on most black markets, but they sometimes accepted this loss when they could not obtain legal permission for exchanges they wished to make. Unemployment also spurred some gambling.[60] Card games were usual because in contrast to mahjong they are not noisy. Cadres had a very delicate job of policing the situation at this unfortunate time.

INCREASED SUPPLIES
AND RENEWED RATIONING IN MID-1960S

Food supplies increased sharply in 1963. By spring, the government was able to remove some commodities from the ration list and there were substantial price reductions for many items.[61] People who were not engaged directly in production still got fairly low allotments; for instance, student rations at the Shanghai Teachers'

60. Edgar Snow, *ibid.*, pp. 535-536, quoted a secretary of the Shanghai People's Congress to the effect that gangsters had been eliminated in Shanghai, although the official conceded that a few prostitutes might be operating "as rare cases." Some interviews with Shanghai people are quoted in the *Hong Kong Standard*, November 19, 1962. The reliability of many similar reports is dubious, but there were severe economic shortages in Shanghai at this time.

An ex-resident of the city informed me that gold in other years sold privately at 10 percent above the official exchange rate.

61. *SHNL*, May 18, 1963.

College in 1963 ranged from 25 to 35 catties of rice per month.[62] Supplies steadily improved into the next year, however. By 1964, it was clear that the shortages had helped strengthen discipline, at least among legal food outlets. The greater availability of goods now helped to drive illegal entrepreneurs out of business. Product quality differed among various retailers, but by this time there was apparently no way for Shanghai citizens to obtain price bargains for most goods by comparison shopping. Rice, flour, and all products containing grain were still on the ration schedules, along with edible oils, sugar, and cotton cloth. Pork and beef came in both rationed and unrationed categories; the premium for the free market varieties differed from 10 fen to 50 fen per catty. Some forms of sugar could also be bought at relatively high prices without tickets, and purchasers of coffee and cocoa were supplied with extra coupons. Lard, fish, and mutton could be had without tickets, as could the really abundant supply of chickens at that time.[63] National Day in 1964 was celebrated with particularly large supplies of food.[64] To commemorate the occasion, some items made out of wheat and rice were taken off the restricted list and could be bought without coupons.

The easing of controls over nonfoods proceeded less quickly. At the end of 1964 in Shanghai, both cotton and woolen cloth were still strenuously rationed.[65] The prices of many nonrestricted utilities and manufactures nevertheless went down, and the cost of Shanghai's electricity for lighting was reduced by the Ministry of Water Conservancy and Electric Power during early 1965. The same period also saw drops in the prices of patent medicines, bicycles, radios, and watches. One resident reported: "Judging by the market during the month preceding the Chinese New Year, when demand is highest, the state control of all prices is complete."[66]

By the spring of 1965, ration controls, even for nonstaples, were gradually beginning to vanish. Cigarettes came off the ticket schedule, the price of soap went down and its availability went up,

62. Interview with a Shanghai person who studied at the Specialized Teachers' University, Huangp'u District, URI, December 1963.

63. *SHNL*, February 12, 1964. The Russian correspondent, long resident in Shanghai, gives enough detail to suggest that he or his wife went to market there every day.

64. *HMWP*, September 30 and October 1, 1964.

65. *SHNL*, December 15, 1964.

66. *SHNL*, February 2, 1965.

and hardgoods like radios and kitchen utensils also had price reductions.[67] The New China News Agency proudly reported that in Shanghai the prices of 139 kinds of manufactured goods dropped "7 percent to 24 percent" from mid-1963 to mid-1965, and that the prices of pork, eggs, and sugar products went down "as much as 30 percent."[68] Even the cloth situation improved toward the end of that year. Although all cotton and most wool items still required coupons, the increased production of synthetics helped to satisfy the demand for cloth. Secondhand suits, often tailored in Western style, were still used to a surprising extent in Shanghai, and traditional gowns could sometimes be seen. As one resident reported, "Especially plentiful are women's fur coats."[69]

By the end of the year, the grain allotment, even for ordinary housewives, was more than 30 catties (about 17 percent in wheat flour).[70] It was proclaimed that "the supply and distribution arrangements had made speculative action almost impossible." Plenitude proved to be the best nostrum against black markets. Lines shortened. It was now "possible for residents to purchase all their requirements without fear of being late."[71]

RATIONING AT THE ONSET
OF THE CULTURAL REVOLUTION

By the spring of 1966, nominal grain rations had not actually gone up much, but the continuing and reliable supply of nonrationed subsidiary foods, including some starches, made it quite easy for anyone with some money to live in Shanghai without legal residence status. Grain and cooking oil were now the only rationed food products.[72] Under these circumstances of abundance, one of the main restraints on immigration to the city had become ineffective. Large rations meant that the need for food would not prevent careers in Shanghai, even for nonregistered persons.

67. *SHNL*, May 28, 1965.
68. NCNA, Shanghai, April 24, 1965. An ex-resident disagreed, saying that food prices had risen slightly since the 1950s, although the tag on manufactured goods had gone down.
69. *SHNL*, October 26, 1965. This is the source that reported on December 15 of the previous year that "Cotton cloth is still scarce and continues to be badly rationed."
70. Interview with a Thai Overseas Chinese from Shanghai, URI, May 1966.
71. *SHNL*, February 2, 1965.
72. *SHNL*, June 8, 1966.

HOUSING AND TRANSPORTATION

The availability of certain physical facilities probably also had an effect on the tendency of people to live and work in Shanghai. Some of these conveniences are rationed through the registration system; others are available to all residents. In China and other Asian countries (even including Japan until recently), expenditure on housing space and uncrowded transportation has not been large, in view of the daily discomforts caused by their inadequacy. To the extent that spending on such items can be considered investment rather than consumption, the return is very slow. The effect on urban migration also tends to counteract other government policies. Above all, good urban housing and transportation are expensive, and they can draw large amounts of money away from other development goals.

THE LONG-TERM DECLINE
IN PER CAPITA LIVING SPACE

Much of Shanghai's housing stock predates World War II. Deputy Mayor P'an Han-nien reported in early 1951 that:

In the whole of Shanghai, there were about 300,000 houses in 1937. At that time, the city's population was 3 million. Now, there are only 246,000 houses left—a reduction of about one-sixth. The population has actually increased by 2 million. The shortage of housing is therefore a very serious problem. . . .[73]

The Japanese war had destroyed buildings, and the civil war had brought refugees. Mayor Ch'en Yi declared in early 1951 that "key areas" would be designated for the construction of new residences for workers.[74]

The attitude of some cadres toward workers' resettlement projects in the cities was quite missionary.[75] This feeling encouraged

---

73. *Shanghai News*, April 29, 1951. P'an's speech, a report on the economic work of the city government, was given at the second session of the second congress of the People's Representatives of All Circles in Shanghai.

74. *Shanghai News*, April 22, 1951.

75. The author's interpretation of an interview with an ex-cadre, Hong Kong, December 1969. The most famous model housing project was the one at Lunghsü Kou (literally, "Dragon Whisker Ditch") in Peking. The pre-Liberation sordidness of this area was a brimstone legend in official circles long after it had been

some of them to build high standards into their blueprints. These designs were generally too expensive to supply the needs of Shanghai's broad proletariat. Idealism combined with a lack of resources to set limits on new construction. The result was a scarcity and stratification of citizens' opportunities to move into new housing.

A study published in Shanghai in 1958 claims that the average housing space per worker in the city increased 48 percent between 1929-1930 and 1956. The average space per family seems to have increased 52 percent over this period. These estimates are, of course, subject to technical questions, and several very able economists have provided somewhat divergent figures.[76] Economists' definitions of residential and commercial house space, and their estimates of depreciation and repair costs, have varied widely. Nevertheless, evidence below will show that the 1930-1956 improvement in space *per capita* must have taken place almost entirely before 1949.

Communist surveys in Shanghai have not attempted to hide the slowness with which the early Communist government directed funds toward housing. Table 3 shows annual percentage increments to Shanghai's residential space between 1951 and 1956, based on an index of 100 at the end of 1949. These figures cover all kinds of new housing, even new shacks. The differentials indicate that the rate of growth was not steady and did not keep pace with the rise in the city's population. Chao Yi-hsiang also gives figures from which it can be calculated that, from 1949 to 1956, the rate of population increase was almost six times the rate of increase in all kinds of housing space.[77]

---

renovated, because of a story about the place by novelist Lao She. With much justification, the Communists felt that their help to the oppressed proletariat in this particular work could be clear and dramatic. The house designs for this purpose tended to be better politically than financially.

76. These percentages have been computed from statistics in Nai-ruenn Chen, *Chinese Economic Statistics*, p. 440, which is based on Chao Yi-hsiang, "Research on Problems of Shanghai's Housing Potential," *Hsüehshu yüehk'an*, No. 4 (April 1958), p. 44. Cf. also Christopher Howe, "The Supply and Administration of Housing in Mainland China: The Case of Shanghai," *China Quarterly*, No. 33 (January-March, 1968). Absolute figures for 1956 housing in Shanghai were: per family, 22.59 square meters; per person, 4.78 square meters. The corresponding rates for 1929-1930 were: per household, 14.89; per person, 3.22.

77. Chao Yi-hsiang, "Research on Problems of Shanghai's Housing Potential," cites a pre-Liberation Shanghai population of 4,140,000 and a 7 million figure for

TABLE 3.

Shanghai Housing Space Increases Above 1949 Level

Year	1949	1951	1952	1953	1954	1955	1956
Index	100.0	101.4	104.4	107.2	109.9	110.5	111.8
Differential		1.4	3.0	2.8	2.7	0.6	1.3

Source: Chao Yi-hsiang, "Research on Problems of Shanghai's Housing Potential," *Hsüehshu yüehk'an* (Academic monthly) (Shanghai), No. 4 (April 1958), pp. 44ff. The differentials have been computed. No figures were offered for 1950, and the lack of qualitative articles on housing in that year suggests new construction then.

Chao provides statistics for three kinds of abodes: "ordinary" houses, workers' apartments, and "simple" houses (*chien wu*) in the slum sections.[78] The Real Estate Management Bureau estimated that 4,000 "ordinary" units had been constructed during the survey period, and their area was estimated at 360,000 square meters. Only 4.6 percent of the space in this category was financed by state agencies. More than half of Shanghai's new housing was of "simple" construction. The survey report was somewhat apologetic about these buildings, and it said that only 38 percent of the better ones were financed by the state. Another announcement of the same period claimed that "1,610,000 square meters of floor space have been built by the government in Shanghai since Liberation, and an equal amount has been constructed by the residents themselves."[79]

Kang Chao, writing in the West, says that Chinese residential construction in all cities fell short of depreciation during the first three years of the Communist era. He indicates that even in later years investment barely met replacement needs.[80] According to a

---

about the same time in 1956. The increase between these dates was therefore about 2,860,000, or 69 percent. The average increase for these eight years was thus 6.7 percent. Chao's index between comparable periods of 1949 and 1956 shows an increase of 11.8 percent in housing space, which implies 1.3 percent per annum. These average yearly estimates for population and housing increase are in a ratio of more than five to one.

78. *Ibid.*

79. *JMJP*, August 13, 1956. This article includes also the claim re government-built housing space in Shanghai since 1949. Presumably the government counted factory dormitories, or at least most of them, in its own sector for this purpose.

80. Kang Chao, "Industrialization and Urban Housing in Communist China," *Journal of Asian Studies*, Vol. 25, No. 3 (May 1966), pp. 386-388.

TABLE 4.

Categories of New Housing In Shanghai, 1949-1956

Categories	Square meterage	Percentage of total 1949-1956 new space	Percentage of units financed privately
"Simple" houses	1,740,000	54%	72%
Workers' tract houses	1,120,000	35%	0%
"Ordinary" houses	360,000	11%	5%
Total	3,220,000	100%	(not published)

Source: Data gathered, derived, rounded, and reconciled from the text of Chao Yi-hsiang, "Research on Problems of Shanghai's Housing Potential," *Hsüehshu yüehk'an* (Academic monthly) (Shanghai), No. 4 (April 1958), pp. 44 ff.

1955 Communist survey of 166 cities, 50 percent of all urban residences were unsafe or too old to be occupied. Under the force of heavy rains or typhoons, these houses sometimes collapsed. Because new housing did not keep pace with replacement needs and population growth, Kang Chao says that living space per capita decreased steadily in the cities of China, from 6.3 square meters in 1949 to 3.1 square meters in 1960. Taking China's actual industrial expansion during the 1950s as a constant, Chao estimates that it would have cost 35 billion yüan to maintain China's 1949 level of urban residence area per head. This money was spent on things other than housing, on types of capital that reproduce more quickly, and a decline in urban indoor living space was the result.

Contrary to what might be expected, the rate of decline was lower in large cities than in small ones. Shanghai had the lowest rate of decrease in per capita space among a group of four cities that Chao compared. The reasons are twofold: first, Shanghai before 1949 was already quite crowded; second, the new industries there (which increased employment and population) were a smaller part of the city's total plant than they were in most other industrializing Chinese places.

The 1955 variation among different parts of Shanghai was also great. The old, central districts averaged 2.69 square meters of living space per person, whereas newly built settlements averaged nearly twice as much, 5 square meters.[81]

William Hollister paints a less grim picture than Chao, because he figures that residential construction in the private sector was larger.[82] Christopher Howe's summary of the work of both these researchers and his careful new estimates[83] provide much more thorough computations than previously attempted. Despite some differences in approach, Howe's and Hollister's results fall broadly within the same range. They conclude that the 1950s may have witnessed roughly a 40 percent decrease in per capita living area in Shanghai. Kang Chao's estimates of that decline may be only a few points higher.

RESIDENTIAL CONSTRUCTION IN THE EARLY 1950s

During the early 1950s, there were three types of organizers of housing construction: the municipal government, industrial unions, and private owners. The Shanghai Housing Administrative Division was the governmental unit inherited by the Communists from the Kuomintang. In September 1951, it began a construction project at Ts'aoyang New Village in P'ut'o District, near the western edge of the city. This was the first of several such villages. Three families had to share each kitchen, but schools, clinics, public bath houses, and other community facilities were put up simultaneously. The new buildings were much sturdier than the structures they replaced.[84] Travellers' reports indicate that the Ts'aoyang residences were quite attractive. Rents were fixed at only 7 percent of the average gross income of the workers who were able to live there, but these were a tiny minority of the city's proletariat.

Many other parts of the city contained two-story tenements, built years earlier, which by the early 1950s were often in need of repair. The Housing Division pushed them over in a few areas, and it

81. *Ibid.,* pp. 392-395.

82. William W. Hollister, "Trends in Capital Formation in Communist China," in Joint Economic Committee, U.S. Congress, *An Economic Profile of Communist China* (Washington, D.C.: U.S. Government Printing Office, 1967), pp. 129 ff.

83. Christopher Howe, "The Supply and Administration of Housing in Mainland China: The Case of Shanghai," particularly p. 79, Table III, line (e), for Howe's "index of per capita living area."

84. *LTP,* December 8, 1951.

financed three-story brick and timber houses to replace them. Where this was done, sewers were also dug, water supplies were put in, and other measures were enforced to assure that communicable diseases could not spread easily. Efforts to repair old residences, and especially old water systems, intensified in 1951. Because these efforts were small in scale, they could not benefit most of the crowded city's families. The construction and repair projects of mid-1951 grew partly from the need to arrange contract jobs and to mobilize Shanghai's many unemployed people.[85]

The government's housing projects were not well financed. Housing Division money for new buildings was controlled mostly by a subordinate organization, which was called the Workers' Housing Repair and Construction Committee, and was oriented toward trade unions. This office took over the Ts'aoyang project. It seems to have operated mainly as an agent of established labor. One of its vice-chairmen was Liu Chang-sheng, the chairman of the city Federation of Trade Unions.[86] Very limited finances were available even to this favored committee.

A campaign in mid-1952 was spurred by official realization that the investment program had not even provided enough housing for especially loyal worker cadres in Shanghai, much less had it solved the space problems of the general population.

In September, a decision was taken to see what could be done, even without large resources. Previously, the government bureaucracy for these matters had been split into two parts. The Housing Administrative Division and its workers' committee had taken care of new construction, whereas the Land Administration Bureau had been Shanghai's major landlord, receiving rents throughout the city and assuming direct control on behalf of the state for "enemy property" (*ti ch'an*) that had been confiscated from Kuomintang refugees in 1949. In September 1952, these two units were merged into the Real Estate Management Bureau, so that all state-owned houses were now under the same office.[87]

Union projects, however, commanded the lion's share of available funds. Standards for these projects were even raised. Clinics,

85. See early pages in Chapter 3 for a description of the unemployment.
86. *LTP*, May 1, 1952. Committee chairman was Tseng Shan; the other vice-chairman (besides Liu) was Fang Yi.
87. *Yi pao*, September 30, 1952.

cooperative stores, bridges, lawns, and new bus routes were added to the residential programs for unionized workers. Not only were elementary schools now to be built, but in the ideal project plan, they were required to be within a ten-minute walk of any house.[88] During early 1953, it was announced that housing begun the previous August for 4,000 families had been completed, even though the accompanying cultural centers, schools, and markets were in this case to be finished more slowly than the living space.[89]

Press reports indicate that this mild construction boom was already losing steam by mid-1953. In July, articles were still announcing that "more than 1,000" (apparently Ts'aoyang's 1,002) workers' homes had been completed the previous year. For the current year, it was said that 21,000 families under the plan had "started" moving into their new flats only in July.[90]

Although most new construction of sturdy residences after 1949 occurred in the public sector, most residential space in the city continued to be privately owned. Indeed, the cadres had enough to manage in the early years without wishing to take on responsibility for Shanghai's whole housing stock. The authorities therefore permitted some private investment in regular, nonshanty dwellings, but most of it was probably for repairs rather than for new space. Kang Chao makes much of the contrast between early-1950s Chinese regulations and the incentives used by Communist East European governments to finance new residential space. The Chinese authorities liked to keep urban rents so low that there was little reason to build new space, even for personal use.[91] As Chao points

88. NCNA, Shanghai, August 29, 1952.
89. NCNA, Shanghai, February 14, 1953.
90. NCNA, Shanghai, July 7, 1953.
91. Kang Chao, "Industrialization and Urban Housing in Communist China," p. 391. An ex-resident of the city reported the use of an old phrase, "private management with public help" (*tzu pan kung chü*) to describe private construction, but there was not much of it. Overseas Chinese landlords could retain higher percentages of rent than other landlords. At some times, even up to the Cultural Revolution, very large Overseas Chinese remittances might give the recipients exceptional rights to purchase real estate for personal use—flats in the city or houses in a special suburban "Overseas Chinese New Village." Other Communist governments have encouraged private construction more than China has done. The Soviet Union supplies low-cost or free building materials, tools, and even blueprints. New private dwellings in Hungary are exempt from property taxes for 15 years, and in Yugoslavia for 30 years.

out, Shanghai contained much of the private capital in China, but from 1950 to 1956, probably no more than 5 percent of the new regular dwellings in that city were built with private money.[92]

The treatment of landlords after Liberation also discouraged private residential construction. The properties of some absentee landlords were expropriated, if only by default, after they fled abroad. The incomes of others who stayed were reduced because of strict rent control. All rents were now paid directly to the city housing authority, which retained the greater part of them and passed on a smaller part to the landlords.

Because residential construction under any auspices in Shanghai was limited, the Real Estate Management Bureau took relatively draconian steps to allocate existing space on a more equal basis. This policy was mostly accomplished by persistent pressure, rather than by the sporadic cyclical campaigns for which China is famous, and it has thus received little scholarly attention although it affected the daily lives of many Chinese people. Local street committees held meetings to encourage, but not force, families with considerable space to move into smaller dwellings. Many agreed to do so. Many who did not agree were criticized, either in their street committees or at their work places. If families owning or renting big houses were unwilling to move, they were asked to sublet rooms. Thus single houses, as well as larger and even small apartments, became divided among many families.

Sometimes people simply refused to move into cramped quarters. If they had informal or local political status, or were very persistent, the housing authorities sometimes gave up trying to persuade them.[93] These procedures (and housing topics in general) received surprisingly little attention in the newspapers from July 1953 to the spring of 1956. Without some measures of this sort, Shanghai's housing problem would have been even more serious to most residents of the city. The amount of capital diverted from resi-

92. *Ibid.*, pp. 386 ff. Kang Chao would put the figure at less than 5 percent, but a Communist survey suggests that it may have been that high. It is small in either case. See Chao Yi-hsiang, "Research on Problems of Shanghai's Housing Potential."

93. Interview with a refugee who had lived in Shanghai during the 1950s, Hong Kong, November 1969.

dential construction by the rent control and house consolidation programs was probably very large.

HOUSING POLICIES IN THE TRANSITION
TO SOCIALISM AND GREAT LEAP

During 1956 and 1957, efforts to provide housing for workers failed to keep pace with rising immigration to the city. The municipal government remained unwilling to allocate large resources to meet Shanghai's housing needs. Because capital returns on housing are slow, business cadres could argue that mass living standards would improve more quickly if the state's limited funds were invested in projects that brought a faster return than housing. Thus, in August 1956, the city announced a seven-year "plan to solve the housing problem." Other needs were more urgent.

This 1956 plan simply assumed a continuation of private residential investment, and it also assumed a stemming of immigration into Shanghai. Both assumptions were highly unrealistic; they neglected the effects of most other official economic policies at that time. On the other hand, the 1956 announcement also called for work to repair houses that had been damaged during World War II.[94] This aspect of the plan was more relevant to the old urban area's real housing shortage than were the union-run schemes preceding it. It promised no huge new financing. Central planners may well have hoped to raise Shanghai's labor productivity and to lower its immigration by reducing the inequalities of life between city and country. One way to do this was to discourage the expansion of residential space in Shanghai. The state therefore refrained from building the high-quantity, low-quality estates that alone could solve Shanghai's residential space problem.

The low investment in housing meant that the average living area per person at the end of 1956 in Shanghai was "about" three square meters. Among workers, only 17 percent had more than four square meters. Among government and factory staff, 40 percent had this much.[95] Although workers' new housing projects accelerated in 1956, their standards remained quite high. They could accommodate employees in some of the newly socialized industries, but

94. *JMJP*, August 13, 1956.
95. Chao Yi-hsiang, "Research on Problems of Shanghai's Housing Potential."

they had no effect on most of the city's population. They were mostly built on rural land at the outskirts of the city, near factories. By April, the Ts'aoyang estate had been expanded to house 30,000 people, and other projects had begun at Chenju, Kanch'üan, Yich'uan, Kuangling, Anshan, Fengch'eng, K'ungchiang, T'ienshan, and even Laoshan on the east side of the Whangpoo River.[96] Thirteen workers' residence areas of this sort were in existence by mid-1956, and five more were on the drawing board. The total number of people housed by the new projects at this time was 200,000,[97] but the total urban population of Shanghai was then about 6.3 million.[98] The union-led projects therefore provided housing for only 3 percent of the city's registered population in 1956.

Enterprises and unions naturally sought permission to use scarce capital to build new residences for their members. Shanghai's *Laotung pao,* a labor newspaper, reported in 1956 that many industrial supervisory bureaus (*kungyeh chukuan chü*) and many centrally run factories (*chungyang kuanhsia ti kungch'ang*) were asking the "construction planning departments" (*chienchu kueihua pumen*) to authorize the use of factory funds to construct employees' apartments.[99] They complained quite openly that work was under way on only 3,000 residential units, and they called for the rate of building to be increased "more than ten times."[100]

Well-entrenched industries did better than the government as a whole in providing new residences, at least for the families of male workers. The Shanghai textile mills' conglomerate could boast in September 1956 that it had built homes for more than 10,000 of its employees' families, that it had arranged living space (apparently in dormitories, some of them undoubtedly of pre-Liberation vintage) for 15,000 single workers, and that it currently had just as

96. These and other "new villages" (*hsints'un*) are noted on a public 1956 street map, picked up by a tourist in Shanghai, which Howard Quan allowed me to photocopy. The data on Ts'aoyang are found in NCNA, Shanghai, April 25, 1956.

97. *LTP,* April 28, 1956.

98. Christopher Howe, *Urban Employment and Economic Growth in Communist China,* p. 34, Table 2, estimates that Shanghai had 6,750,000 people total, of whom 400,000 were rural, at the end of 1956. This would leave 6,350,000 people or less in urban districts in the middle of the year. There are stunning difficulties in estimating total populations, even for a place like Shanghai.

99. *LTP,* July 5, 1956.

100. NCNA, Shanghai, July 6, 1956.

many new family units under construction as the Real Estate Management Bureau of the whole municipality was then building.[101]

While industries and unions were seeking to construct new housing for workers, the Shanghai authorities were attempting to link housing and transportation policies in a more rational way. During 1956, the government intensified its efforts to move workers closer to their jobs. The campaign was justified largely on the grounds that it would save commuting time. Yet it also reduced the load on the municipal transportation system and, somewhat surprisingly, helped save residential space. People could often be given smaller quarters when they moved closer to their jobs. At the municipal level, a Housing Adjustment Committee was established to propagate this movement through offices that ran the work units. For example, the Education Bureau quickly registered more than 2,000 teachers, who volunteered either to take jobs in schools nearer their homes, or to move their homes nearer their schools. The East China Textile Management Bureau "adjusted" 315 families at the very beginning of this campaign, and the Shanghai Tobacco Company moved 530.[102] Local "residence exchange stations" (*chufang chiaohuan so*) were set up under the Real Estate Management Bureau to promote this work among still more people.[103]

The city government determined that 130,000 daily commutes in Shanghai were too long. The exchange stations therefore set out to rearrange that many jobs or residences. It was never announced whether they had achieved this high target. The house exchange program was, after all, only one of many projects during the busy postsocialization period in Shanghai, and the municipal government may have lacked sufficient personnel to execute it thoroughly.

The city also had inadequate resources for the maintenance and repair of existing housing. By 1957, the Real Estate Management Bureau had acquired huge tracts of run-down tenements but could not find good managers for its property. It was suffering major paper losses as a result of nails and holes in apartment walls. This issue was duly raised in the Shanghai People's Congress. Some of

---

101. NCNA, Shanghai, September 13, 1956.
102. *HWJP*, November 18, 1956.
103. *LTP*, November 29, 1956.

the representatives insisted that new and strict regulations be set up to protect the city's property.[104]

Not only did residents fail to maintain the socialized buildings; there was also wholesale evasion of rent payments. Chao Yi-hsiang complained:

> Shanghai residents still have a general habit of not paying their rents. They never ask for reductions in the price of rice, coal, fish or meat. They consider it a shame not to pay their water and electricity bills. But they think it is a real glory not to pay their rents.[105]

Management problems of this sort probably dampened any enthusiasm that Party leaders had for heavy state involvement in housing construction and ownership.

By early 1957, the influx of peasants to Shanghai was completely outstripping the supply of new residences in which they could live. The *Laotung pao* in early 1957 reported that residential construction in the approximately seven-and-a-half years since Liberation had been 3,170,000 square meters, accommodating 600,000 people.[106] The new construction planned for 1957 was 450,000 square meters. This represents only a 7 percent increase above the previous annual average for the years since Liberation, but it was a decrease from the plans of 1956.

At the same density of people per square meter as had existed in previous post-Liberation housing in Shanghai, these 450,000 square meters would house 85,170 new people. Yet the *Laotung pao*

104. *HMPWK*, January 14, 1957. Tenants, after poking holes in their dwellings, sometimes put varnish or plaster over them. The government did not take full responsibility for the city's new joint state-private Shanghai Real Estate Corporation, which took charge of repair operations. Newspapers were frank to point out that municipal resources for renovation were limited. *HMPWK*, February 19, 1957, said: "Houses needing repair are too numerous, and the present amount of capital allotted for them is limited. There are difficulties in the supply of construction materials, and the labor power available for this purpose is insufficient. Therefore it is necessary to progress with the repairs in a planned manner, step by step. It is hoped that the residents will cooperate in this."

105. Chao Yi-hsiang, "Research on Problems of Shanghai's Housing Potential."

106. *LTP*, January 6, 1957. Contrast *LTP*, April 28, 1956, which gives an increment of 200,000 persons in state housing alone since Liberation. The figures in the text imply an average space per person in post-Liberation buildings of 5.2 square meters. They also imply an average of about 420,000 square meters of new construction per year.

said in another report that Shanghai's population had increased by 700,000 between May 1956 and January 1957.[107] The annual rate of increase for this eight-month period was thus 1,050,000 people. In other words, the city's housing authorities were *planning* to accommodate about 8 percent of Shanghai's immigrants in 1957, *if* the rate of that immigration could be held to its late 1956 levels and if natural increase were ignored. In fact, Shanghai's rate of population growth rose sharply during 1957.[108]

The municipal government did little to relieve the shortage of housing. During the Hundred Flowers campaign, Real Estate Management Bureau chief Wang Wei-heng made a mild criticism of his department: "Over the past few years, the Real Estate Management Bureau has solved many problems for the upper ranks, but it has solved few problems for those citizens who really have housing difficulties."[109] He pointed out that there were many means by which cadres could obtain rooms for their families and could forget about the rest of the population. He implied that the Bureau needed more funds. When more money was provided, access to new housing remained stratified. In June 1957, the Shanghai Railways Union boasted that it was putting 850 workers into new homes each month. Even a great many such efforts could not have solved Shanghai's housing shortage.

The immigration of 1957 was severe enough to help inspire a general decentralization of housing authority to the district level. For example, the Luwan District People's Committee set up a "self-construction, public help" (*tzuchien kungchu*) program for its bureaucratic staff. District officials who wanted to build houses for their families paid 30 percent of the cost down. They received five-year loans to cover the 70 percent balance. The district committee began with a plan to supply only brick and wood for the construction of 32 double-story duplexes. Each story housed a single family and thus provided exceptionally private accommodations for the period. The original, limited subscription ran out quickly. By April 1957, the local committee had been able to provide financing for somewhat more than 100 such duplexes.[110]

107. *LTP*, March 14, 1957. The figure 8 percent below is 85,170 divided by 1,050,000.

108. See information presented in Chapter 2 about peasant immigration in 1957.

109. *HWJP*, June 7, 1957.

110. *HMPWK*, March 29, 1957.

Chapei District is another example of the decentralization process. The area had suffered severely from Japanese bombing during the war, and it had more shack residences than any other city district. As late as 1958, 60 percent of its area was covered by sheds in places that the bombs had cleared. These shantytowns used land inefficiently. They accommodated only 247,000 households, or about two-fifths of the district's population, even though they occupied three-fifths of its area. Another 53,000 slum households contained about 9 percent of the population, and about 300,000 households (roughly half of the district's population) had more adequate housing.[111]

In 1957, Chapei District set up a Shack Areas Reconstruction Committee. This group planned to raze the district's slums within "three to five years" and to replace them with four-story buildings. Construction began in 1958 on 40,000 square meters of state-financed, district-administered projects. Another 8,000 square meters were financed privately. Progress was slow. From May to November, only 1,000 households moved out of sheds into the new villages.[112] Interviews indicated that when slums were cleared in Shanghai, management of the land was transferred to bureaucratic and productive organizations (not to the previous occupants, who were compensated in other ways). The new buildings were often used as dormitories and apartments for the families of cadres and workers in the area. Residential, educational, and economic space were more distinctly separated from one another in the new arrangements than in previous ones. Shopping centers and sometimes even large factories took the land which had previously been covered with shacks. Both the function and the population of the area changed.

The previous inhabitants and squatters on razed shackland sometimes resented their eviction, and the government made efforts to placate them. One ex-cadre was defensive about the state's policy in this matter. He said that the municipal government took full responsibility for resettling squatters displaced by housing projects. If they had legal residence status in Shanghai, they were not

111. *HWJP*, April 4, 1958. See also *Shanghai p'enghu ch'ü ti p. ench'ien* [The transformation of Shanghai's slum districts] (Shanghai: Shanghai Shehui K'ohsüeh Yüan, 1965), the back cover foldout, for an extremely useful map of the distribution of shacks.

112. *HWJP*, November 26, 1958.

put back on their old land but were sent to other houses that could be arranged for them. Their new rents were the lowest that the Real Estate Management Bureau could allow, and much of the rent proceeds were marked for maintenance, to keep their new houses habitable. No formal contract was signed between the ex-squatters and the Real Estate Management Bureau; as the ex-cadre explained, "This was all under the whole people's collective ownership of socialist China; therefore no contract was needed."[113] It is probable that any squatters who were allowed to stay in Shanghai were pleased to have new quarters, and the move in some cases may have regularized their legal status in the city.

Because of a general weakening of residential controls during the Great Leap Forward, and because economic units enjoyed a good deal of independence in hiring policy at this time, immigrant workers were able to build some new housing for themselves. These homes were mostly in one-story structures near the outskirts of the city.[114] Also at this time, some better financed, four-story apartments were put up in connection with major new industrial investments. By mid-1959, it was claimed that one-tenth of Shanghai's population was living in residences built since Liberation, although the quality and space varied considerably.[115]

113. Interview, Hong Kong, December 1969. Information in the previous paragraph comes from another interview with a nonofficial ex-resident of Shanghai, Hong Kong, November 1969. Some of my notions about resettlement contracts are derived from visits to the urban "village" studied by Mr. and Mrs. Graham Johnson in Chuen Wan, Hong Kong, 1968. The Johnsons' research describes a well-integrated, urban Hakka community that had moved under Hong Kong Government aegis to a new site. There they were provided with new housing, new clan temples, and other amenities.

According to a Hong Kong Government survey taken between late 1963 and middle 1965, 16 percent of the tenants who were to be evicted from condemned buildings *stated* their *intention* to move after eviction to staircases, boats, rooftops, and other squatter settlements. The percentage of them who actually moved into such premises was probably larger. See also D. J. Dwyer, "Urban Squatters: The Relevance of the Hong Kong Experience," *Asian Survey* X, No. 7 (July 1970), pp. 607-613; and Sheila K. Johnson, "Hong Kong's Resettled Squatters: A Statistical Analysis," *Asian Survey* VI, No. 11 (November 1966), pp. 643-656.

114. Ian Davies told me that he saw great numbers of such structures, reportedly and apparently built during the Leap, on the main rail route out of Shanghai toward Hangchow.

115. NCNA, Shanghai, July 29, 1959. There is evidence that slum area populations grew quickly. *JMJP*, July 23, 1960, said that the number of "children" on

The urbanizing effect of the Leap was not limited to Shanghai. By the end of 1960, more than 120 large and medium-size Chinese cities had set up new housing projects. In addition, 160 new small cities "for workers" were established.[116] Among Shanghai's varied suburbs, which greatly expanded their population during this period, the largest new satellite towns were Minhang and Wuching on the Whangpoo River, south of the metropolis, where electronic and fertilizer factories were established in old market towns.

IMPACT OF THE POST-LEAP YEARS

Housing, like all other sectors of Shanghai's economy, was severely affected when the Leap's production boom subsided. When rural transport broke down, construction materials ran out even for projects already under way. Work on new sites was postponed. Edgar Snow, visiting Shanghai in 1961, reported that old shacks still existed, for example, in Fankua Lane (an area he had known before Liberation). Snow's guide said that most of the squatters did not want to leave their homes.[117] This was just as well, for they would not easily have found other urban housing.

Mengtzu Road increased by 2,856 between Liberation and 1960, when the total road population was 8,147. The article did not specify how "children" were defined, but population growth can nevertheless be deduced from these data. Assuming that the adult population did not decline during this 11-year period, the total population in 1949 on Mengtzu Road could not have been more than 5,291 persons (8,147 minus 2,856). The average growth rate of this area due only to the increase of children was therefore at least 5.0 percent per year and probably more. If adults are included, the full annual growth rate in this area must have been well above 5 percent. In addition, the averaging technique used above obscures the likelihood that growth was higher after the housing project was under way than before it started.

116. NCNA, Peking, December 29, 1960. The supply of water in Shanghai is too large to deter immigration or investment. A light freshwater bore is regularly pushed out of the Yangtze up the Whangpoo by tidal action. This water is less polluted than what comes down the Whangpoo at ebb tide. The most important water purification works is therefore below (northeast of) the main city, in Yangp'u District, and it provides a practically unlimited supply.

117. Edgar Snow, *The Other Side of the River*, p. 542. Snow stopped in one of the Fankua shacks, which he found surprisingly clean. It had a radio. Three generations, apparently consisting of seven people, lived in the house; there were two wage earners, reporting salaries of 68 and 60 yüan, which seem high if they were supposed to be typical. The grandmother said that she did not want to move.

During the early 1960s, unemployment and food problems made the household registration system somewhat touchy to enforce, even though the same factors made job opportunities and rations all the more important to individual citizens. By reinvigorating its campaign to move workers into quarters closer to their work places, the Shanghai government clearly hoped to regain some of the control over urban population that it had lost during the Leap. In June 1960, the Shanghai Party Committee formed an office specifically for resettlement near jobs. By August of the next year, more than 70,000 workers had been resettled.[118] Most of these commuters had previously lived more than fifteen *li* from their factories; they had spent more than two hours each day going to and from work.

Improvement of Shanghai's public transport system was also on the government agenda in the early 1960s. The major transport change came in 1962, when a program was initiated to convert all of the city's trams to trolley buses. Operating expenses for these electric buses were slightly higher than for trams, but the buses were faster and less noisy.[119] They were popular and crowded. As one resident put it, "All vehicles are overcrowded at all times."[120] To reduce this problem, the working hours of many institutions were staggered. Some schools, for example, began classes at 7:00 A.M.[121]

As housing shortages caused by the Great Leap were gradually alleviated, the government was able to step up its efforts to replace the temporary shacks. Most projects begun in the 1960s had support from specific offices within the bureaucracy, as for example, villages for seamen, postal employees, and railway workers.[122] The local model for post-Leap slum clearance, however, was built by the Real Estate Management Bureau at Fankua Lane, Chapei District,

118. *JMJP*, August 4, 1961.

119. *SHNL*, September 28, 1963. When tram tracks were removed, the ground floors of some buildings were torn out to make more space for traffic. By the mid-1960s about 200 trolley buses, with another 200 cars towed behind them, travelled 16 routes throughout the city. Whenever one of them broke down, later ones could circumnavigate and did not have to queue in line, as the old trams had very frequently done. Subways, which would also be run by electricity and might use power efficiently, cannot easily be built in Shanghai because the soil is soft and the water table high.

120. *SHNL*, October 28, 1961.

121. *SHNL*, October 8, 1964.

122. NCNA, Shanghai, October 29, 1963.

the area Edgar Snow had visited. The first stage of work on the Fankua project began in October 1963, and it lasted until March 1964.[123] In mid-July 1964, newspapers indicated that only 45 families had moved into the newly built five-story buildings.[124]

One report on the Fankua estate said that its inhabitants had been "rickshaw pullers, beggars, and war refugees" before Liberation.[125] However this may be, they were certainly doing better than most of Shanghai's poor by 1964. Money for the new buildings was provided out of government funds, and squatters were compensated whenever their houses had to be razed. Before demolition of the old dwellings, the government moved residents into temporary quarters on Kungho New Road and Chunghua New Road. It was reported that although 2,000 households had been removed from the area before construction, only 1,000 would return afterward. Half of the evicted families therefore went to new addresses on a permanent basis. In view of the excellence of the Fankua houses, whose pictures were published widely, these 1,000 households may not have been the poorest that had lived in the area before. Other lucky families from elsewhere also joined them in the new estate. The total space of the projected buildings was 20,000 square meters—i.e., 20 square meters per household. If most of these households were not too much larger than the city's average of about five, and if Kang Chao's estimate is accurate that the average space per person in Shanghai in 1960 was 3.1 square meters, then it is clear that the new dwellers in Fankua Lane were better housed than most Shanghai residents. If they were really all squatters before, then their economic rise was quick indeed.[126]

Several new construction projects were undertaken during the post-Leap recovery period, but most funds in 1964 were devoted to projects that had started during the Leap and were still behind schedule. The general policy of slow space growth and high construction quality did not change. One report of mid-1964 said

123. *HMWP*, October 13, 1963, and March 21, 1964.

124. *HMWP*, July 16, 1964. It was announced that the project had been completed by the "401 Engineering Team of the Fourth Construction Engineering Company." This was apparently a corporation under the municipal government.

125. NCNA, Shanghai, July 20, 1964.

126. *Shanghai p'enghu ch'ü ti piench'ien*, pp. 78-79. A few of the old huts in Fankua Lane were not demolished but were preserved for educational purposes.

that only 2,000 workers' families had "recently" moved into new housing. The sites and business connections of the new buildings were also familiar: in the satellite town of Minhang, beside some factories in Yangp'u District, and along Wuk'ang and Kaoan roads in the western part of the city.[127]

As the economy revived, public enterprises were again encouraged to sponsor residential projects with their own money. City government projects regained momentum slowly. All the new housing estates provided more space per household than previous construction had done. For that reason, the families that moved into them were generally larger. Ts'aoyang, for example, now had 12,000 households with a population of 64,000,[128] an average household size of 5.3 persons. It would be difficult to measure the extent to which new construction induced the immigration of cadres and unionized workers' family members from the countryside. Shanghai's housing problem was still not solved, but many of the estates built after 1963 were clearly attractive to the people who could move into them.

Decentralization trends persisted, as low levels of government assumed responsibility for providing Shanghai residents with many services that had been supplied before by small private enterprises. In the mid-1960s, every service bureau of the municipal apparatus established branches throughout the city, at the district level, and often even in neighborhood committee areas. Many bureaucracies in this period recruited volunteers or part-time representatives even on local lane committees.

These low cadres operated nurseries, kindergartens, libraries, informal mediation courts, bulletin boards, matrimonial counseling services, and first aid centers. They helped assemble data for the ration and public security systems. They also ran small economic enterprises, such as barbershops, communal restaurant-kitchens, and baby-sitting services. They sometimes set up service repair stations to mend shoes and socks, to retread rubber shoes, fix broken umbrellas, piece together porcelain, reset circuit breakers, rebristle toothbrushes—in short, to perform any number of minor services that hardly require the attentions of a national conglomerate trust.

127. *KJJP*, April 30, 1964.

128. Chang Feng, "New Housing Estates for Workers: Report from Shanghai," *PR*, No. 8 (February 22, 1963), p. 14.

Even very small enterprises often functioned best under nominal public supervision. Basic-level committees and representatives provided that kind of legitimation for them. Residents' committees also became the chief collecting agencies for public utility companies.[129] In addition, they were charged with helping the Real Estate Management Bureau collect rents and maintain houses.

By the early 1960s, most large residential buildings in Shanghai had "dependents' committees" (*chiashu weiyüanhui*). One of the main functions of these organs was to foster an ethic of maintaining the state's property in good repair. Municipal housing authorities increasingly stressed that it was necessary to "walk on two legs" to keep up the supply of residential space. When finances and building materials were scarce, new construction alone could not possibly provide enough room, and repair work was important. A *People's Daily* article pointed this out in 1962, adding bluntly that the second "leg," i.e., housing maintenance under the aegis of local committees, should be strengthened. The newspaper advocated that more money be spent on repairs.[130] Periodic campaigns for this purpose were carried out by the Real Estate Management Bureau during the spring cleaning that preceded each Chinese New Year.[131] District-level authorities also called sporadic meetings to urge household heads to keep up the buildings in which they lived.[132]

Complaints concerning maintenance could flow in two directions. By late 1965, the Real Estate Management Bureau's branches had responded to tenants' grumbles by admitting some responsibility for house maintenance. It was announced that the mid-level "repair companies" (*hsiuchien kungszu*) would be funded to do this work. A "three-in-one" (*sanchiehho*) organization was established in these companies to unite their leaders, technicians, and repair workers. All their employees were officially implored to be polite to tenants. The *Hsinmin wanpao* insisted that maintenance men "listen also to the opinions of the residents," making repairs "according to the opinions and demands of the residents . . . whenever possible."[133]

129. *SHNL,* November 13, 1961.
130. *JMJP,* May 9, 1962.
131. A 1964 example is cited in *HMWP,* January 26, 1964.
132. *HMWP,* April 6, 1965.
133. *HMWP,* October 13, 1965.

By the mid-1960s, the Shanghai government could proudly announce that it had overseen the building of enough new workers' housing since 1949 to accommodate 1 million people.[134] The only difficulty was that Shanghai's population had increased by a substantially larger number, which cannot be cited exactly because it has not been published.[135] The redistribution of available space provided some urban residents with better accommodation than they could have found there previously. The housing shortage in any case seems not to have kept many potential immigrants out of the city.

BIRTH CONTROL

Birth control must be treated at least briefly in a discussion of careers in Shanghai, because the vast amount of personal time and energy it frees from the raising of families can be used in work for collective goals. Its most immediate effect is on young men and women just beginning their careers, but it also relieves population pressures on food and housing. All of these aims are more important in a capitalized area like Shanghai than they would be in rural areas.

FAMILY PATTERNS IN THE EARLY 1950s

Birth control can be organized more easily in cities than in the countryside, even when the basic urban birthrate is very high. The

134. *HMWP*, April 29, 1964.

135. On some comparable problems of estimating local populations without data, see Ezra F. Vogel, *Canton Under Communism*, Appendix I. Also, Christopher Howe, *Urban Employment and Economic Growth in Communist China*, p. 34, notes that figures cited for 1965 are identical with those published in 1959. Howe in "The Supply and Administration of Housing," p. 78, calculates a population for Shanghai based apparently on the boundaries of the city before February 1958. He then makes some guesses about what the Shanghai birthrate might have been in various years (annually 2.8 percent for 1958-1959, 1.5 percent for 1960, 0 percent for 1960-1961, 2 percent for 1963-1965), but he explicitly makes no allowance for net migration. He concedes that "this may seem unrealistic in the light of scattered references to migration in this period," and he invites readers to insert their own estimates and adjust the final results accordingly. His estimate of Shanghai's population, within this area, comes out to 8.2 million people in 1965. This may be low, but it is the most carefully calculated guess any economist has published to date.

rate in Shanghai during the 1950s was phenomenal—well above the national average of somewhat more than 2 percent per year. Immigrants to China's largest city have been concentrated in especially young and fertile age groups, and the Shanghai marriage rate alone in the mid-1950s was 1.6 percent to 2.0 percent per year. This is about double the figure for most countries.[136] Other evidence suggests that the birthrate in green suburban areas near the city (from which population transfers to the urban area are important) was higher in the 1960s than in the 1950s.[137]

"City-limit sociology" (to use Gideon Sjoberg's splendidly disdainful phrase) is useless for studying long-term urban population trends. Because immigrants to Shanghai come mostly from the countryside, peasant birth customs undoubtedly affect natural increase inside the city. It has been quite difficult to define this relationship specifically, or to determine how effective urbanization may have been in breaking down the traditional Chinese big family ethic. In 1937, Olga Lang studied the comparative forms and functions of families in Shanghai, Peking, Tientsin, and rural areas.[138] Shanghai showed more departure from traditional patterns than did the other cities in her survey. In later years, no further studies of this quality have been published, and we can only guess that Shanghai residents may still be more "modern" than their country cousins. Studies of other countries make clear that the differences between urban and rural life patterns need not be great. Oscar Lewis, studying some peasant immigrants to Mexico City and the village from which they came, found amazingly little urban effect.[139]

One of the differences between urban and rural households that might nevertheless have affected Shanghai birth practices is family

136. See Kang Chao, "Industrialization and Urban Housing in Communist China," pp. 385-386.

137. Michael Freeberne, "The Specter of Malthus: Birth Control in Communist China," *Current Scene* 2, No. 18 (August 15, 1963), p. 1, quoting *HMWP* of May 1963.

138. Olga Lang, *Chinese Family and Society* (New Haven, Conn.: Yale University Press, 1946).

139. For a summary of Oscar Lewis's ideas on this, see his "The Folk-Urban Ideal Types," in Philip M. Hauser and Leo F. Schnore, eds., *The Study of Urbanization* (New York: Wiley, 1965), pp. 494-495. To cite an old slogan of urban science, *Stadtluft macht frei* may not be true after all.

size. The average household (*hu*) in Shanghai had slightly less than five persons in 1950.[140] The typical Shanghai "family" in a Western sense is probably smaller, because the term *"hu"* apparently includes residence institutions such as dormitories, which bring up the average. Evidence suggests that the number of persons per household in workers' sections of Shanghai changed hardly at all between 1929-1930 and 1956.[141] Average household size was clearly larger within the city than outside of it. The approximately 4.9 persons per *hu* in Shanghai during the mid-1950s can be compared with a 4.3 average in the rural areas of surrounding Kiangsu.[142]

In 1948, Shanghai had 124 males for every 100 females. The

140. A 1950 urban census showed that Shanghai had 1,015,000 households containing 4,981,000 people. *Shanghai chiehfang yinien* (Shanghai: Chiehfang Jihpao She, 1950), p. 14. This makes 4.9 people per household. Another 1950 study gives slightly different figures that lead to the same conclusion: *Yinienlai ti Shanghai kungan kungtso* (Shanghai: Shanghai Shih Jenmin Chengfu, Cheng Kung Pao, 1950), p. 261, says that the city had 1,042,257 households containing 4,973,128 people—almost 5 people per household. Christopher Howe, "The Supply and Administration of Urban Housing," p. 76, reports that the average household size in Shanghai in 1966 was only 4.7 persons.

141. Calculation by an indirect method yields a very slight rise of 2.2 percent in the average size of workingmen's households. Nai-ruenn Chen, *Chinese Economic Statistics*, p. 440, quotes a 1957 Communist article, based on 1929-1930 and 1956 surveys in Shanghai, that Shanghai average workers' *housing* space per *hu* was 14.89 square meters in 1929-1930 and 22.59 square meters in 1956. He also gives per-person rates: 3.22 square meters (1929-1930) and 4.78 square meters (1956). Some divisions and subtractions yield +0.022 for a proportional change, which is almost no change at all, in the persons per household for these samples. It is quite possible that institutional *hu* became larger and familial *hu* smaller between these two periods, so that the average remained fairly constant. On the other hand, *Shanghai p'enghu ch'ü ti piench'ien*, pp. 69-70, cites Granny Jen's household in Yangshup'u District's Chunglien Village, which before Liberation had only four members and afterward had ten. Maybe Granny Jen's establishment, and others like it in the parts of Shanghai where immigrants came, were just unofficial versions of the authorized, enterprise dormitories whose expansion may have coincided with a diminution of ordinary families.

142. This conclusion had to be milked from recalcitrant data by the following method: *1967 feich'ing nienpao* (1967 yearbook on Chinese Communism) (Taipei: Feich'ing Yenchiu Tsachih She, 1967), Chapter 8, pp. 1015-1016, says that rural Kiangsu in October 1958 had 1,420 communes with an average of 6,121 households per commune. Etsuzō Onoye, "Regional Distribution of Urban Population in China," *The Developing Economies* VIII, No. 1 (March 1970), p. 114, says that the rural population of Kiangsu in 1958 was 37,749,000. In October 1958, only 1

regional average for East China as a whole, which is mostly rural, was 103 males per 100 females.[143] Both figures may be lower for the Communist period, although extensive data have not been found on this topic.[144]

Government policies have also indirectly affected Shanghai's birthrate. The land reform changed old marriage and family patterns in rural areas. The reform may, for example, have led to earlier and more secure marriages among poor peasants, thus spurring the birthrate upward. In theory, the 1950 Marriage Law granted divorces freely whenever both husband and wife wished to leave one another. In fact, this law was intended more for rural and backward parts of China than for places like Shanghai, where a total of only 145 divorces was granted in 1955 and 1956.[145] Conservative enforcement of the Marriage Law in large cities may have discouraged the marital plans of prospective partners.

Improvements in applied medicine during the first few years of Communist rule in Shanghai created a classic case of generally rising birthrates and generally declining death rates. Of the children who were born, increasingly fewer died. By 1956, Shanghai's infant mortality rate was less than half that of 1952.[146] This rate was subject to some fluctuation; in 1955, for example, it showed a

---

percent of China's rural households were not communized at least nominally, and since the basis of their refusal was more social than geographical and the dissident households were probably both large and small, it may be reasonable to distribute this small correction over most provinces equally. From these considerations, the text's 4.3 persons per rural household can be derived mathematically.

143. Stanford University China Project, *East China* (Subcontractor's Monograph HRAF-29, Stanford-3) (New Haven, Conn.: Human Relations Area Files, 1956), Vol. 1, p. 86.

144. W. R. Geddes, *Peasant Life in Communist China* (Ithaca, N. Y.: Cornell Society for Applied Anthropology, 1963), suggests on the basis of a brief survey of one East China village that female infanticide had not yet completely vanished by the mid-1950s. Presumably it has done so by now.

145. *HWJP*, January 11, 1957.

146. Specifically, in 1956 a reported 3.1 percent of children born in Shanghai died before age one, as compared to 8.1 percent in 1952. (The 1955 rate for rural areas even near the city was almost 11 percent, much higher than the urban figure.) See, for the figures here and in the text, Nai-ruenn Chen, *Chinese Economic Statistics*, p. 137, which relies on data supplied by the Ministry of Health to S. Chandrasekhar, and by the State Statistical Bureau to R. Pressat.

puzzling rise,[147] but the general trends of infant mortality, birth, and death rates all combined to give Shanghai an increasingly large natural increase in population.

ECONOMIC REASONS FOR BIRTH CONTROL
IN THE MID-1950s

China's birth policy has sometimes been described as if it emerges from an academic debate. In practice, the policy has many immediate and concrete motivations. Even if the rationing and employment authorities of Shanghai had not wanted to reduce the city's population, certain kinds of enterprises still had a huge financial interest in lowering pregnancy rates among their female employees. One example can show the business cost of not having birth control in Shanghai's largest light industry, textiles, where most of the employees are young women.

A newspaper reported that, among the 4,500 workers in the No. 9 Shenhsin Cotton Textile Mill, an average of 1,122 babies was born per annum in the mid-1950s. Pregnancies and pregnancy-related leaves cost 11,220 woman-days per year (i.e., 10 days during each pregnancy). About 120 of these expectant mothers miscarried each year and were given a month off work. After the birth of a child, the mother was granted 56 days. From the point of view of a business cadre in this factory, pregnancies and births caused an average loss of 77,652 woman-days each year. This meant that the equivalent of 260 workers (6 percent of the female labor force or about 5 percent of the total textile labor force) were permanently idle on the payroll because of pregnancies.[148]

Economic enterprises had the financial and organizational resources needed to conduct a birth control campaign. Especially after the transition to socialism, loyal Communists who had been placed in managerial posts had the political influence to bring

---

147. Deaths below one year of age were more than 4 percent of births in 1955, instead of 3 percent which would have continued the downward trend. This aberration also applies to the 1955 statistics for Harbin and Hofei. Reports from rural areas are mixed, but the most reliable one, based on a small sample, indicates a 1955 drop in the rate of children born and allowed to live: W. R. Geddes, *Peasant Life in Communist China*, p. 15. The reasons for these birthrate reductions of 1955 are not clear, but the food shortage of that year may be partly responsible.

148. Calculated from figures in *WHP*, January 23, 1958.

TABLE 5.
Birth and Death Rates in Shanghai, 1952-1957
(Percentage of Total Population)

	1952	1953	1954	1955	1956	1957
Birthrate	3.8%	4.0%	5.3%	4.1%	4.0%	4.6%
Death rate	1.2%	1.0%	0.8%	0.8%	0.7%	0.6%
Difference	2.6%	3.0%	4.5%	3.3%	3.3%	4.0%

Source: Figures for birth and death rates, given differently by S. Chandrasekhar and Roland Pressat, are identical when rounded to the nearest tenth of a percent. Chandrasekhar's and Pressat's data are presented together in another form in Nai-ruenn Chen, *Chinese Economic Statistics* (Chicago: Aldine, 1967), p. 136.

about this kind of program. Both managers and ideologues preferred contraception to abortion.[149] After the 1955 food shortages and intensification of rationing, contraceptives were readily available in Shanghai, and were often supplied without cost to employees by their companies.

Some of the large new commodity trusts were particularly eager to publicize birth control, because their wage costs rose sharply after the transition to socialism, when relatively generous pregnancy leaves became standardized for state companies. The Shanghai Tobacco Company, for example, had 14,500 women employees in 1957 and an annual "company birth rate" of 3,000. The No. 2 Cigarette Factory alone had 2,700 women workers, and one child was born for every six of its employees per year. Many of the women workers had large families: 200 had four children, 120 had five, 100 had six, and 90 had more than six children.[150]

149. For arguments against abortion, see *KJJP*, September 27, 1962. The Chinese Communists object to abortion more on medical grounds than on moral ones; but by the 1970s abortions have become common in cases where childbirth would threaten the mother's health.

150. Another article in *HMWP*, February 10, 1957. Grandparents play a traditional child-raising role in China, but this does not liberate mothers from all responsibility.

An ex-resident of the city said that birthrates correlate inversely with "cultural level," i.e., the parents' years of schooling. He also said that proletarian families are generally larger than bourgeois ones.

Shanghai businesses in this situation also called on the Public Health Bureau to intensify birth control measures, since their main potential and replacement labor pool consisted of unemployed female city residents without children. In March 1957, the Bureau called together the heads of all hospitals and district-level sections to decide that every clinical unit in Shanghai must have a department to advise on contraception.[151] It was resolved that "contraception propaganda" (*piyün hsüanch'uan*) was "an important task of the city's public health work."

The campaign began in factories, offices, and schools, although it was not generally carried out in residents' committees during 1957. As a matter of policy, the campaign was supposed to be directed "especially toward males." To coordinate the program, the Bureau set up a Contraception Guidance Office, as well as several specialized "research small groups" (*yenchiu hsiaotsu*).[152]

Official publicity promoting birth control was temporarily suspended during the antirightist campaign, not because the policy had been abandoned but because the demographers and liberals who favored birth control were then under attack for their *other* political opinions. By January 1958, the Shanghai *Wenhui pao* was again reporting that birth control propaganda was being "carried out among the masses by the municipal Women's Federation, the Federation of Trade Unions, the Public Health Bureau, and other relevant departments." The contraception clinics continued to exist, and their supply of drugs was "increased."

BIRTH CONTROL IN THE GREAT LEAP FORWARD

With the advent of the Great Leap Forward, the birth control campaign sharply intensified among applicants for marriage licenses. According to Shanghai registration records of 1953-1955, 70 percent of newly married couples were in the eighteen- to twenty-five-year-old age group. In 1958, couples applying for licenses were given lectures on the value of late marriage and serious birth control. With the cheerful optimism so typical of this Leap period, officials declared that they thought these procedures would reduce the city's birthrate from about 4.5 percent per year to 2 percent per year by the end of the second five-year plan.[153]

151. *HWJP*, March 2, 1957.
152. *HMPWK*, March 4, 1957.
153. *WHP*, January 23, 1958; and *CFJP*, January 7, 1958.

The Leap's openness also encouraged hope that other measures might control births if these policies should perchance fail to meet their target. At the Shanghai People's Congress in January 1958, resolutions were passed to propagandize contraception during the second economic plan and to use *hsiafang* and other means to reduce the number of urban residents to 7 million (from the then current 7.2 million) by 1963.[154]

The Leap also put great emphasis on the improvement of facilities for children. After 1958, families could raise more children with less strain. By mid-1959, Shanghai had 26,000 nurseries and kindergartens and 1.5 million pupils were cared for in primary schools during the daytime.[155] The general Great Leap mobilization of labor also staffed many cinemas, children's palaces, science centers, parks, theaters, sports schools, and children's homes to occupy their spare time. These facilities had effects that counteracted the birth control program to an unknown extent.

BIRTH CONTROL AFTER THE LEAP

When food shortages set in after the Leap, the Party was faced with a delicate situation. On the one hand, birth control was more urgently needed than ever. On the other hand, there were many other, more immediate public uses for the Party's limited political resources. Birth control was approved in Shanghai throughout this period, but it was not a high-priority matter because its most obvious results could not be produced quickly.

In mid-1959, the *Jenmin jihpao* had already declared, "We insist on family planning, but generally speaking we think it is a good thing to have a large population."[156] In 1960, demographer and birth control proponent Ma Yin-ch'u's dismissal from the presidency of Peking University was announced but there is no evidence that birth control was criticized in principle or that the supply of contraceptives was stopped. The ideas behind the Great Leap, which gave great importance to uneven technological change and labor productivity if not birth control, were in fact rather congruent with most of Ma's theory. The National People's Congress in April 1960 specifically approved birth control for heavily populated

154. *WHP*, January 7, 1958.
155. NCNA, Shanghai, May 29, 1959.
156. *JMJP*, April 4, 1959, quoted in Michael Freeberne, "The Specter of Malthus," p. 4.

regions such as Shanghai, and for all parts of China not inhabited by minority peoples. By 1963, birth control had become increasingly tied up with more general social policies. The campaign was not "resumed," because it had never been abandoned either in principle or in practice.[157] The style of the program changed somewhat, possibly because the relevant government cadres hoped that reforms would make it more effective. For example, in Shanghai in early 1963 the Huangp'u District Health Education Hall was sponsoring elaborate exhibits to encourage "planned child-bearing" (*chihua shengyü*).[158] The Shanghai branch of the prestigious Academia Sinica was given special responsibility in this program, and by October it had trained four groups of cadres in contraception work. The Academy was also charged with the task of doing scientific research in "various methods of contraception," testing their effectiveness and propagating the best measures.[159]

The most important emphases in birth control work during the mid-1960s were on "late romancing" (*wan t'an lienai*) and "delayed marriages"(*ch'ih chiehhun*). The political implications of this propaganda became more explicit than before, and lower-level resources were now also brought into play. The Chingan District People's Bank General Affairs Office, for example, was one of many organs to assume responsibility in this campaign:

Education for late marriage is carried forth by first teaching these young people about revolution as a way of life, so as to set up the "will to revolt." Before now, these young people have not worked hard. They have liked to play around after office hours. But now they work very hard at their jobs, and after hours they join groups to study the works of Chairman Mao, or else they attend night universities, cadre culture schools, or specialized training classes for the bank business. They also participate in militia training, in all kinds of ball games and dramas, and so forth.[160]

157. This interpretation places less emphasis on ideology than does Leo A. Orleans in "A New Birth Control Campaign?" *China Quarterly*, No. 12 (October-December 1962), pp. 207-210. Even his article contains the double-edged explanation: "A number of hypotheses have been suggested to explain the 1958 policy reversal. Birth control, of course, conflicted with the propaganda of the 'leap forward,' but that propaganda could have been tailored to incorporate birth control." See also Orleans's *Every Fifth Child: The Population of China*.
158. *HMWP*, March 7, 1963.
159. *HMWP*, October 26, 1963.
160. *HMWP*, September 23, 1964.

In Chapei District, birth control inspection teams were sent by the local People's Consultative Conference to 118 lanes, factories, shops, schools, and offices to propagandize in favor of late marriages and few children.[161] The campaign in Ts'aoyang New Village emphasized the feminist aspects of this movement. A working mother explained the bitterness of having a son too early:

I was married at the age of twenty and had a son within less than a year. He is a financial and physical burden to us. At the end of the day I am all worn out, and I cannot get enough sleep to prepare myself for work. Mentally I am backward, since I have no time to improve myself by reading newspapers. . . . To have a son means to hinder progress and damage socialist revolution and national construction.[162]

Moreover, under the new social system, a son would be of less use to his mother and father than his ancestors had been to their parents. The economic and career motivations for birth control were very evident in statements urging later rather than fewer births: "After Liberation, early children certainly do not mean an earlier happiness [retirement] for their parents. . . . They bring no advantage at all, either to their parents or to the State. . . ."[163]

Motherhood and children were hard enough for the cadres to politick against, but love was a truly formidable rival for economic construction. Fan Cheng-ch'ing, a young workman at the No. 5 Chunghua Rubber Factory, pointed this out in answering the question, "Does it matter whether one has a girl- or boy-friend too early?"

Only those who actually experience anything can tell how it is. I was very young when I decided to try to get in love. When I did, I completely neglected political study and technology, and I didn't care whether I acquired better and faster skills. . . . To fall in love too early would wear away one's revolutionary will power and hinder progress. We young people should guard against this bourgeois idea and way of life.[164]

The municipal government and state enterprises were well aware of the amount of time parents must spend to raise children. They realized that birth control would free parents' time for careers, and

161. *HMWP*, November 1, 1963.
162. *CFJP*, November 19, 1964.
163. *CFJP*, January 13, 1965.
164. *CFJP*, November 13, 1964.

their policies reflected this understanding. Business cadres seemed to feel that Shanghai should concentrate on production, and that the rest of China could raise children for the future labor force.

RESIDENCE AND GUIDANCE

This chapter has assessed the effects of Shanghai's residential controls—its household registration and rationing systems, housing and transport policies, and birth limitation programs—on the structure of available urban careers. Household registration also relates to other government policies discussed earlier: it is a prerequisite for admission to any Shanghai school. The household book, or a change in it, is also the legal essence of rustication. No fully privileged employment in Shanghai can be obtained without a valid local register. This population inventory system is the administrative key to managing the resources that enable Shanghai's government to encourage some career options and discourage others. Because this system also restricts citizens' freedom, it stirs some resistance and is not uniformly effective in all situations. Food rationing, for example, worked well in Shanghai after its establishment had been coordinated with the police-run registration system and had been given urgency by the 1955 food shortages. In years like 1958 or 1966, however, when these conditions were less salient and few types of foods had to be seriously rationed, the household incentives to socialist careers were less important.

The partial, probabilistic kind of pressure on careers, which official policies can structure by means of this whole set of incentives, provides economic and social planners with powerful means of increasing capital funds and directing individual energies for community purposes. Social overhead costs in the city can be reduced by this valuable system. Residential career guidance both saves state money and increases the social efficiency of individual labor.

GUIDANCE AND PROSPERITY:
A CONCLUSION

The preceding chapters have shown that government policies in the form of educational programs, patriotic rustication plans, employment procedures, and residence registration all had effects on individuals' career motivations in Shanghai. The government in general has extended primary and lower middle school education to the masses and has greatly restricted even technical education at higher levels. *Hsiahsiang* campaigns have urged urban youths to adopt rural careers. Differential salary scales and other job benefits have favored workers in industries selected for development. Residence policies have allowed some people to maintain their homes in Shanghai but have also discouraged many unskilled peasants from moving into the city.

At first glance, none of these things alone may be a very spectacular matter. These policies influence personal decisions, but no single guidance measure in this set is irresistible. On many day-to-day issues, individuals in Shanghai sometimes could refuse or evade doing what the government wanted. When this happened, they truly made "policy" and had "power" themselves. Nevertheless in a probabilistic way, most career choices in Shanghai were influenced by the government policies described in this book. These programs operated over large numbers of people. The fact that they often functioned indirectly, and with exceptions, does not mean that they were weak. Their development effects for the nation and their other effects on individuals were both quite real. These nets caught fish, even though they had holes.

207

A GUIDANCE SYSTEM AND ITS LINKAGES

To what extent do these policies constitute a system? If they can be called by that name, what are the system's variables? What linkages hold it together?

A search for the things that clearly changed in correlation with the changing effectiveness of the career guidance system must start from discussions in the previous chapters, which show how specific guidance policies evolved over time. The chapters emphasize that education, citizenship, employment, and residence policies varied from one year to another. Contrary to conventional practice, this analysis has not stressed the periods of political campaigns very strongly over other times. No matter what periodization is used, the following question is implicit in the task of the project: was there coordination, during each of these periods, among policies in the education, citizenship, employment and residence fields?

A preliminary answer lies in the official desire that everyone in China devote all personal energies to communal betterment. This, however, is as much a stable assumption of the guidance system as a variable in it. A more dynamic reason for the coordination of these policies was that the government used each of them, during each time period, to countervail the effects of current economic problems. These policies constitute a system not only because they inherently reinforced each other by establishing an official right to govern careers but, even more important, because changes in policy administration were affected by the same thing in each period: the current state of the city's economy. Shanghai's economic health was a major factor in determining the administration of four resources for individuals (education, respectability, employment, and urban residence), which were also incentive resources for the government to use in guiding careers. A brief discussion of each of these, and of the linkages connecting them, must precede an analysis of the relation between the effectiveness of the career system and the general level of urban prosperity.

FOUR FACTORS AFFECTING THE GUIDANCE SYSTEM

The chapters above have often referred to Shanghai's net rate of population increase and to the net rate at which the city provides new occupations (either jobs *or* places in school). The population factor includes both net immigration and natural increase. The chapters of this book concerning respectable urban citizenship and residence regulations show the intensity of official efforts to control that growth. The occupational rate of change, covering both employment and education opportunities, is also subject to official manipulation for development purposes. The chapters concerning government constraints on the availability of schooling and jobs show the scope of cadres' efforts to arrange occupations to promote national economic growth.

If the Shanghai city fathers could easily orient the city's people to social tasks by government fiat and high policy, they would face fewer challenges than these chapters have described. The difficulty for the officialdom is that individual citizens generate personal notions of how and where to spend their lives. Thus a third factor, "government policy," does not affect the "population change" and "occupation change" factors in simple, straight-line ways because of a direct link between the latter two, and also because a fourth factor (an economic one, called "urban supply" below) intervenes between them and policy.

In the first place, the demographic and occupational rates in Shanghai are not fully independent of each other. People come to the city if they expect they will find something to do there. Individuals' incentives to urban immigration are a difficult topic to research for Shanghai, but the subject must be treated because it constitutes a link between Shanghai's jobs and people that, by definition, is not subject to communal power. The direct "occupations"-"population" linkage, i.e., the fact that people want to be in Shanghai if they can find a slot there, dilutes the effect of "policy" on both of these factors.

In the second place, the chapters above suggest that there is a fourth factor—namely, the level of general commodity "supply" to the city—which affects both population changes and employment changes but has not been subject to official control for career guidance purposes. Because this economic factor has been less steady than the incentives of people to move into Shanghai, its alterations have largely determined the effectiveness of career guidance policies over time. Thus the state of Shanghai's economy is the key factor affecting the strength of linkages within the career guidance system.

THE OCCUPATIONS-POPULATION LINKAGE

The attraction of Shanghai for immigrants was primarily economic. Changes in the supply of big-city jobs, or in the number of Shanghai school places which might lead to them, affected the opportunities of people to come to the urban area. Government policies increasingly determined the number of occupational slots in the city, but in general these policies were aimed at raising Shanghai's production by methods less roundabout than career guidance. The main constant, invariant link between the supply of occupations and urban population was thus not mediated very effectively by government policies; it was the desire of people to come live in the city.

There is some direct evidence to suggest the nature of this centripetal attraction to Shanghai and also some comparative, international evidence. As one ex-resident of the city explained:

They come mainly for material benefit. A worker is usually paid higher wages in Shanghai than in other cities, not to mention the rural areas. And in Shanghai he can enjoy the facilities of China's most modern city. There he will have more rationed food, cooking oil, and sugar. He can buy a greater variety of commodities than is available even in Peking. And because Shanghai is more developed in all respects, the people enjoy more freedom of ideology, so to speak. Even the meetings in hours after work are fewer than elsewhere.[1]

Although it is not currently possible to poll Shanghai immigrants on their reasons for moving there, data from cities in other countries indicate the general importance of economic motivations for urban migration. It may be that the causes of Korean migration into Seoul cannot be precisely equated with the factors that make people move to Shanghai because of cultural and political differences between the two situations. Also, the relation between interview responses and basic causes is not a sure one. Nevertheless, the figures from Seoul at least suggest the kinds of motives that are important in similar residence decisions.

Economic reasons explain most of the cases in Seoul for which the motives were not so complex as to make simple categories fail. The Korean surveyor conscientiously filed the mixed responses— in which economic and occupational motives often played a role

1. Interview with an ex-resident of Shanghai, Hongkong, November 1969.

TABLE 6.
Percentage Distribution of Immigrants into Seoul
by Cause, 1963 and 1964

Reasons	1963 January-June	1964 January-June
Economic		
(1) to look for a job	16	13
(2) to take a job	9	8
(3) to change jobs	3	2
Educational		
(1) to change schools	3	2
(2) to graduate to higher school	8	4
Social		
(1) marriage	4	3
(2) family discord	——	——
Other		
(Miscellaneous)	56	70
TOTAL	ca. 100	ca. 100

Source: H. Chung, "An Analysis of Urbanization and its Problems," *Journal of Population Study* 1 (1965), p. 159 (The Institute of Population Problems, Seoul), translated by Kim Hyung Man, "Urbanization in Southeast Asia and the Far East: A Comparative Study of the Origin, Growth, Social, Economic, and Physical Development of Selected Metropolitan Areas with Special Reference to Planning Policies" (Ph.D. diss., University of Sydney, 1969), p. 209. Percentages are rounded from the original and do not total 100 percent. Family discord was not cited as a cause in 1963 or 1964.

—under a broad residual category. Among the cases that could be realistically placed under clear headings, more than two-thirds were explained by economic factors. Another fifth of the precisely motivated migrations could be assigned to educational causes.[2] An

2. To calculate the broad terms "majority," "two-thirds," and "another fifth" for this text, Chung's two surveys were averaged. The exact percentages come out respectively at 63 percent, 68 percent, and 22 percent, but these precise numbers must be taken with a grain of salt, not only because they are used to suggest things about Shanghai, but also because the "others" category in the table no doubt includes cases that were partly determined by occupational or educational factors.

unspecific, cultural attraction of the city seems to be pervasive, but the special importance of economic motives is also evident.

Another study of the same problem in Djakarta supports the same broad conclusion. At least two-thirds of the respondents cited economic reasons for their migration into that big city. If surveys could be conducted in Shanghai or other Chinese Communist cities concerning the motives for immigration, the findings might differ somewhat from those obtained in Seoul and Djakarta, but economic and occupational causes would probably predominate among Shanghai immigrants, too.

Kang Chao has identified some specific economic factors that may affect urban immigrants' motives. Writing about China as a whole, he points out that, in the period before the Great Leap, peasants' real incomes rose slightly but workers' real incomes went up more. Migrants may have been attracted to cities because the income differential was increasing, because rural cadres encouraged certain families to leave villages, and because urban employees received family allowances, free medical care, and other benefits that were less available in the countryside. Chao believes that the "pull factors" bringing people to cities were predominant in the early 1950s. He also states, with less evidence, that "push factors" were predominant after peasant incentives to stay on the land had been weakened by collectivization.[3] More detailed research would be necessary to prove this last conclusion. At least in Shanghai, the 1956-1958 period affected hiring routines in ways that suggest the continuing importance of "pull factors." Nevertheless, economic motives were significant and Chao's specification of them is valuable.

Further evidence for the importance of occupational motivations for migration lies in the fact that some social conditions in Shanghai did not differ vastly from those in the surrounding countryside. Population density was one such condition. Shanghai is only the most crowded place in a very crowded region. According to the 1954 census, the city had about 6,575 people per

---

Chung's table is not easy to interpret, but it is a credit to his realism that he did not try to overspecify the responses of his informants.

3. Kang Chao, "Industrialization and Urban Housing in Communist China," p. 384.

TABLE 7.
Reasons for the Immigration of Male Household Heads into Djakarta, 1955
(Percent citing each reason)

Reason	From rural areas	From other urban areas	Total
Financial pressure	43%	29%	34%
Income improvement	20%	12%	17%
Dissatisfaction with previous job	12%	12%	12%
Official transfer	6%	19%	10%
Family reunification	9%	9%	9%
Continuation of schooling	5%	5%	7%
Security problems	2%	2%	2%
Conduct of trade	2%	2%	2%
Return to family home	1%	1%	1%
Health reasons	0%	0%	0%

Source: R. J. Hearn, ed., *The Urbanization of Djakarta* (Djakarta: Institute for Economic and Social Research, University of Indonesia, 1955) (reprinted from *Ekonomi Den Keuangan Indonesia* 8, No. 11 [November 1955]), p. 36. The categories of the survey are not mutually exclusive, and some titles have been rephrased. The meaning of the original term "financial pressure" is not entirely clear in English. The "total" column refers to a general sample of immigrants already in the city. The columns do not always total 100 percent vertically, because some respondents failed to reply or to answer clearly. All percentages have been rounded from the original.

square kilometer.[4] At the same time, the population density of Kiangsu Province as a whole was 436 people per square kilometer—the highest rate for any Chinese province and 37 percent more dense than that of second place Shantung.[5] The next highest

4. *KMJP*, January 11, 1954, cited in Stanford University China Project, *East Asia*, p. 79. A denser figure of 8,500 persons per square mile in Shanghai is given in *Chinghu tich'ü tzuliao mulu* (Taipei: Kuochia Anch'üan Chü, 1967), p. 20. This higher statistic is apparently derived on the basis of pre-1949 city limits that left out some of the partially built-up suburbs.

5. See the table in Etsuzō Onoye, "Regional Distribution of Urban Population in China," p. 110. This information is based on surveys in 1953, 1954, and 1957, during which time the order of the densest provinces did not change. The most

densities occur in Honan, Chekiang, and Anhwei. In other words, the five most dense provinces form a thick and continuous belt around Shanghai. Life in the city was crowded, but life in the countryside from which most immigrants came was not characterized by solitude either.

Factors of this sort, which may have affected immigration rates, are not subject to quick changes. The linkage between the number of urban occupational places and the size of the city's population was real, but insofar as this relation was a matter of individuals' wills rather than of government plans, it did not alter greatly from one time to another. The low-level politics outlined in this book deal with tensions between personal desires and public imperatives. In order to find out what made the former change, we must locate a factor less constant than the desire of peasants to live in the city.

THE GOVERNMENT POLICY-URBAN SUPPLY LINKAGE

Both the availability of urban occupations and the number of urban people were influenced by (a) government policies concerning them, (b) some direct linkages between them which the government could not control, and (c) the level of material supply from the countryside to Shanghai. The general state of the urban economy, as represented by urban supply, was only partially subject to official control for career guidance purposes. In any case, it had a higher priority than the guidance system, which was usually regarded as a policy that should be instrumental to urban prosperity rather than more important.

The level of urban commodity supply is meant to be a broad category. It includes consumption goods, which are rationed and then filtered through the household procedures, thus affecting the city's population size. It also includes capital and raw materials supplies for industries, which provide Shanghai people with jobs. In theory, inland demand for the city's products

---

populous province, Szechwan, in the mid-1950s already had 70 million people, nearly half again as many as the next one, Shantung. Because of the large vacant areas in western Szechwan, however, that province ranked only eleventh on the list for density. Another good way to measure population pressure on land would be to use per capita grain production as an indicator. This index, however, is less stable from year to year for reasons of weather.

might also be a variable constraint on the career guidance system in the same way, but distribution of Shanghai's goods either did not arise as a problem or was so concurrent with trends in urban supply that it need not be treated separately. The supply of materials that Shanghai used to create jobs, produce goods, or support residents is a very general, inductive, synthetic category whose specific forms have cropped up many times in this book's explanations of how the major kinds of guidance policy worked.

What then was the exact relationship between urban supply and career-control policy? Was it direct, or inverse, or otherwise? Three variables are implicit in this question. The first one is independent, comprising government policies in the educational, citizenship, employment, and residence fields. The second, an intervening variable, concerns the general level of material supply to the city. The third variable is dependent; it is the output of this system, the degree to which official guidance plans are effective. Previous sections of this book suggest that the variables align with each other in the following main ways:

(1) When supplies to the city were at a low level, for example during the "bad years" of the post-Leap period, then career control was relatively low. Local authorities could not, at such a time, politically afford to enforce strict discipline or household laws. *Hsiahsiang* was at a low ebb; it could not be fairly administered because the residence registers were in bad order. Birth control was voluntary and low on the list of political priorities. Rationing existed, but the black market was booming because the official stores did not have much food to distribute. Government housing budgets had nearly ceased to exist, and unauthorized housing was economically important. Few new jobs were available within the city because materials shortages kept current factories running at only partial capacity, and unemployed people had to be occupied in special schools; moral education was difficult to carry out when the pupils had empty stomachs.

(2) When supplies for the city were at a moderate level, the government had more means to restrict personal mobility, but the people did not have so much that they could evade the restrictions easily. In the recovery periods of 1956-1957 and 1963-1964, educational opportunities were made available to selected students. There was some technical rustication, and proposals for residen-

tial rustication involved both material and ideal attractions to the volunteers. Birth control had strong institutional support. The government had rations to give, but ration cards were still necessary because there was no great surplus. Some housing was built; some new jobs were available; and official efforts in the realm of public faith had some success.

(3) Finally, when the resources for urban consumption increased still further, as in the mid-1960s, population controls began to suffer despite the political campaigns to strengthen them. The *hsiahsiang* movement, whose technical and residential justifications were now indistinguishable, became increasingly strident, until finally (in the summer of 1966) everyone was so busy within the city advocating rustication that almost no one moved out to stay. Jobs were somewhat available, but placement in them was now so systematized that the recruitment structure generated almost as many political problems as a shortage might have done. Rationing declined in importance and restrictiveness as food supplies increased. New housing was built but remained in short supply. Birth control devices were easily available but, for many people, so were the means to support large families. Moral education was in surfeit; for all its enthusiasm, it became too unspecific to direct behavior effectively. As a result, the intense patriotic campaigns of this period tended to be sporadic and temporary at low levels and to lack the support of material awards or sanctions.

In other words, as soon as the city's supply of goods became really adequate, career control in its many aspects tended to decline. The three conditions stated above might be summarized graphically. The relation between urban supply and career guidance can be thought of as a hump-shaped curve. When the city's people were either quite badly off or very well supplied, then the government had little leverage over many important aspects of their daily lives. It could regulate them best when the local economy's resources were in a moderate range of supply.

Conversely, individuals had more low-level power and mobility when the government was preoccupied with commodity shortages, or also when real prosperity lowered the value of the material incentives that the regime could offer for socialist careers. This story is the same, no matter whether it is told from the viewpoint of the government or of the people. The state had most power in daily affairs, and the citizens had least, when economic prosperity was medium. Individuals somewhat increased their freedom of career choice, and the government had fewer means to resist them in these personal matters, when the urban economy was doing either quite well or quite badly.

PROSPERITY, CAREER CONTROL, AND URBAN IMMIGRATION

This statement about a nonlinear relation between urban supply and career guidance suggests some corollaries. Just one example of them will be given here.

It might at first be thought that migration to a city would always increase as a function of greater commodity supplies there. Shanghai data, however, suggest that this relation may be less simple, at least in contexts where the government has great political will and has socialized the economy. Control of net urban immigration is a form of career guidance. As commodity supplies move from low to medium levels, these resources may increase official capacities to restrain urban households faster than they increase the households' capacities to resist. If residence control is thus related to urban supply in a hump-shaped manner, and if net immigration is related to residence control in a linear inverse way, then it follows mathematically that there would be a U-shaped relation between net immigration and urban supply.

Other corollary suggestions of this sort might be derived from the ideas presented above. None of them could yet be proven for any city of the People's Republic of China in a quantitative fashion, because the political stringency that makes such a guidance system work also makes social surveys about it impossible for an outsider to conduct. Nonquantitative evidence on these matters is readily available, however, and much of it is presented above. To the extent that inductive generalizations of this sort are true, they show some unexpected interactions of strong government policies with changing economic prosperities.

THE NEED TO SHIFT GUIDANCE STRATEGIES

Moderate economic shortage was a usual condition of effective low-level career guidance in Shanghai before the Cultural Revolution. By the mid-1960s, however, many people in the city enjoyed a reasonably high and stable standard of living. The food ration system had lost almost all of its restrictive function, and residence control was consequently weakened. Many kinds of coupons had been used only during the difficult post-Leap period. Later these chits were not needed, and rationing by ordinary money and prices was sufficient to put demand within range of supply. Households could get along conveniently for some time, even if some of their members were not registered at the police station. Local investment had revived, and generally good progress had been made toward raising both industrial and agricultural output in East China.

Even though the subsequent political movement disrupted some factories temporarily, food and raw material supplies from rural areas to Shanghai were fairly well maintained. Administrative decentralization was promoted during the Cultural Revolution. More hiring authority was vested in small- and middle-size enterprises, which newspapers of the period described as technologically more useful for China's growth than large businesses and the "trusts" imputed to Liu Shao-ch'i had been. A stable and high general level of urban supply boded to continue into the future, despite the fact that it dipped slightly during the most turbulent months of the Cultural Revolution. This had basic implications for urban career guidance policy in China.

If the government wished to continue determining urban population and occupation changes under good economic conditions, it would need to find new, nonmaterial incentives to buttress its weakening monopoly over the economic resources that had previously been used to this end. The Cultural Revolution, and the assertion of political will and propaganda that went with it, began to supply this need.

Some alternatives to the idealistic guidance movement existed, but they were very unattractive. Most traditional methods of career control—personal identity cards, restrictions on transport tickets, internal passports, and careful enforcement of the visit-reporting laws—were unpopular and obviously repressive. The Communist government has in general not wanted or even been able to use these methods very much.[6] It is unclear whether such measures

6. This paragraph was largely suggested by an informant, Hong Kong, January 1970.

can be completely avoided as China's urban economy becomes relatively stable. There have been scattered reports of their imposition in recent years, but if they ever must be used extensively in place of the incentive mix of earlier years, they will threaten the enthusiasm of the revolution.

FEWER MATERIAL MEASURES, MORE IDEOLOGICAL PERSUASION

The simplest option for the government has been to lift the restraints that proved unworkable in a prosperous setting. As early as 1965 in Shanghai, this had already begun to happen. A resident in the city reported at that time:

The past years have been very trying for those school leavers who were unable to receive immediate placement. . . . This year is much easier in this respect. Practically all have been given employment . . . and a considerable number have joined the now fast developing part-work and part-study factories.[7]

A second and related government option was to have idealistic and evangelical campaigns play a stronger role in accomplishing some of the guidance goals that stricter official distribution of food and jobs might have achieved in times of scarcity. The government has moved in this direction. For example, upper third-year students from Ts'aoyang Middle School (in the favored housing project of the same name) sent themselves forth to the countryside with a flurry of vows affirming their patriotism. The diary of one girl student reported that on August 3 she stayed up all night to study an editorial in the *Jenmin jihpao*. On August 4, she arrived to live in "Uncle Chin's" peasant home and to "hang Chaiman Mao's portrait on the brightest and cleanest wall." On August 6, she spent all day planting rice seeds: "In the afternoon the sun was hot, and since there was no wind, the water six inches deep felt boiling under the sun. . . . My knees were in the mud. On account of small animals, my legs itched. But when I saw the poor and lower-middle peasants working for more than ten hours each day without becoming tired, I did not feel any need to take a rest." On August 7, she carried a Mao quotation board to the fields.[8] For all its passion, this was only a campaign for short "double-

7. *SHNL*, October 26, 1965.
8. *HMWP*, August 18, 1966.

snatch labor" (*shuangch'iang laotung*). A few days later, this girl
and all her classmates were back at school in Shanghai.

THE ADMINISTRATIVE PROBLEMS
OF NONMATERIAL INCENTIVES

Despite their value in arousing enthusiasm, ideological campaigns
have produced some difficulties. One difficulty was that youths
who responded to these campaigns had to be granted Party recognition, and some of them naturally hoped for attendant career
rewards. For example, in the expanding commodities markets of
1964-1965, the Shanghai No. 9 State Cotton Mill took on more
than 1,300 young people, almost 40 percent of whom soon afterward asked to join the Youth League. The article describing them
did not mention their family backgrounds, but "some cadres
thought that these people were too young . . . they were ignorant
and could not play a useful role in the League." In particular,
some reluctant older workers "did not consent to taking these
young people into the League" and were worried that the "level of
consciousness of the present young applicants" was too low.[9]
Many of these youths had avoided long-term residential *hsiafang*,
and some were from bourgeois families. They nevertheless were
good and talented workers and won some Party support. "The
educated youths have really grown very fast and are so energetic
that they can overtake those ahead of them." Nevertheless, resentment against their co-option did not cease even after the official
tolerance for the youths was obvious.

[Some workers] imposed a large number of "additional qualifications"
on the applicants. They think that youths who have not been recommended by their organizations, apprentices and temporary workers who
have not become regular workers, youths who still need to master difficult
production techniques, and even youths who are diminutive physically
are all not qualified to join.[10]

9. *CKCN* 21, No. 1 (November 1, 1965), translated in *SCMM*, No. 504, p. 7. The
Shanghai No. 9 State Cotton Mill is probably the same as the No. 9 Shenhsin mill
of an earlier period.

10. *Ibid.* League members are all supposed to be within the eighteen to twenty-
five age range. Young Pioneers are all supposed to be aged seven to seventeen.

Despite such opposition, the factories needed these youths' energies in a time of economic expansion and honor could not be kept from them.

Hsiahsiang was also still a way for individuals to escape their heritages. Now that the material sanctions for failure to volunteer for rustication were ineffective, this symbolic aspect of the *hsiahsiang* appeal became more important. When youths were sent down, details about their backgrounds ordinarily were kept secret. Only personnel officials had convenient access to the files in which such information was stored. Basic kinds of data about people, for example their family backgrounds, were often common knowledge in groups that worked and lived together, but the practical meaning of such facts depended very much on broad ideological campaigns. Sometimes even ex-members of the KMT could hope to redeem themselves through labor in the countryside. At least before the Cultural Revolution, they would often not be molested if they worked well and offered ostensible support to the Party line. There is a certain irony in the effects of movements like the Socialist Education Movement and especially the Cultural Revolution. On one hand, such campaigns condemned many individuals because of their family histories. On the other hand, the *hsiahsiang* they symbolically supported gave bourgeois-background people (especially youths) reason to regard themselves as native proletarians, because now the young "capitalists" had as much experience at manual work as did their working-class peers. When an "educated youth" wrote an article for the youth newspaper *Chungkuo ch'ingnien pao* about his experience in Shanghai's Ch'ingp'u County, he headlined it, "It is Very Honorable to Be a Peasant," and this glory clearly redounded as much to himself as to the peasants.[11]

For many Shanghai graduates who continued to go "down" to the countryside, the ambiguity of the moral campaign became bothersome only when their bourgeois, or at least urban, backgrounds hindered what they had hoped to do for themselves in the rural areas. Some of them were dissatisfied with rustication partly because they came to realize that even good volunteer work could not erase their class status in a sure way, for all time. Those who

11. *CKCNP*, December 24, 1963.

were persuaded to take their political stigma seriously found that they could not get rid of it. In addition, the Communist Party could not always keep its implicit promises to Shanghai volunteers. Its long-standing peasant and minority group branches in rural areas had to be served on many specific local issues, lest peasants harm public security and production in those places. Altruism and careerism were as thoroughly mixed in the motives of Shanghai *hsiahsiang* volunteers as among youths anywhere. Many of them wanted to serve all their values, both spiritual and material, and when they could not, they were frustrated.[12]

A further problem of ideological campaigns like the *hsiahsiang* movement was youths' realization that rustication might be permanent and might not lead to promotion. For instance Tung Chia-keng, an officially designated model young intellectual, refused to take his entrance exams for promotion to a university and instead volunteered for agricultural production. He was much eulogized in the press, but at least some Chinese middle school students reportedly felt sorry for him, and for others like him, because the lack of university education was thought to limit such persons' career prospects.[13] One middle school graduate made public assurances that he would be glad to respond to the Party's call, *if* he failed his university entrance exams.

The worst specific complaints about *hsiahsiang* concerned the difficulties that volunteers had in reversing decisions to rusticate themselves. An ex-cadre, who remained quite loyal to the ideals of the government, said bluntly:

In the *hsiahsiang* movement from its beginning, and especially after 1958, there were some deserters. They said they were not used to the life and work of the places to which they were sent. After they had applied several

12. This interpretation was suggested to the author by the remarks of some interviewees, e.g., by a graduate of the Electrical Manufacturing School at Minhang, who reports on the 1960-1965 period; URI, July 1966. Salaries of electrician volunteers to South China, Sinkiang, and Tibet were only about 35 to 45 yüan. Some of the later complaints were economistic in the sense that volunteers for distant *hsiafang* missions might feel that they deserved more material support for such self-sacrifice.

13. This example is not from Shanghai. See "Make Many Preparations: Let the Motherland Make Its Choice," *Yangch'eng wanpao* [Canton evening news], June 27, 1964, translated in *URS* 36, No. 16 (August 14, 1964), pp. 198-199.

times for transfer back to their original places, and after they had been refused, they would sometimes leave their work units by themselves and would go home. Because they had no permission from the leading organs to do this, they were usually unable to get their household registrations back, and they would become unemployed.[14]

The tribulation of volunteers who changed their minds was public knowledge in Shanghai. Organizers of the official movement were aware that many potential pledges were lost to the cause of residential *hsiahsiang* because these decisions were difficult to reverse. Potential volunteers would hold off until they were sure that they would not later regret their public commitment to obey the state's assignment.

To answer these doubts, Shanghai's local governments in the mid-1960s occasionally made use of a very exceptional document: "household guarantee certificates" (*huk'ou paocheng shu*). These were given to rustication volunteers who would not go to the countryside unless their right to return to residence status in Shanghai was guaranteed on paper. It is unclear how much credence rusticates and their parents put in these documents, or how many certificates were issued in Shanghai. The report of their existence comes from interviews, not from publications. Nevertheless, the offers of such certificates may have persuaded some young people to volunteer, even when the promised right to return home was not very clear or well believed.[15] Any unauthorized returnee from rustication was visited by street cadres, who would urge him and his family to reconsider his decision about leaving the countryside. The defector's urban residence status could not easily be restored. But when the city's general economic prosperity made low-paid jobs somewhat available and rations adequate, these policies created more frustration than compliance.

14. Interview, Hong Kong, October 1969.

15. Interview, Hong Kong. December 1969, with an ex-red guard who had done some *hsiafang* labor. He had been to Shanghai and said he knew definitely that "organs of the Shanghai People's Congress" had issued some "household guarantee certificates." The author has been unable to find documentary confirmation of this report. These papers were issued sparingly, and they may not have been fully legal documents.

THE CAREER GUIDANCE SYSTEM
IN THE CULTURAL REVOLUTION

The career control system for youths, particularly in its residence and rustication aspects, was possibly the most explosive specific cause of the early Cultural Revolution in Shanghai. This major political earthquake of course had many complex causes, not all of them local. Beginning in late 1966, many workers participated, who had no rural experience. The close relation between the *hsiahsiang* campaign and the low-level motives for Cultural Revolution has nevertheless been obscured, because patriots could attack residence and rustication policies only indirectly. They could criticize the ways in which *hsiahsiang* was administered, not the substance of the policy, which is difficult to assail from any public point of view.

Former rusticates and potential graduates, now together dubbed "red guards," marched through the city in the summer and fall of 1966 to make "revolution," but their goals were as complicated as their actions were passionate. Some youths ceremoniously burned their household registration certificates in public.[16] They accused municipal Party leaders of having lied to them about rustication procedures. Certain high officials, who had been most intensively engaged in *hsiahsiang* propaganda during the Socialist Education Movement, were attacked sharply during the Cultural Revolution, even though some others in the Party Propaganda Department became active on new revolutionary committees and were not hurt. Yang Hsi-kuang, the main education czar in the city's Party apparatus, was accused of having put so many "demons and monsters" in Shanghai educational institutions that 80 percent of the various committee members in universities were "representatives of capitalism"[17] "Red guard fighters" from Futan University and workers from a related factory jointly struggled against Yang in person, to show that he was "an agent in Shanghai of China's Khrushchev."[18] Shih Hsi-min, the main secretary dealing with

16. *Ibid.* Documentary confirmation of this part of the report is also not available. There are, however, published evidences of an anarchist strain in some Shanghai ideologies that are consistent with this interview.

17. *WHP*, May 20, 1968.

18. *WHP*, August 27, 1968.

rustication for the Shanghai Party Committee, was declared to be a "docile tool" of Liu Shao-ch'i.[19]

Street level cadres could not avoid the effects of this resentment. For many years, they had been pressured from above to carry out all residence policies, including *hsiahsiang*. They were in charge of recruitment because no higher level could effectively do the job. In the summer of 1966, when certain streets in Hungk'ou, Huang-p'u, and Yangp'u districts "accepted applications" for *hsiahsiang* to Sinkiang, some youths registered for the program.[20] It is doubtful that many actually went to the frontiers. Students preferred to "make liaison" (*ch'uanlien*) in other places, and residence control became impossible because touring red guards had to be provided with facilities and food. In early 1967, Radio Shanghai repeatedly mentioned that "lane cadres" had been attacked by travelling students. Directors of street offices (*chiehtao panshih ch'u chujen*), Party branch secretaries (*tang chihpu shuchi*), and all higher cadres were officially declared liable to criticism if they had committed errors. In fact, even lower functionaries were often attacked, too.[21] Target restrictions and exhortations that "the practice of making liaison must be checked immediately"[22] had only a gradual effect on youths, who caused the old career guidance system to become a dead letter in the Cultural Revolution.

That large movement serves as a natural watershed and ending for this book, for a particular strategy toward career controls collapsed then. When career guidance policies were restored in 1968, their effectiveness depended more on ideological campaigns, and less on any increased organization of resource flows, than had been the case before. From the government's viewpoint, few new returns were to be gained from improved control over the distribution of material resources. Career guidance definitely did not

---

19. *Kungjen p'inglun* [Workers' review], No. 5 (June 1-10, 1967), translated in *SCMM*, No. 622, p. 1. Ch'en Lin-hu, who was associated closely with *hsiafang* but was active in government organs rather than Party ones, survived the events of 1967-1968 and became a member of the Shanghai Revolutionary Committee. No distinction between Party and government is made here. From the viewpoint of citizens in low-level politics, these two are for the most part indistinguishable.

20. *HMWP*, May 31, 1966.

21. *CNS*, No. 161 (March 16, 1967), p. 3.

22. *WHP*, August 18, 1967.

end with the Cultural Revolution—in some ways, it was strengthened in later years—but the basis for further refinements of this system changed importantly at that time.

CAREER GUIDANCE AND SOCIAL DEVELOPMENT

There have been recurrent strains between public patriotism and individual interests in Shanghai. At no time could either official policies or private hopes determine all behavior there in a watertight way. Each of these seats or "levels" of power in China can be taken seriously. Sovereignty is not a behavioral idea, not even for the People's Republic of China. Some of the real "policy directives" in that country do not emanate from government offices but are equivalent to citizens' motives. At the same time, important evasions of nationally approved procedures do not show that the Chinese system was lacking in a sense of common purpose. The social science of power and hierarchy has recently paid much good attention to what actors do as well as to what they say. It should also begin to take the public behavior of nongovernmental actors into as full account as that of governments. If this were done, hierarchy would turn out to be a more complex topic than is usually admitted. The changing nature of the daily power that affects most people's lives, and the economic and other influences on it at various times, could then be given the attention they deserve.

This approach is at least as interesting in specific forms as it is in the abstract. Whenever the Shanghai government attempted to impose a career control under economic conditions that militated against compliance, some behavior commonly arose to provide a partial, countervailing effect. The new institution was often indistinct and scattered among many kinds of action, but for some cases a specific change can be pointed out. In the Great Leap and its immediate aftermath, for example, privation succeeded prosperity with such speed that there was no time to establish a guidance system of the sort that usually obtained at middle levels of prosperity. Rural people first flocked into Shanghai to take jobs which Leap and pre-Leap economic reorganizations had created. When the government tried to assert employment controls, and when unions wanted to define Shanghai's local proletariat in a more limited way, the economic system reacted by creating hundreds of thousands of temporary jobs, most of which were not even governed by written contracts.[23] When shortages came and the government hoped to maintain a strict ration system, people to a startling extent simply went to restaurants, where most dishes were still not rationed. When the restaurants were regulated more rigidly, the black market swelled as much as supplies would allow.[24] In some ways, this kind of control was a game in which policy and society constantly vied to keep one step ahead of each other.

At many other times, the government's guidance policies had their effects in a simple manner, as officially intended. Cat-and-mouse relationships have been seen quite often in the chapters above. They are indeed real, but they explain only part of what was happening in Shanghai. There can be little doubt that most residents of the city regarded their motives as more patriotic than this description alone would imply. Often Shanghai people were quite willing to play by the official rules for residence in the city, either because they considered it their social duty to do so, or else because it was the easiest way. If much of the discussion in this book implies that they were alienated from government policy, that is true in a strictly technical sense. By definition, they did not make that policy directly, and there is much circumstantial evidence that they saw its effects on their lives as being independent of their motives—even when they agreed with it for its worthy social purposes.

Nor would it be at all correct to suppose that leaders of the Shanghai Party saw in this set of guidance techniques only a means to control people, as if that were the main intention of their socialist government. Their appeal to revolutionary objectives was not just an effort to use norms to regulate behavior. Supervision of careers was not their final purpose. The business value of occupational and residential policies for spurring the economic development of China was obvious to them. In fact, the guidance of personal energies by these policies may have contributed to the growth of China's industrial economy in exactly the same way

23. See Chapter 3 above.
24. On restaurants and illegal immigration, see *Current Scene* I, No. 6 (July 10, 1961), pp. 3-4.

that a tax system served the same end. If the science of econometrics extended so far, the contribution of the career guidance system to China's growth in various years might even be computed. The extent of that contribution is unsure and is beyond the scope of this book. Probably the most fruitful future research on career guidance systems will concern their economic efficiencies and inefficiencies.

All the policies discussed here were intended to foster China's development as a strong society. These methods, in combination, were immediately repressive of individuals, but the regime often justified them on grounds that they contributed to national goals. Surely the cadres knew that such policies deeply and daily affected many people. They knew also that restrictions of current freedoms were sometimes unpopular. Their motives, like the motives of the citizens with whom they dealt, were permeated by a sense of tradeoffs, a sense of what is lost when other things are gained. The Communists must be given credit for not uniformly fudging this point. They call their regime a "dictatorship" and have a particular understanding of what that word means. It may be more justifiable to them because Marxist historical theory tells them it is temporary.

Economic changes, more than any other kind in the long run, may serve by steps to lessen the gap between legitimate individual and collective interests. Recent experiences in the West suggest that this will not occur with much speed, but maybe it is good that nothing foreign is likely to dampen Chinese hopes.[25] Social growth is slow, and individual lives are short. Tensions between the ideals of public spirit and freedom have made for lively politics in Shanghai.

25. See Arthur M. Okun, *Equality and Efficiency: The Big Tradeoff* (Washington: The Brookings Institution, 1975).

BIBLIOGRAPHY

Newspapers, especially local ones from Shanghai, are by far the most important sources of data for this book. Nearly all of these papers are available, at least in microfilm form, at the library of Union Research Institute in Hong Kong. (The only significant exception is a run of *Laotung pao* issues, which is not at URI but can be seen at the Library of Congress, Washington, D.C.) These sources were supplemented by interviews and by other materials at Universities Service Centre, Hong Kong, and at the University of California's Center for Chinese Studies.

The main Communist Party organ in Shanghai, *Chiehfang jihpao*, supplied information on official attitudes and policies. The true goldmines, however, were less formal papers directed toward Shanghai's large non-Communist, ex-bourgeois readership. These papers, no less than any others in China, have a duty "to carry out the Party line." They are, however, supposed to do that job in the most interesting way possible, so that their talented non-Party readers will be inspired to comply with government policies in practical ways and, indeed, will be inspired to read newspapers at all. Articles in the bourgeois-directed press are often livelier and more informative (in social science terms, more behavioral) than the sweeping rationales, ideals, and directives to be found in local Party organs.

The most famous of the Shanghai bourgeois papers is *Wenhui pao*. *Hsinwen jihpao* and *Hsinmin wanpao* proved to be even more useful on particular economic and educational topics during many periods. A third category of local newspaper, of a kind that lies between the Party organs and the formerly bourgeois press, consists of journals that are dependent on specialized organizations. The most important examples are the Shanghai Federation of Trade Union's *Laotung pao* and the local Communist Youth League's *Ch'ingnien pao*. During 1967-1968 there were of course the famous Red Guard tabloids.

Local newspapers in all these categories have been exported from China during the 1960s only under ban of a loosely enforced Chinese law. China specialists (no matter what their politics) regularly use materials obtained by others in this manner. These newspapers carry livelier and more realistic information on the creativity of the Chinese local scene than do the exportable, better censored publications.

The footnotes and bibliography do not cite all the theoretical or comparative works that could be mentioned in many contexts. Below is a list only of reference publications that were required in the writing process. Some important books in the field are thus omitted. Periodicals are separated from books. Specific articles in magazines or collections are cited separately only when they are quite important in the text.

PERIODICALS AND NEWSPAPERS

Ajia keizai [Asian economies]. Monthly, Tokyo, 1960 onward.

Asian Survey. Monthly, Berkeley, Calif., 1961 onward.

Chanwang [Prospects]. Irregular, Shanghai, 1948-1959.

Chiaoshih pao [Teachers' news]. Irregular, Peking, during 1950s.

Chiehfang jihpao [Liberation daily]. Daily, Shanghai, 1950 onward.

Chiehfangchün pao [Liberation army news]. Irregular or daily, Peking, 1955 onward.

China News Analysis. Weekly, Hong Kong, 1955 onward.

China News Service. Irregular press dispatches, many cities, until mid-1950s.

China News Summary. Weekly, Hong Kong, 1964 onward.

China Quarterly. Quarterly, London, 1960 onward.

China Reconstructs. Monthly, Peking.

China Topics. Weekly, Hong Kong, 1961 onward.

Chinese Literature. Monthly, Peking, 1951 onward.

Chungkuo ch'ingnien [China youth]. Semimonthly, Peking, 1948 onward.

Chungkuo ch'ingnien pao [China youth news]. Almost daily, Peking, 1951 onward.

Ch'angchiang jihpao [Yangtze daily]. Daily, Hankow, 1950-1959.

Ch'ingnien pao [Youth news]. Daily, Shanghai, 1953-1961.

Ch'ün chung [The masses]. Weekly, Shanghai, 1946-1947.

Current Background. Irregular, Hong Kong, 1950 onward.

Current Scene. Weekly, Hong Kong, 1961 onward.

Eastern Horizon. Monthly, Hong Kong, 1966 onward.

Extracts from China Mainland Magazines. Irregular, Hong Kong, 1955-1960. Succeeded by *Selections from China Mainland Magazines* (see below).

The Far Eastern Economic Review. Weekly, Hong Kong, 1946 onward.

Foreign Broadcast Information Service, *Daily Report, Communist China*. Daily, Washington, D.C., 1963 onward.

Futan [Aurora]. Monthly, Shanghai, 1956-1961.

Hsinchiang jihpao [Sinkiang daily]. Daily, Urumchi, 1951-1959.

Hsinmin pao wank'an [New people's evening gazette]. Daily, Shanghai, 1954-1966.

Hsinmin wanpao [New people's evening news]. Daily, Shanghai, 1954-1966.

Hsinwen jihpao [News daily]. Daily, Shanghai, 1952-1959.

Hsüehhsi [Study]. Monthly or semimonthly, Peking, 1949-1958.

Hsüehshu yüehk'an [Academic monthly]. Monthly, Shanghai, 1957-1963.

Hungch'i [Red flag]. Monthly or semimonthly, Peking, 1958 onward.

Issues & Studies. Monthly, Taipei, 1964 onward.

Jenmin jihpao [People's daily]. Daily, Peking, 1949 onward.

Jenmin shouts'e [People's handbook]. Annual, Peking, 1950-1966.

Joint Publications Research Service, Irregular, Washington, D.C., 1957 onward.

Journal of Asian Studies. Quarterly, Ann Arbor, Mich., 1956 onward.

Kuangming jihpao [Bright daily]. Daily, Peking, 1949 onward.

Kungjen jihpao [Workers' daily]. Daily, Peking, 1949 onward.

Laotung pao [Labor news]. Daily, Shanghai, 1956-1957.

Mengya [Sprouts]. Monthly, Shanghai, 1956-1964.

New China News Agency. Many telegraphic dispatches daily, various cities, 1949 onward.

Peking Review. Weekly, Peking, 1958 onward.

Selections from China Mainland Magazines. Irregular, Hong Kong, 1960 onward.

Shanghai chiaoyü [Shanghai education]. Monthly, Shanghai, 1957-1966.

Shanghai kungshang tzuliao [Data on Shanghai industry and commerce]. Irregular, Shanghai, 1951-1952.

Shanghai News. Daily, Shanghai, 1946-1952.

Shanghai saomang [Shanghai illiteracy elimination]. Weekly, Shanghai, 1957.

Shanghai wanpao [Shanghai evening news]. Daily, Shanghai, 1966.

South China Morning Post. Daily, Hong Kong, 1881 onward.

Survey of the China Mainland Press. Daily, Hong Kong, 1950 onward.

Takung pao [*L'impartial*]. Daily, Tientsin. Peking, Shanghai, Hong Kong, 1902 onward.

Union Research Service. Irregular, Hong Kong, 1955 onward.

Wenhui pao [Literary news]. Daily, Shanghai, 1945 onward.

Yi pao [Further news]. Daily, Shanghai, mid-1952.

BOOKS AND ARTICLES

Almond, Gabriel A., and Sidney Verba. *The Civic Culture*. Princeton, N.J.: Princeton University Press, 1963.

Baum, Richard, and Frederick C. Teiwes. *Ssu-ch'ing: The Socialist Education Movement of 1962-1966*. Berkely: Center for Chinese Studies, University of California at Berkeley, 1968.

Berliner, Joseph S. *Factory and Manager in the U. S. S. R*. Cambridge, Mass.: Harvard University Press, 1957.

Bernstein, Thomas P. "Cadre and Peasant Behavior Under Conditions of Insecurity and Deprivation: The Grain Supply Crisis of the Spring of 1955." In *Chinese Communist Politics in Action*, edited by A. Doak Barnett. Seattle: University of Washington Press, 1969.

Breese, Gerald. *Urbanization in Newly Developing Countries*. Englewood Cliffs, N. J.: Prentice-Hall, 1966.

Chao, Kang. "Industrialization and Urban Housing in Communist China." *Journal of Asian Studies* 25, No. 3 (May 1966).

Chen, Nai-ruenn, ed. *Chinese Economic Statistics: A Handbook for Mainland China*. Chicago: Aldine, 1967.

Chesneaux, Jean. *The Chinese Labor Movement: 1919-1927*. Translated by Hope Wright. Stanford, Calif.: Stanford University Press, 1968.

Chinghu tich'ü tzuliao mulu [Catalogue of materials for the Nanking-Shanghai region]. Taipei: Kuochia Anch'üan Chü, 1967.

Chunghua Jenmin Kunghokuo yukuan kungan kungtso fakuei huip'ien [Compendium of laws and regulations relevant to public security work in the People's Republic of China]. Peking: Ch'ünchung Ch'upan She, 1957.

Cohen, Jerome Alan. *The Criminal Process in the People's Republic of China, 1949-1963: An Introduction*. Cambridge, Mass.: Harvard University Press, 1968.

Dahl, Robert. *Who Governs? Democracy and Power in an American City*. New Haven, Conn.: Yale University Press, 1961.

Donnithorne, Audrey. *China's Economic System*. London: George Allen and Unwin, 1967.

Dwyer, D. J. "Urban Squatters: The Relevance of the Hong Kong Experience," *Asian Survey* X, No. 7 (July 1970): 607-613.

Eckstein, Alexander, Walter Galenson, and Ta-chung Liu, eds. *Economic Trends in Communist China*. Chicago: Aldine, 1968.

Eckstein, Harry, and David E. Apter. *Comparative Politics: A Reader*. New York: The Free Press, 1963.

Elliot, Elsie. *Avarice, Corruption, and Bureaucracy in Hong Kong. Volume I*. Hong Kong: published by the author, 1972.

Etzioni, Amitai. *Modern Organizations*. Englewood Cliffs, N. J.: Prentice-Hall. 1964.

Fainsod, Merle. *How Russia Is Ruled.* Rev. ed. Cambridge, Mass.: Harvard University Press, 1963.

Falkenheim, Victor Carl. "Provincial Administration in Fukien, 1949-1966." Ph.D. dissertation, Columbia University, 1971.

Feich'ing yenchiu ts'achih she (Institute for the Study of Chinese Communist Problems). *Yichiuliuch'i feich'ing nienpao: shihch'inien lai feich'ing tsunglan* [1967 yearbook on Chinese Communist situation from 1949 to 1966]. Taipei: Institute for the Study of Chinese Communist Problems, 1967.

Freeberne, Michael. "The Specter of Malthus: Birth Control in Communist China." *Current Scene* 2, No. 18 (August 15, 1963); 1-20.

Gardner, John. "The Wu-Fan Campaign in Shanghai: A Study in the Consolidation of Urban Control." In *Chinese Communist Politics in Action,* edited by A. Doak Barnett. Seattle: University of Washington Press, 1969.

Geddes, W. R. *Peasant Life in Communist China.* Ithaca, N. Y.: Cornell Society for Applied Anthropology, 1963.

Geertz, Clifford F., ed. *Old Societies and New States: The Quest for Modernity in Asia and Africa.* New York: The Free Press, 1963.

Gray, Jack, and Patrick Cavendish. *Chinese Communism in Crisis: Maoism and the Cultural Revolution.* London: Pall Mall Press; New York: Praeger, 1968.

Hauser, Philip M., and Leo F. Schnore, eds. *The Study of Urbanization.* New York: Wiley, 1965.

Hoffman, Charles. *Work Incentive Practices and Policies in the People's Republic of China, 1953-1965.* Albany: State University of New York Press, 1967.

Howe, Christopher. "The Supply and Administration of Housing in Mainland China: The Case of Shanghai." *China Quarterly,* No. 33 (January-March, 1968): 73-97.

―――. *Urban Employment and Economic Growth in Communist China, 1949-1957.* Cambridge, England: Cambridge University Press, 1971.

Hu, Chang-tu, ed. *Aspects of Chinese Education.* New York: Teachers College Press, Columbia University, 1969.

―――. "Communist Education: Theory and Practice." *China Quarterly,* No. 10 (April-June, 1962): 84-97.

Hunter, Neale. *Shanghai Journal.* New York: Praeger, 1969.

Johnson, Sheila K. "Hong Kong's Resettled Squatters: A Statistical Analysis." *Asian Survey* VI, No. 11 (November 1966): 643-656.

Kim Hyung Man. "Urbanization in Southeast Asia and the Far East: A Comparative Study of the Origin, Growth, Social, Economic, and Physical Development of Selected Metropolitan Areas with Special Reference to Planning Policies." Ph.D. dissertation, University of Sydney, 1969.

Lang, Olga. *Chinese Family and Society.* New Haven, Conn.: Yale University Press, 1946.

Lee, Rensselaer W., III. "The *Hsia Fang* System: Marxism and Modernization." *China Quarterly,* No. 28 (October-December 1966): 40-62.

Lewis, John Wilson. "Commerce, Education, and Political Development in Tangshan, 1956-69." In *The City in Communist China,* edited by John Wilson Lewis. Stanford, Calif.: Stanford University Press, 1971.

_____. *Leadership in Communist China.* Ithaca, N. Y.: Cornell University Press, 1963.

Loh, Robert, as told to Humphrey Evans. *Escape from Red China.* New York: Coward-McCann, 1962.

McFarlane, Bruce. "Visit to Shanghai." (Sydney, Australia: apparently at the University of Sydney, 1968). A section of his mimeographed travel notes.

Munro, Donald J. "Egalitarian Ideal and Educational Fact in Communist China." In *China: Management of a Revolutionary Society,* edited by John M. H. Lindbeck. Seattle: University of Washington Press, 1971.

Murphey, Rhoads. *Shanghai: Key to Modern China.* Cambridge, Mass.: Harvard University Press, 1953.

Namier, Lewis. *1848: The Revolution of the Intellectuals.* Garden City, N. Y.: Doubleday-Anchor, 1964.

Ning T'ao et al. *Shanghai Wuching huakungch'ang ti tansheng* [The birth of the Wuching Chemical Factory at Shanghai]. Shanghai: Shanghai Jenmin Ch'upan She, 1965.

Okun, Arthur M. *Equality and Efficiency: The Big Tradeoff.* Washington: The Brookings Institution, 1975.

Onoye, Etsuzō. "Regional Distribution of Urban Population in China." *The Developing Economies* VIII, No. 1 (March 1970): 93-107. Tokyo: Institute of Developing Economies.

Orleans, Leo A. " Birth Control: Reversal or Postponement?" *China Quarterly,* No. 3 (July-September, 1960): 59-73.

_____. *Every Fifth Child: The Population of China.* Stanford, Calif.: Stanford University Press, 1972.

_____. "A New Birth Control Campaign?" *China Quarterly,* No. 12 (October-December 1962): 207-210.

Palmer, R. R. *A History of the Modern World.* Rev. ed. New York: Knopf, 1960.

Parsons, Talcott. *The Structure of Social Action.* Cambridge, Mass.: Harvard University Press, 1937.

Richman, Barry M. *Industrial Society in Communist China.* New York: Random House, 1969.

Russett, Bruce M. et al. *World Handbook of Political and Social Indicators.* New Haven, Conn.: Yale University Press, 1964.

Salaff, Janet. "Revolution in the Streets." *Far Eastern Economic Review* LXI, No. 35 (August 29, 1968): 391 ff.

————. "The Urban Communes and Anti-City Experiment in Communist China." *China Quarterly*, No. 29 (January-March 1967): 82-110.

Schlesinger, Joseph A. *Ambition and Politics*. Chicago: Rand McNally, 1966.

Schurmann, Franz. *Ideology and Organization in Communist China*. Berkeley and Los Angeles: University of California Press, 1966.

Shanghai chiehfang yinien [One year of liberated Shanghai]. Shanghai: Chiehfang Jihpao She, 1950.

Shanghai shehui k'ohsüeh yüan, Chingchi yenchiu so, Ch'engshih chingchi tsu [Shanghai Academy of Social Sciences, Economic Research Institute, Urban Economy Group]. *Shanghai p'enghu ch'ü ti piench'ien* [The transformation of Shanghai's shack districts]. Shanghai: Jenmin Ch'upan She, 1965.

Shanghai Shih Tsung Kunghui Tiaoch'a Yenchiu Shih [Shanghai General Labor Federation, Investigation and Research Office]. *Kunghui ch'ingkung kungtso* [Youth work in the unions]. Shanghai: Laotung Ch'upan She, 1951.

Skinner, G. William. "Marketing and Social Structure in Rural China." *Journal of Asian Studies* XXIV, Nos. 1-3 (November 1964-May 1965): 3-43, 195-228, 363-399.

Snow, Edgar. *The Other Side of the River: Red China Today*. New York: Random House, 1961.

Stanford University China Project. *East China*. 2 vols. (Subcontractor's Monograph, HRAF-29. Stanford-3). New Haven, Conn.: Human Relations Area Files, 1956.

Taubman, William. *Governing Soviet Cities: Bureaucratic Politics and Urban Development in the U.S.S.R.* New York: Praeger; 1973.

Tien, H. Yuan. "Population Control: Recent Developments in Mainland China." *Asian Survey* 2, No. 4 (July 1962): 12-16.

Townsend, James R. *Political Participation in Communist China*. Berkeley and Los Angeles: University of California Press, 1967.

Tung, Robert. "People's Policemen." *Far Eastern Economic Review* 53 (August 18, 1966): 319-321.

United Nations, Department of Economic and Social Affairs. *Future Population Estimates by Sex and Age: Report IV, The Population of Asia and the Far East, 1960-80*. No. 31, ST/SOA/series A, 1959.

van der Sprenkel, Otto, Robert Guillain, and Michael Lindsay, eds. *New China: Three Views*. New York: John Day, 1951.

Vogel, Ezra F. *Canton Under Communism: Programs and Politics in a Provincial Capital, 1949-1968*. Cambridge, Mass.: Harvard University Press, 1969.

Wakeman, Frederic, Jr. *Strangers at the Gate: Social Disorder in South China, 1839-1861.* Berkeley and Los Angeles: University of California Press, 1966.

White, Lynn T., III. "Changing Concepts of Corruption in Communist China: The Case of Shanghai, 1949-52" (Unpublished article.)

————. "Leadership in Shanghai, 1955-1969." In *Elites in the People's Republic of China,* edited by Robert A. Scalapino. Seattle: University of Washington Press, 1972.

————. "Local Autonomy in China during the Cultural Revolution: The Theoretical Uses of an Atypical Case." *American Political Science Review* LXX, No. 2 (June 1976): 479-491.

————. "Low Power: Small Enterprises in Shanghai." *China Quarterly* (forthcoming).

————. "Shanghai's Polity in Cultural Revolution." In *The City in Communist China,* edited by John Wilson Lewis. Stanford, Calif.: Stanford University Press, 1971.

————. "Workers' Politics in Shanghai." *Journal of Asian Studies* XXXVI, No. 1 (November 1976): 99-116.

Whyte, Martin K. *Small Groups and Political Rituals in China.* Berkeley and Los Angeles: University of California Press, 1974.

Wu Shao-ch'üan. *Tao nungts'un ch'ü* [Going to the villages]. Shanghai: Shenghuo Shutien, 1947.

Yinienlai ti Shanghai kungan kungtso [Shanghai public security work over the past year]. Shanghai: Shanghai Shih Jenmin Chengfu, Cheng Kung Pao, 1950.

INDEX

237

Design: University of California Press Staff
Composition: University of California Press
Lithography: Thomson-Shore, Inc.
Binder: Thomson-Shore, Inc.
Binding: Holliston Roxite Vellum B 51501

Text: Compset/500 Baskerville
Display: Compset/500 Baskerville
Paper: Book Mark, basis 50